MINORITY RULE

MINORITY RULE

ADVENTURES IN THE CULTURE WAR

ASH SARKAR

BLOOMSBURY PUBLISHING

LONDON · OXFORD · NEW YORK · NEW DELHI · SYDNEY

BLOOMSBURY PUBLISHING
Bloomsbury Publishing Plc
50 Bedford Square, London, WC1B 3DP, UK
Bloomsbury Publishing Ireland Limited,
29 Earlsfort Terrace, Dublin 2, D02 AY28, Ireland

BLOOMSBURY, BLOOMSBURY PUBLISHING and the Diana logo are
trademarks of Bloomsbury Publishing Plc

First published in Great Britain 2025

A catalogue record for this book is available from the British Library

ISBN: HB: 978-1-5266-4833-4; TPB: 978-1-5266-4832-7; EBOOK: 978-1-5266-4827-3;
EPDF: 978-1-5266-4829-7

2 4 6 8 10 9 7 5 3 1

Typeset by Newgen KnowledgeWorks Pvt. Ltd., Chennai, India
Printed and bound in Great Britain by CPI Group (UK) Ltd, Croydon CR0 4YY

To find out more about our authors and books visit www.bloomsbury.com
and sign up for our newsletters

For product safety related questions contact
productsafety@bloomsbury.com

For Mum

I hope this is enough to convince you
that I've got a real job.

CONTENTS

Introduction

We know, deep down, that something is wrong. Our material conditions – the pay in our pockets, the roof over our heads, the stuff that we buy, the services we rely on, the planet that sustains us – are getting worse.

A friend, in the middle of a painful breakup, informs her letting agent that they'll need to take her ex off the tenancy contract and put it in her name instead. They email back promptly: new name means new contract, which means an extra £300 a month in rent to keep up with market rates (and, supposedly, to compensate the landlord 'for the disruption'). Just what you need in the midst of heartbreak. This is not unusual. Hardly a week goes by without hearing from someone saying that their landlord has hiked the rent; either they find the money somewhere or they move out. In April 2024, the average UK rent had increased by 8.9 per cent since the previous year[1] – far above the 3.4 per cent rate of headline inflation over the same period. Almost three million people, despite being in full-time work, are in problem debt, according to a report by StepChange, Britain's largest debt advice service.[2] Housing costs more. Food costs more. Bills cost more.

Even the National Health Service, once a byword for British excellence, is on a downward trend. Since 2010, waiting lists have ballooned, and medical staff (tempted by better pay and conditions elsewhere) have left in droves.[3] Navigating the corridors of a labyrinthine hospital just outside of London to find my sister after she'd had an episode of bad health, I learned that it had received £140 million just ten years ago; and yet there were signs of dilapidation all around. The paint was flaking, bits of ceiling crumbling from where water had intruded, the corners of steps hastily patched up with hazard tape from where they'd fallen into disrepair. The smell of chips permeated the air. I finally found my sister, wheezing into tubes: she was still on the same trolley that she was wheeled in on the day before. When staff turned up, they were cheerful and efficient, but plainly overstretched. There are too many people much sicker than my sister, and too few to treat them. I wonder who would have helped her go to the bathroom or plugged the loose cable of her nebuliser back in if I hadn't taken the day off work. But the mere fact that she was seen at all, that she eventually got a proper bed, and that she didn't come back with a secondary infection means this counts as a positive experience in the NHS.

On the way back home, outside the underground station, I saw a homeless woman with purpling bruises on her face, her arms stick-thin. Later that day, I watched a man scream obscenities at a younger woman, substance use problems written all over her. London, the fifth-richest city in the world, teems with people who need the care of the state and aren't getting it. Eight in ten primary school teachers in England say they've had to spend their own money to buy items for kids who are showing up to school hungry, or without proper clothing.[4] Half of all young mothers report skipping meals to feed their children.[5] Politicians cut ribbons at food banks, heap praise on charitable efforts and say little about the causes of hunger. Were they to speak, they might be expected to do something about it.

Happiness slumps. Year by year, the percentage of people (and especially, younger people) reporting that they experience some sort of anxiety ticks upwards, and all the self-care in the world is unable to make a dent.[6] We can practise active listening and setting healthy boundaries all we like, but the ground on which we form connections with others feels increasingly unstable. We drift through jobs, relationships and crappy houseshares, while floating somewhere amongst perfumed clouds the world's billionaires add the equivalent of Italy's entire GDP to their wealth in just a single year.[7]

Anxiety is not merely an affliction of 'generation rent'. Even those with property to their names have reason to feel uneasy. Our population is ageing, but the joys of longer life are cut with the fear that we might not be looked after as we grow older and more frail. There are more than five million unpaid carers in England and Wales;[8] in the United States, about 14 per cent of the population provide unpaid care to the elderly.[9] Women of my mum's age increasingly find themselves sandwiched between the care needs of their parents and those of their children or grandchildren. For anyone who isn't wildly rich, or so utterly destitute that even our atrophied welfare state is compelled to kick in, being cared for in old age is no sure thing. The NHS has a legal duty to cover care if you're diagnosed with cancer. Dementia? Good luck pal. Meanwhile billionaires pour money into reversing the signs of bodily ageing and trying to upload their consciousness into digital immortality.

Drought in southern Europe and further afield – including Morocco and Brazil – jacks up the price of tomatoes, olive oil and sugar. In 2022, temperatures soared above 40°C in the UK for the first time since records began. The next year saw the UK rack up its second highest temperature in our recorded history. The North Sea was on average several degrees warmer in 2024 than it had ever been before. We huff at each other and mumble platitudes about how mad it all is. When the rain pours down in sheets, ruining crops in the fields, we all make the same joke about how we could use a bit of global warming. Even the art of British understatement becomes absurd in the face of a global existential crisis. 'Did you hear about so-and-so?' 'Yeah, they had to flee their hotel in Greece because of the wildfires.' Holiday ruined, what a shame. The ordinary, humdrum language of life struggles to contain an increasingly chaotic reality. Some things – like that there were more excess deaths in England during the hottest day of the summer in 2022 than there were British Forces personnel killed in the Afghanistan and Iraq wars combined – are simply not said at all.

And what about all those goods that we're burning the planet for? Clothes and phones, both designed to be replaced at the earliest opportunity. A top from Shein rips on the second wear, and I try not to think about the woman who sewed it. Technology connects us to more people than at any other point in human history, and yet loneliness hollows us out from the inside. For fun, I spend hours on an app that makes me hate myself. I watch a genocide[10] unfold on infinite scroll, the shredded limbs of children following selfies and engagement announcements. My best friend swipes a catalogue of men that'll ghost her. Instagram, Hinge, TikTok, Twitter[11] – it's like trying to live on the empty calories of Skittles because they approximate the sweetness of fruit. Satisfaction is fleeting; fulfilment is elusive. This isn't social connection. Capitalism, in commodifying every second of our waking lives, has managed to come up with a form of leisure that's even more alienating than labour. We gaze at blue screens and yearn for the warmth of people. The sons and daughters of the Global North, dead-eyed and flat, scroll consumer products that will provide neither fulfilment nor joy.

Rough sleepers are curled up against storefronts, unsheltered and freezing on some of the most valuable real estate in the world. Rivers and coastlines are pumped full of human faeces, drinking water teems with microplastics and chemicals whose effects we don't understand, and there is no democratic lever to fix it. A full-time job no longer guarantees a life above the poverty line. In real terms, we're getting paid less, squeezed more by rents, and are suffocated by a sense of societal decline.

Capitalism, says a certain sort of person, has lifted more people out of poverty than any other system ever. But for most people holding this book, our time is defined by inequality, insecurity, lack of community and information overload. These are collective conditions, but they leave us feeling atomised and abandoned. The silent question, for lots of people, is 'why are things like this?' In previous centuries, enough people asking that out loud might result in an uprising. Instead, we in the Global North are curiously deadened. So if the system is failing to result in making it better every year to be a human being – if we're not getting happier, or feeling that the trajectory we're on is a good one – why are we paralysed by inaction? That is the question that this book is trying to answer.

I'm not the first to attempt to grapple with this. Like a lot of people, the first politics books I read were all trying to explain the origins of the deeply unequal world that I lived in. I got my first copy of *The Communist Manifesto* when I was thirteen. It wasn't because I was particularly interested in German political theory, or had heard much about Karl Marx and Friedrich Engels. I just spent a lot of time loitering in bookshops at that age, hoping to cultivate an aura of wistful intelligence and catch the eye of a boy who'd go for that kind of thing. None did. But slowly, my pocket money transformed into a bookshelf of political texts in my bedroom.

I learned about something called *The Feminine Mystique*, pronouncing Betty Friedan's name wrong well into my twenties. I read *The Beauty Myth* – both furious at how a male-dominated society manipulates girls into starving themselves into ghostliness and quietly stung that I didn't have the willpower to do the same. I got my hands on the work of Frantz Fanon and considered the morality of political violence for the first time. I thought about the version of history I learned – that Britain had benignly administered an empire, until it didn't fancy having one any more – and contrasted it to the reality of bloody struggle. I encountered, for the first time, the idea that the race and gender identities that we're born into might be constructed in the interests of programming a profoundly unequal society.

And, though I didn't meet the sensitive scholar of my dreams at Palmers Green Bookshop, I did begin one of the political relationships which has defined my life. Instead of becoming someone's girlfriend, I became a Marxist.

When I got to university, there was no shortage of people interested in these ideas. And, returning to the works of Marx, I felt again the revelatory thrill of reading *The Communist Manifesto*. A slim, breathless pamphlet, *The Communist Manifesto* was intended to be passed from hand to hand amongst workers. In 1847, when it was written, Europe was in the throes of political revolution. But the upheavals that swept the continent were baby potatoes compared to what Marx and Engels predicted were coming down the line. There would be a proletarian revolution – the overthrow of the ownership class by the working class – and it would be caused by capitalism itself.

Marx and Engels came up with a model for understanding how history-defining change, like the French Revolution, happens in a society. Sorry to the Oxford debating nerds out there, but it's not a battle of bons mots in the marketplace of ideas. Instead, Marx and Engels theorised that social transformation happens when an economic class becomes strong enough, or big enough, to overthrow the one above it. Got a merchant class that's making money, but locked out of the aristocratic chambers of state power? Say goodbye to feudalism, and hello to liberal democracy.

Political systems are a product of economic interests, not abstract ideas. Though individuals may change the course of history, it's only the distribution of class forces in a society that puts them in a position of opportunity to do so in the first place.

Marx and Engels understood their present moment of mid-nineteenth-century capitalism as being defined by the private ownership of the means of production (i.e. the resources needed to create goods and services). Rather than being geographically tied to landowners, workers sold their labour-power (i.e. their capacity to do work) to that ownership class, in return for wages. They moved to the new urban centres of industry, to labour in dark satanic mills. These workers, with nothing to sell but their time, were labelled the proletariat. The ownership class, meanwhile, was dubbed the bourgeoisie.

You don't need a doctorate in political theory to see that, despite writing in the early bloom of capitalism, Marx and Engels predicted much of the harvest. In the rich West, we live surrounded by the morbid symptoms of capitalist devastation. That's why we can't shake the feeling that something is deeply and profoundly wrong. Wasn't capitalism meant to catapult us, rich and optimistic, into a brighter future?

Perhaps you view all these problems as merely an unfortunate series of coincidences. Or maybe, like Marx and Engels, you connect the dots between the presence of extreme wealth for the very few and the process of impoverishment for everyone else.

Marx predicted globalisation, foreseeing that the insatiable need for new markets would see the bourgeoisie slip the surly bonds of their home nations and spread over the face of the earth. Corporations, international banking institutions and supply chains have made capitalism a planet-spanning and tightly interconnected system. He understood that the tendency of competition was monopoly, that smaller businesses would fail and that corporate giants would feast. In 1999, Amazon made up just 5 per cent of the American e-commerce market; by 2023 it was nearly 40 per cent.[12] And as Jeff Bezos' growing share of a growing e-retail sector became ever more dominant, high street stores shuttered and once thriving neighbourhoods became ghost towns. Capitalism has been ceaseless in its drive to extract profit from the gifts of nature; now, even the human attention span is a product that can be parcelled up, bought and sold. Our personal information, online habits and meta-data are valuable commodities. Capitalism has, in the name of economic development, created ecological wastelands.

What Marx and Engels thought would happen was that, with the tendency amongst the bourgeoisie being for the big fish to gobble up the small fry, a greater percentage of wealth would end up concentrated in fewer hands. The middle classes would be squeezed out of assets and would join the ranks of the proletariat. Polarisation of economic classes would grow as the proletariat got bigger. But they got one massive thing wrong. They thought that, eventually, the proletiariat would be pissed off enough to overthrow the bourgeoisie and seize the means of production for themselves. The engines of industry would be collectively, rather than privately, owned. In this way, they theorised, capitalism produces its own gravediggers – it creates the very class of people that will end it.

This – spoiler alert – did not happen. Though inequality today between those who own assets and those who don't is growing, and in the UK, property affordability is at its worst level since 1876,[13] revolution feels further away than ever. Why? In essence, this is what *Minority Rule* is going to show: how culture, politics and unequal stakes in the economy combine to fragment, weaken and inhibit working-class power. We're not lumped with falling wages, a degraded environment and a generalised sense of hopelessness because humans spontaneously got worse at improving society. It's because wealth

8

concentrations warp politics and stunt our ability to shape society for the better. Because if you can't see the world clearly, you can't change it. I'll show you how the media and much of our political class collaborate to make identity-driven conflicts – the so-called 'culture wars' – the most prominent issues of the day. We'll see how trivial non-events are blown up out of all proportion to fuel a culture of distraction. I'll examine the tactic of weaponised grievance, which manufactures a false conflict between class equality and racial justice, and breaks down the possibility of a united working-class movement. And finally, we'll look at how the most ardent defenders of predatory capitalism politically profit from the very problems they create, by shoehorning perceptions of a very real social decline into a narrative about racial demographics. All of these tactics are in the service of facilitating one of the biggest wealth grabs the world has ever seen.

Throughout this book, the idea of 'class consciousness' will crop up again and again. What I mean by this is how people think of their social status and economic conditions, who they feel themselves to have common cause with and who they perceive as their opponents. And what we'll see is that there are huge, ideology-producing machines which work to inhibit, splinter and weaken class consciousness based on economic status and steer resentment instead towards an extreme fixation on culture and identity. I'll show you how the left embraced an individualistic and competitive model of victimhood; how the media machine functions to pump out trivial outrage-bait; what makes the political class so obsessed with the pursuit of headlines; the way stoking of anti-immigration moral panics and the atrophying of working-class institutions like trade unions and council housing produced a right-wing shift in the political consensus; and how a manufactured demographic panic directs working-class anger horizontally and downwards rather than up at elites.

Media and politics work on cues and misdirection. Like a magician pointing the way they want us to look while the rabbit disappears, we have been encouraged to focus our anger on a new set of villains. Who are these villains? Just open a newspaper to find out. Our villains are asylum seekers (note: don't call them refugees, that makes them sound too human), coming to these shores on unsafe dinghies purely for the hell of it. They're the 'lefty lawyers' wielding human rights law to stop deportations. They're Just Stop Oil, Insulate Britain or Extinction Rebellion – inconveniencing the public, winding everybody up by reminding us of climate devastation. Transgender people, who want nothing more than to lurk in toilets and cause distress. In fact, they're the woke more generally: 'wokies', 'tofu-eating woke-rati', 'woke students', 'woke warriors' and the 'out of touch metropolitan elite'. These nebulously defined individuals range from diversity and inclusion managers to anyone who pipes up and makes you feel like a bit of a bigot. You can throw in Black Lives Matter too. Not black people, you understand, that would be racist: just those who protest when black people are killed by police.

Activists, whether protesting against climate change or racial injustice, are routinely described as 'selfish', 'shrill', 'disruptive' and 'hypocritical'. The feeling is that they've somehow hijacked your eyeballs, forcing you to pay attention – not to their cause but to them as individuals. They are too noisy, too visible, and demand an unfair share of attention. Their outsize presence in the attention economy is presented as evidence that progressive harpies wield too much power and influence (despite being on the losing side of every General Election between 2010 and 2024). The overarching narrative is that, by virtue of their place in the attention economy and the hyper-visibility of their identities, these groups and individuals want to impose what this book will call 'Minority Rule'.

Minority Rule is the paranoid fear that identity minorities and progressives are conniving to oppress majority populations. It's a meta-narrative, a big story told through countless speeches, TV segments, articles, videos, books, policy papers and social media posts. It articulates the idea that the power of ordinary people has been curtailed, stolen or attacked by an elite minority. But instead of that elite minority being defined in material terms (as in, the real ruling minority of hedge-fund managers, press barons, landlords, corporations and oligarchs), they're defined as a mishmash coalition of ethnic minorities, graduates, sexual and gender minorities, environmental activists and people who live in cities and regularly drink frothy coffees. This isn't because anyone really thinks that these types of people are actually the driving force behind wealth inequality, but because these minorities are opposed to the cultural values and interests of those who've been dubbed 'the white working class'. This is the thesis of Douglas Murray (*The Madness of Crowds*), Matthew Goodwin (*The New Elite*) and pretty much anybody who writes for *The Spectator*. They're telling a story about institutional capture – you, the decent and silenced majority, have been oppressed by identity and political minorities who've seized control of the levers of culture. You are being ruled by minorities.

The Minority Rule story – that majority interests are threatened by minorities – is used as political cover to justify authoritarian and antidemocratic measures that threaten everyone. The unpopularity of climate groups like Extinction Rebellion, Insulate Britain and Just Stop Oil has been used by the UK government to push through sweeping anti-protest legislation. Asylum seekers crossing the Channel are cited by leading Conservatives as a reason to leave the European Convention on Human Rights.[14] Jair Bolsonaro's scaremongering about trans and gay people in Brazil served as a distraction while he used

the courts and police to crush political dissent. And the permanent state of culture war in the US, with the Black Lives Matter
movement, LGBTQ people and others being accused of imposing 'ideologies' like Critical Race Theory on the population, has
culminated in five individuals on the Supreme Court overturning abortion rights for millions of women. Ah well: at least those
judges weren't drag queens reading storybooks to children.

Minority Rule works to obscure, prop up and extend *actual*
forms of minority rule. It directs working-class anger away from
wealth and political inequalities, and towards identity minorities
who've been made into scapegoats. Financial elites are missing
from this big story (unless they're a corporation like Sainsbury's
or Budweiser, who've done something 'woke' like support Black
History Month or partner with a trans influencer). The scaremongering of Minority Rule breaks down the power of the working
class by fragmenting them into warring identity groups – white
working class pitted against ethnic minorities, trans people
against women, city against small town. By leveraging paranoia
and resentment in media and politics, the ruling class use the
Minority Rule story to fragment the economic majority (those of
us who have to live off wages, and not asset wealth) into culturally opposed minority groups. Those who would otherwise see
common cause with others of a similar class position are made to
think of them as villains, and themselves as victims.

The explanation for how this occurred is a complicated one
with deep roots. But bear with me.

In order to account for the failure of the status quo to deliver
rising standards, it's important to look at how politics has
changed over the last eighty-or-so years. Politics, in essence, has
become a spectator sport. Party political membership has fallen,
as has trade union membership. Big protests – against racism,
austerity or climate change – flare up every few years. But the
number of people consistently engaged in political activity is

really quite small, and the number of people with the power to easily influence political results is even smaller.

Lyndon B. Johnson supposedly once said that the first rule of politics is learning how to count. And in a democracy like ours, people don't determine a government: places do. It doesn't matter if you win a seat by seven votes or 70,000; get enough constituencies, and baby, you're in government.

Younger people, by which I mean the under-forty-fives, are stacked up in electorally useless cities. If you live in a place like Tottenham, Manchester Gorton or Liverpool Walton, nobody cares about your vote. Sorry. It's a done deal, you live in one of the surest bets in the country. The Conservatives know you're not worth bothering with, and Labour can focus on people living in constituencies with tighter margins. The voters worth the most are the ones who can be tempted from one party to another. That way, you're not just gaining a vote, you're taking one away from your closest rival. In football terms, you'd call that a six-pointer. Everybody else can go hang.

Where we experience politics most of the time, outside of the context of an election, is where we spend increasing amounts of our time: screens. We scroll endlessly, argue with relatives and strangers, share articles and videos, and post like our lives depend on it. Though polling shows trust in media falling, thanks to the twenty-four-hour news cycle and the dizzying speed of online content churn, we consume more of it than ever.

The image that we get of the world through the media is warped and distorted, like a hall of mirrors. Issues which are huge, such as the climate crisis or demographic ageing, are small in comparison to who's up and who's down this week in Westminster. Panels of pundits and talking heads aren't assembled to talk about why living standards are falling, but, rather, whether an Oxfam cartoon depicted a well-known children's author as a transphobe, whether *Fawlty Towers* is racist, and whether Prince Harry should be stripped of his titles after running off with Meghan Markle. The grotesque inflation of these trivial issues relative to the systemic and existential crises facing our society constitutes nothing less than reality manipulation. We are being robbed of our right to see the world around us clearly.

Attention, as well as being a commodity that can be monetised through digital platforms, is a psychological wage. We know this from when we are children: think of the heaven of basking in the glow of an attentive parent or teacher. To be recognised is to be told that you matter, that your life has worth and that you have a place in the world. There's nothing unhealthy about that. But our media and politics leverage the psychological wages of attention in a way that is utterly corrosive and warping. Though there is no shortage of content that flatters 'ordinary Brits' and 'hard-working Americans', this isn't to let us know that we're loved. It's more about telling us who is hated. The message of who is good, moral and decent is conveyed through repeated propagandising about who is deviant, dangerous and illegitimate.

This is where identity politics, and how it has been weaponised against the very movements which generated it, comes in. Identity politics was originally formulated in the 1970s, during a wave of black radicalism, feminist consciousness-raising and trade union activism, as a way to incorporate feminist and anti-racist critiques of society into a wider anti-capitalist framework. It wasn't so much about individual identity – the question of 'who am I?' – but looking at how collective experiences of race, capital and gender form the basis of a movement against both material and social inequalities.

But this changed sharply from 1979 onwards, when Margaret Thatcher, Ronald Reagan and their accomplices in billionaire-controlled media established a new political paradigm. Corporate profit was presented as one and the same as the public good. As the great cultural critic Stuart Hall wrote in his famous paper 'The Neoliberal Revolution', Thatcher's mission was 'to break trade union power – "the enemy within", as she put it'. Instead of promoting the values of cradle-to-grave welfarism, people were herded towards 'new, individualised, competitive solutions: "get on your bike", become self-employed or a shareholder, buy your council house, invest in the property-owning democracy'.[15] A neoliberal consensus emerged across the West, and the idea that governments had responsibility for the distribution of wealth, the provision of essential services like water and energy, and the size of the financial sector relative to manufacturing, was laughed out of town. By the 1990s the grand ideological battles of history had supposedly ended, socialism was defeated and everyone (in the words of John Prescott) was middle class now. Talk of class politics, of workers struggling against the forces of capital, was as retro as pipe-smoking and donkey jackets. The power of government was dwarfed by the power of the markets.

The big questions of how to run an economy, like whether there should be price controls on certain goods, or particular industries owned by the state, receded from political view. And in this context, identity politics left behind anti-capitalist values. The goal was no longer to overthrow an unjust and hierarchical system, but to be represented better within it.

While issues might involve activist or interest groups as they did before, such as Black Lives Matter, Extinction Rebellion or Stonewall, these groups are now dragged into a media battle between identities and their assigned values. The success of your cause isn't measured in policy wins – it's measured in airtime. Politics takes place within a competitive attention economy. So a news story about Sainsbury's supporting Black History Month is folded into a war between 'woke' graduates versus 'the white working class', the demand for trans equality is framed as trans activists versus women, and anything to do with anti-black racism (whether it's a protest about police violence, or statues of slavers) is BLM versus everybody else. Identity politics has come to describe the fight about how we see ourselves, rather than what kind of society we want to have.

This form of individualised and liberal (as in, perfectly comfortable with the existence of capitalism) identity politics has, to be fair, been somewhat successful. Though more diverse representation hasn't delivered the post-racial, post-bigotry utopia that some may have dreamed of (and certainly hasn't addressed issues like incarceration, wealth inequality, exploitation or state violence), it has resulted in profound cultural shifts. In a matter of decades, a great deal has changed in some aspects of the lived experience of identity minorities.

Racists can no longer be entirely confident that bandying around slurs in the workplace will be totally consequence-free; there is greater awareness and sensitivity around the language used to describe minority identities; there has been a great deal of de-stigmatisation around same-sex relationships. The kinds of faces and identities visible in film, television, music and advertising are a lot more diverse in terms of race, gender and sexuality than they used to be. I don't want to belittle the emotional impact of this change for people who aren't used to seeing their identities presented in a positive light. As W. E. B. Du Bois pointed out, to only see yourself as a figure of 'crime or ridicule'[16] is a form of oppression. While wealth inequalities grow ever wider, there has been – at least – some redistribution in the psychological wage of attention.

But this can be manipulated. Though identity minorities are objects of fear and derision, presented as an enemy within for wanting to impose Minority Rule, they're also given a degree of social prestige by being acknowledged as minorities. Recognised identity minorities like people of colour, some of those with disabilities or LGBTQ people get the consolation of attention. While this attention doesn't necessarily convert into justice or systemic change, it does at least establish a sense of public importance. That's not nothing in our information-saturated, discourse-obsessed attention economy. As a way of muddying the waters, dividing the working class and driving a backlash against some of the cultural gains made by minorities, right-wing elites have developed a strategy that I call the Minority Game.

The Minority Game involves minority identities being disparaged but also weaponised against one another. Women are simultaneously the sharp end of the spear in transphobic moral panics and characterised as censorious and finger-wagging in the wake of the #MeToo movement. During Jeremy Corbyn's tenure as Labour leader, antisemitism became the cause célèbre of the racist and reactionary right, who accused the socialist wing of politics of being an existential threat to Jewish people in the UK. The very same individuals who argued that accusations of racism are used to shut down free speech (see Melanie Phillips' claim that 'Islamophobia is a fiction to shut down debate')[17] also insisted that the left were an illegitimate political force, institutionally and irredeemably antisemitic because of their sympathy with Muslims and the Palestinian cause (see Melanie Phillips again: 'Jeremy Corbyn isn't the cause of left-wing Jew hate, he's the result of it').[18] While identity minorities are presented as wielding illegitimate or disproportionate cultural power (moral panics around cancel culture spring from this central narrative), and should be mistrusted or ignored, the silent majority are bestowed the social capital that comes from identity politics. They're framed as being the 'real' victims of identity-based oppression.

This is encouraged by a media which wants you to identify with stock characters who participate in the culture war. Power dynamics are reversed, so that those with wealth, power and status are depicted as being bullied and terrorised by people without it. The newspaper columnist is a victim of social media users, the aristocrat pal of the Queen is a victim of an anti-racist lynch mob, the multi-millionaire novelist is besieged by transgender women. By being recognised as a victim, you can direct anger towards other individuals or groups. This is very useful for elites, who can dress themselves up as the downtrodden, or present themselves as speaking on their behalf.

The white working class are set up in competition with people of colour demanding racial justice, despite the fact that white working-class people are oppressed on the basis of their class. Anti-racists are accused by conservatives of marginalising the white working class by taking up media space and visibility. All the while, those in power get away with imposing the economic policies which have impoverished the working class in the first place. The working class, therefore, have their power as the majority of the labour market undermined, because they are presented as a minority group in society. And anti-racists are also undermined, for the very same reason that they're advocating for minority groups in society. This is the purpose of the Minority Game: to lift language from the collective struggle of minority identity groups, make it impossible to organise politically around shared interests, and use the language of identity politics to undermine and attack progressive political projects.

This book isn't an academic examination of the forces that shape our society. It's a way of making sense of the work that I do. If I sound bitter about the state of contemporary journalism, it's because I'm a frustrated idealist. When I was a student, the likes of Naomi Klein, Gary Younge, Amy Goodman and Stuart Hall were the people who made sense of the world for me. These writers took their responsibilities to their audience seriously; they took the political repercussions of their work

seriously. People need facts and analysis to be able to understand what's going on around them. Writing, at its best, is a profound act of consciousness-raising. But the fact that so many
journalists view this duty as secondary to career advancement,
that they are happy to act as the mouthpieces and outriders of
elite interests, makes me feel physically ill. It's an abuse, and
an abdication, of that sacred responsibility to arm your readers
with the truth, so that they can wield it against power. The first
step towards a better future comes from being able to see your
present conditions with ruthless clarity.

Michel Foucault, turning a famous aphorism on its head, said
that politics is war by other means.[19] You're not trying to score
points in a genteel debate. You're trying to win a war. It's not a
surprise that Vladimir Lenin was obsessed with applying military thinking to political struggle – he understood that achieving
the strategic objective of a working-class revolution involved
drawing together a variety of interrelated tactics, such as the
day-to-day activities of trade union organising, parliamentary
manoeuvring and local agitation.

Other people, much more clever than me, are doing the work
of thinking through tactics and strategy for the left. Instead,
what I'm going to do in this book is dissect the right's political
tactics for pursuing their strategic objective, which is basically
preserving an economic system that is destroying your well-
being, your community and the very planet you live on. In this
book, I argue that the right's strategy is this: to subvert, diffuse
and redirect class conflict – which, along with technology, is the
most powerful engine of social transformation in our history –
into culture war.

There are people who'll accuse me of just trying to make you
angry. They'll read a couple of pages where I'm spelling out how
the media is hoodwinking you, how politics is being poisoned,
and how workers are being robbed of their wages, and suggest

that I'm just as bad as someone who wants to blame migrants, or trans people, for all the world's ills. At the risk of playing into the image of the crude banshee they have in their heads, that's a load of bollocks. There's a big difference between being prodded and poked into a perpetual state of confused agitation on the basis of lies and being stirred to anger because of how the world really works. It used to be that elites wanted to keep populations apathetic and disengaged from politics. But in an age of media saturation, they've worked out that constant, misdirected rage is indistinguishable from paralysis. It's the quality of focus which turns anger into a catalyst of change.

Over the next seven chapters, I'm going to show you how the paranoid fantasy of Minority Rule upholds a *real* minority rule, by keeping us divided and competing against one another for attention. By examining media, politics and finally the economy, I'm going to explain how our perception of reality is manipulated to sustain a deeply unequal status quo. I'm going to examine how the weaknesses in progressive arguments about identity politics helped set up the traps created by the right in their mobilisation of the Minority Game. I'll look at how news and current affairs media has pumped bullshit into the public conversation, and what that's done to our political leadership. I'll break down how class and race have been presented as mutually exclusive categories, and how a misleading portrayal of the 'white working-class' has been weaponised against left-wing political projects. You'll see how scaremongering about Minority Rule has created the conditions for an authoritarian power-grab in the UK and America. And lastly, I'm going to show you what all of this paranoia, confusion, violence and victim-blaming upholds – a global system of extraction that robs us all of health, happiness and our fair share.

Where, then, to begin? Rather than reaching back into decades past, I want to start by thinking about the movement I've been a part of since my teens. It's a loose constellation of people known as 'the left', who politically commit themselves to the cause of equality, justice and social transformation, but aren't necessarily interested in standing for elected office themselves.

I want to take criticisms of this movement seriously, regardless of whether these criticisms come from friends or foes, and not just because it's the mark of a weak culture to hide from your own failings. What we'll see in the next chapter is that the left unwittingly forged the political weapons being used against it by our political opponents. We created an inverse hierarchy, where those most recognised as victims wield the most power. But the problem is we defined a victim as being anyone who claimed that status, rather than agreeing on any kind of material unit of measurement. Without meaning to, the left opened the door for powerful people to tactically present themselves as victims – and tie us up in the knots of our own obsession with grievance.

How the 'I' Took Over 'Identity Politics'

It was when the silver-haired climate activist called every-one in the room 'a bunch of fucking cunts' that the wheels began to come off. Over 200 people, broadly on what you might call the 'radical left', had gathered in the main hall of an arts centre in Liverpool to debate strategies for social change (the event was titled, in Lenin's famous formulation, 'What Is To Be Done?'). It was October 2023, and I was there to facilitate the discussion – introduce speakers, select audience members to contribute, push the chat in a constructive direction – in what the organisers hoped would be a blend of Spanish-style mass assembly and Ancient Greek direct democracy. The evening was part of The World Transformed, an annual festival founded in 2016 for the left to meet, organise and strategise. Its organis-ers are some of the most inventive and committed activists I've ever met, united by an unshakeable belief in the power of people and DIY. Around the room, I could see the faces of friends I'd known since the 2010 student movement; veteran trade union-ists in their sixties sat next to dewy-skinned Zoomers. Though the left is often maligned as homogeneous, it was exactly this kind of kaleidoscope of people, from a range of places and back-grounds, that for me summed up what it meant to be part of the movement. Since the defeat of Jeremy Corbyn, and the lonely panic of the pandemic, the left was hungry for a new direction, for a new plan to change the UK for the better. I thought the event would be a piece of cake.

That was, until Roger Hallam stepped up to the lectern. The co-founder of Extinction Rebellion and Just Stop Oil, Hallam had transformed the face of the environmental movement by embarking on a campaign of civil disobedience in the UK: a combination of attention-grabbing stunts and mass mobilised protest intended to force politicians to take action on catastrophic global heating. The government and the police promised a heavy-handed crackdown in response, and Roger Hallam – along with other activists – have been jailed multiple times. Before the event got underway, I'd jokingly called him 'climate Gandalf'. He resembled Tolkien's wizard not only because of his long, grey hair, but also in his single-minded sense of mission and his often abrasive urgency. Hallam didn't want to debate his strategy. He wanted to shame and shock people into signing up to it. Which is why (if I had to make an educated guess) his answer to my opening question of what the left was getting wrong, was that everyone in the room was 'a bunch of fucking cunts'. Hallam didn't raise his voice, or jab his finger. He said it sadly, as though this were the most disappointing fact in all the world.

To be fair, he certainly succeeded in shocking people. After Roger Hallam ceded the mic and the floor was opened to contributions, nearly every hand I took from the audience was followed by a comment disputing Hallam's characterisation of them. Look, I get it: nobody likes being called a cunt. I wasn't exactly thrilled about it either. It felt like a crude attempt to strong-arm people into doing what he wanted, without trying to persuade them why it was the most effective thing to do. But, I hoped, the hubbub about Hallam's use of coarse language would subside. Surely, a roomful of adults who'd gathered because they want to change the world would get over a man in his late fifties doing a choice bit of swearing?

Alas, it was not to be. Rather than dying down, the furore grew – amplified through the lens of identity. An activist sitting near the front spoke up in alarm about the 'white anger' in the room, and how it 'terrified' her. Her comrades nearby clicked their fingers to signal approval. A group of people of colour in their early twenties returned after a short break to say that they'd discussed it and that this was clearly an unsafe space for minorities. Valiantly, a few people tried to redirect conversation back to the matter at hand – what was the best strategy for social change? Should people unionise their workplaces, wherever they are, or should they identify more strategic sectors? Was the Labour Party a useful vehicle to organise in? Had the government's backsliding on climate commitments proved the Extinction Rebellion theory of change wrong? But the event was, unfortunately, truly derailed. People couldn't stop talking about how upset they were. Someone stood up, visibly close to tears – Roger Hallam had 'brought violence' into the space, they said. They had been harmed by it, they continued, everyone had been harmed by it.

As they spoke, I found myself thinking about the cost paid by revolutionaries of the past. Bobby Seale, bound and gagged in a courtroom at his own trial. Fred Hampton, shot dead by the Chicago police in collaboration with the FBI. Trotsky, living his last days behind the boarded-up windows of a house in Mexico City, bullet holes lodged in the brickwork from an unsuccessful assassination attempt.[1] If we couldn't cope with a stern climate activist calling us a bunch of fucking cunts, what hope had we of taking on the state?

If this had been a one-off, I wouldn't bother sharing the story with you. But that same weekend in Liverpool, at a discussion about socialism and the climate crisis, one panellist insisted

that 'we should dismantle all our movements that aren't majority people of colour'. Her words were greeted with nods of
approval – the left loves it when you make the raddest point
possible, particularly if it's about the centrality of minority communities to political success. But when you really think about
what she said, it's bananas. We should, in a country that's over
80 per cent white British, literally stop and demolish any political movement that isn't at least 51 per cent black and brown, and
expect to somehow win? With strategies like this, we deserve
to lose. The left has a persistent habit of immobilising itself
over matters of identity. Rather than injustices of race, gender,
sexuality, disability and gender identity being a catalyst for collective action, they're all too often brought up as reasons *not*
to work together for the cause of social change. And because
we've embraced a version of identity politics in which individual experiences trump collective realities, the right has been able
to appropriate it as a weapon for their own political ends.

There are some people, including dear friends of many years,
who are probably a bit annoyed that I'm writing this. They're
concerned that, by talking critically of the progressive left's
relationship to identity politics, I'm giving ammunition to our
political opponents. That's a fair concern to have. There's no
shortage of left-wing-firebrands-turned-right-wing-pundits to
suggest that yes, there's a strong correlation between getting
a publishing deal and then noisily disavowing everything you
once believed in. But what I'm about to say doesn't come from
a disdain for anti-racism, feminism, disability rights and the
fight for LGBTQ liberation: it comes from wanting to see those
causes achieve their goals. That means no more denial, and no
more defensiveness.

So, it's time to be brutally honest about something that's
been happening on the left: we have absorbed the tenets of liberal identity politics. We have nurtured a culture that's deeply

individualistic, where to be seen as a victim, to be able to claim a marginalised identity position, gives you social capital. That capital, unlike its monetary equivalent, isn't transferable outside left- and liberal-leaning environments. It doesn't prevent you from experiencing discrimination, injustice and even violence in the world outside. But within left- and liberal-leaning spaces, victimhood – a close friend of lived experience – gives one a perch from which to speak with authority. It's understandable that people want to 'correct' for injustices by giving people from certain communities a boost, a better hearing, a bigger platform. But that well-intentioned effort can result in something that's counter-productive, even corrosive, to the cause of liberation. Instead of fighting to liberate ourselves from harm, we end up attached to the social status that being a victim brings. We maintain a comically low threshold for harm, and a prohibitively high threshold for trust in other people. We turn individuals into standard-bearers for their entire identity community: whatever follows the phrase 'speaking as a…' is treated as nothing less than the gospel. We isolate ourselves, insisting that other struggles are simply too different to link up with our own. Attention is treated as currency, and a finite one at that. We are not comrades but competitors in a mad scramble for recognition.

It wasn't always like this. In the twentieth century, anti-racists and feminists were ruthlessly materialist in their analysis. No, that doesn't mean that they were 'materialistic' in the sense of coveting luxurious objects. But they believed that you could understand society through a scientific method. Materialism is the idea that it's real-world conditions that shape consciousness, and not the other way around: so if you want to understand a person, or a whole community of people, you should look at the distribution of wealth, resources and access to power. But in recent years, we've retreated from that way of seeing the world. We don't speak of *the* truth any more, but *my* truth. Subjective judgements – when uttered from the throne of victimhood and given the title of 'lived experience' – are given sacred status. To question someone's lived experience is to undermine their very identity. We've chucked the idea of material truth out of the window, in favour of agreeing with whatever is most emotionally and socially convenient. We've abandoned the idea that we might, for all our differences, live in a shared reality. Identity is no longer a starting point for understanding the political and economic forces that shape the world around us. It has become the cage that keeps us isolated.

Why does this matter? Firstly, it makes the left much less effective at contesting politics. By making a virtue of marginalisation, breaking ourselves down into ever-smaller and mutually hostile groupings, we make it impossible to build a mass movement capable of taking on extreme concentrations of wealth and power. Secondly, we have opened the door to victimhood being appropriated by the right. Because we've jettisoned the idea that identity politics has a relationship to material conditions, and have instead made a secular religion of individual, subjective experience, we've unwittingly crafted a playbook of grievance for reactionaries to wield against us. It's no good pretending that there aren't weaknesses in this kind of identity politics that permeates the left, because those weaknesses are being exploited by our opponents.

What this chapter is going to show you is that identity politics has been appropriated, weakened and warped to become a force that actively inhibits the causes it's meant to advance. I'll look at the liberal turn, where a once explicitly anti-capitalist movement has been so profoundly blunted that their rhetoric has been absorbed by Coca-Cola's Diversity, Equity and Inclusion training. I'll show you how concepts like 'lived experience' have been blown out of all proportion, so that it's impossible to describe a shared social reality. And I'll look at the impact of the progressive left becoming obsessed with the discursive over the material, to the point of elevating language to an absolutely obscene status and creating a cult of subjectivity, obsessed with individual victimhood rather than collective material conditions. And insistence on the separateness and competing needs of struggles, what I call irreducible difference, means that we just split ourselves into smaller and smaller groups – and the reactionary right have pounced on these weaknesses, exploiting the power of weaponised grievance.

The Origin of Identity Politics

The term 'identity politics' was coined by the Combahee River Collective, an organisation of American black feminist thinkers and organisers founded in 1974, who were participating in the anti-racist, feminist and lesbian struggles of the time. Members included Audre Lorde and Barbara Smith, whose works still form the foundation of black feminist politics. *The Combahee River Collective Statement*, published in 1977, was a combination of searing critique and righteous manifesto. Naming themselves after a raid on slave-owning plantations led by Harriet Tubman during the American Civil War, the collective argued that black women had been expected to subordinate their own struggles to the liberation of others for too long. White feminists had failed to account for the impact of racism on black experiences of womanhood, while misogyny still ran rampant in anti-racist and black power movements. Though some white lesbians might argue for separatism – that is, women basically ghosting the other half of the species in every sphere of public and private life – the Combahee River Collective said that was impossible for black women. They argued that black women don't have the luxury of just cutting themselves off from their male counterparts, as they're both under attack from racism. The task for black feminists was to fight on every front at once: to struggle together with black men against racism, whilst they also struggled against black men about sexism. 'Our politics evolve from a healthy love for ourselves,' they wrote, 'our sisters and our community which allows us to continue our struggle and work.'[2] And this was what they termed 'identity politics'.

But while the Combahee River Collective viewed their experiences as black women as the starting point of their political analysis, their vision of liberation wasn't just about identity. They viewed their enemy as being the same elites who were responsible for the exploitation of workers, the work of empire and the war waged on the Global South. They came to the conclusion that the liberation of marginalised groups depended on bringing down capitalism and imperialism, and not just by changing how different groups interact socially. The Combahee River Collective identified themselves as socialists, 'because we believe that work must be organized for the collective benefit of those who do the work and create the products, and not for the profit of the bosses'.[3] While they agreed with some elements of Marxist thinking, they warned against conceiving of the working class as 'merely raceless, sexless workers'. As black women, they had been first-hand witnesses to how race and sex exerted a kind of gravitational force on people's working and economic lives. They refused to separate race from class 'because in our lives they are most often experienced simultaneously'.[4] Systems of oppression did not remain neatly distinct from one another – rather, they were interlocking, and it was that very interaction between capitalism, imperialism and patriarchy which created the conditions of our lives. Although their politics were rooted in their own oppression, the Combahee River Collective also knew that political work had to form coalitions with organisations of people that were not like them. Indeed, they did not see black feminism as being solely for black women: the Combahee River

Collective asserted that it was 'the logical political movement to combat the manifold and simultaneous oppressions that all women of color face'.[5] In some ways, the phrase 'identity politics' was misleading: the Combahee River Collective weren't interested in identity so much as the vantage point that being black women at the bottom of the labour market gave them on how the world really works. The Combahee River Collective's formulation of identity politics was unambiguously anti-capitalist, collective, and international in its scope.

How the 'I' took over 'Identity Politics'

Today, though, identity politics in most of its articulations is confused, atomised and oddly unambitious. Instead of talking seriously about bringing down capitalism, we're seeing identity politics invoked to police relatively trivial social interactions (like whether saying the word 'cunt' constitutes 'violence'). Though recent years have seen an increase in real-world organising work, whether through the Black Lives Matter movement or feminist activism centred on abortion rights in Ireland and the United States, a certain kind of identity politics has been popularised through the work of denunciation. 'Calling out' problematic behaviours, or the elaborate performance of checking/announcing your privilege, might be understood as cultural gestures which have absorbed the idea that the personal is political, at the expense of remembering that the political is still political.

As Emma Dabiri put it in *What White People Can Do Next*, today's identity politics are centred around allyship as opposed to solidarity: and just what that allyship really is, nobody can tell you with any real precision. There's a generalised trend of 'being chastised to transfer your "privilege" to a "black" person', but the advice on how to do that is foggy, unhelpful and distinctly individual. People are instructed to 'call out racism, take a pay cut, only support "diverse" brands' – but as Dabiri writes, each of these actions is interpersonal, Instagrammable, and 'all neatly contained within a neoliberal framework'.[6] It's about building a personal brand, rather than a collective movement.

The liberal turn in identity politics has been driven by three major preoccupations: the notion of *irreducible difference* between identity groups, the idea that identity groups have *competing interests*, and that *lived experience is a form of unassailable political authority*. And these features have in turn made elements of liberal identity politics rich material for appropriation and weaponisation by the forces of reaction in the form of grievance politics.

Lived experience is one of those ideas that has become notably voguish in the last few years. In short, it refers to personal knowledge of the world gained through firsthand experience. That's not a bad thing, and is a source of valuable information. Turning to lived, firsthand experiences of the world has led to important work being done in diverse fields. Lived experience has been the jumping-off point for research into the physical health impacts of chemical hair relaxers on black women,[7] centring patient experience in mental health care, and arguably the #MeToo movement was the product of women sharing their lived experiences of sexual harassment and violence.

But how this often plays out in practice is that lived experience is presented as an unassailable form of moral authority – when a person makes a statement about the world, and says it's their 'lived experience', you can't question whether what they're saying is actually true. If it's your 'lived experience' that a climate activist saying the word 'cunt' is threatening, or that an all-white yoga class is traumatic, who is anyone to say that it's not? And if you're identifying yourself as being victimised in some way, who can say that it's not the case?

For what it's worth, I think that lived experience should be allocated the same value as witness testimony in a court trial.

It's important, it shouldn't be automatically thrown out and it deserves a fair hearing. But it's not unimpeachable. You have to weigh up whether this person's account matches up with corroborating evidence, whether they're credible and whether the conclusions you're drawing can be reasonably inferred from the experience being recounted. But in the current political climate, such considerations are interpreted as an intellectual assault on the identity of a marginalised person. And as we'll see, this is ripe for weaponisation.

What about the notion of *irreducible difference*? Throughout history, marginalised groups have been named and categorised in ways not of their own choosing. Gay men, for instance, have been variously called inverts, sodomites, catamites, Uranians – and that's before you get into slurs, such as faggot, queer and poof. The language of race has been imposed on black people (capitalisation optional) in both politics and law, from terms like 'coloured' and 'Negro' to 'black', 'black British', 'Afro-Caribbean' and 'African American'. The term African American is used so widely in the US to mean 'person of African descent' that I was once gently chastised by an American student for identifying characters in Joseph Conrad's *Heart of Darkness* as black, rather than African American (the novel is set in Congo, which as far as I know is not in the Midwest). Some of these terms have been largely abandoned, and consigned to the dustbin of history, for being degrading, imprecise or simply archaic. Others have been reclaimed in acts of defiance, notably the word 'queer', and deployed to insist that marginalised groups have the right to change an unjust society, rather than merely conform to it. How identity groups are defined and named has always been a deeply political, and fiercely contested, social process. To have a name thrust upon you is a feature of your disempowerment. The question of how to identify shared conditions between people who are from different backgrounds, but are all marginalised on the basis of race, becomes a particularly sticky issue.

In the UK, between the 1970s and 1990s, anti-racist efforts were often coordinated under the umbrella of 'political blackness'. To be politically black, in this school of thought, didn't necessarily mean that you were part of the African diaspora. Instead, anyone who experienced discrimination on the basis of skin colour could claim to be politically black. The British Black Panthers included South Asian people, and organisations like Southall Black Sisters and the Newham Monitoring Project all operated on a similarly politically black basis. The purpose of political blackness was twofold – the first was to build power by unifying Britain's ethnic minorities under a single banner, and the second was to undermine the idea of race as something that's real and fixed, as opposed to an idea that's constructed and killable. The framework of political blackness began to fall out of fashion in the 1990s, but the concept had been rooted in the specificities of UK race relations: it wasn't just slavery that accounted for the presence of non-white communities in the UK, but the fact that British colonialism spanned Africa, the Caribbean and Asia. Most non-white immigrants to the UK after the Second World War were simply branded 'coloured', and as my grandmother was fond of saying, if a sign said 'No Blacks, No Irish, No Dogs', it didn't mean that Indians were welcome.

But for many black people, the adoption of the term 'politically black' by Asian, Arab and other minoritised communities undermined the specificity of their political and historical experience. What's more, this sharing of the term 'black' when anti-black prejudice was also sometimes rife in such communities felt like an especially insulting form of erasure. While some organisations in the UK still use the term 'black' to include all people of African, Arab, Asian and Caribbean heritage, it's not something that's nearly as common these days. One replacement that has seen use in the UK since the 1980s is 'BAME', which stands for Black, Asian and Minority Ethnic. BAME didn't emerge out of radical organising, nor was it supposed to be an identity that people related to in an organic way: it was a way for the government and other organisations to monitor inequalities between white Brits and their counterparts of colour. Like political blackness, BAME has been sharply criticised for failing to capture the diversity of experiences and differences in outcomes amongst different minority groups.

At the same time that political blackness was in the ascendant in the UK, another term was being developed in the United States: 'people of colour' (commonly abbreviated to POC). Though its use dates back to slavery, where it was used to distinguish free individuals of mixed African and European heritage from enslaved people,[8] and though Martin Luther King deployed the phrase 'citizens of color' in his 'I Have A Dream' speech, it wasn't until the 1970s that it was widely used in the context of anti-racist organising as an umbrella term for people of African descent, Native Americans, Hispanics, Arabs, South Asians and East Asians.[9] But like some of the criticisms directed at 'political blackness', the term people of colour has come under fire for trying to lump together diverse experiences of racism and racialisation within a single bracket. In 2020, not long after the murder of George Floyd at the hands of police ignited protests around the globe, NPR's *Code Switch* podcast hosted a discussion that solicited listener contributions about whether it was time to retire the phrase 'people of colour'.[10] Some people felt that it didn't capture the experience of people whose features could be considered whiter, or white-passing, than other racial minorities. One listener said that its attempt to contain both black and non-black communities felt like an erasure of her experiences as a black woman: 'I feel that the term POC is nonsense, and I think it's a way for non-Black people to sit comfortably in their anti-Blackness because they're so afraid to say Black. So they come up with these terms that make them feel comfortable, with their whiteness or their adjacency to whiteness. And I get irritated – not irritated, vexed – when people refer to me as POC or BIPOC ['black, indigenous and people of colour', a broader term]. Like, no, absolutely not. I'm Black, don't play me.'[11] Here, we get to the logic of *irreducible difference*. People's experiences of race and racism, according to this view, are simply too different to be held within a single language container.

The framework of irreducible difference is a close cousin to the sense that different identity groups, or liberation struggles, actually have *competing interests*. This isn't something which is necessarily explicitly stated, but it's the logic on which many arguments about how marginalised people interact with one another plays out. These debates, unsurprisingly, often take their most embittered, counterproductive and occasionally outright deranged forms on social media. As pointed out on *Pod Save America*, I don't think that you'd see someone arguing in real life that Anne Frank had white privilege,[12] or that telling someone to 'touch grass' (i.e. stop arguing on the internet and go outside) is ableist.[13]

Like irreducible difference, the rationale of *competing interests* can have its origins in legitimate and reasonable critiques. But there is a difference between examining how communities have been placed in competition with one another, and saying that our interests are mutually exclusive. Often, this is what underpins a demand for 'prefigurative' politics, i.e. the insistence that movements, organisations and individuals involved in social justice have to be free of oppressive dynamics before they can get moving on their chosen cause, which often leads to them spending so much time working on their own internal culture that they don't do anything public-facing. Rather than the Combahee River Collective's emphasis on *simultaneity* (that because they experienced racism and sexism at the same time, they would fight them at the same time) there is a feeling of paralysis: that unless you do everything, you can do nothing. People are held responsible for what goes on in 'their' community, and told that good allyship means tackling oppressive behaviours amongst those who share identity characteristics with you. In one article from 2016, titled 'How to tackle anti-blackness as a non-black PoC', readers are advised to 'speak to your own community' and 'generate platforms where black voices need to be heard'.[14]

While certainly well-intentioned, this is exactly the kind of vague and imprecise advice Emma Dabiri critiques in *What White People Can Do Next*. It upholds the idea that people with shared identity characteristics aren't just a community because of their shared experiences, but that they're a community in the sense of all having social access to one another. In this view, we're all individual envoys for a particular tribe, to whom we report back at the AGM. It isn't dissimilar to the logic that demands Muslims root out extremists in their midst, regardless of whether we know any or not. And this simply isn't how community works. We're dispersed by geography, language, class, religion and political values. But instead of imagining anti-racism as something that brings dispersed individuals and communities into contact with one another, it's presented as work that's done in discrete and hermetically sealed groupings.

Indeed, the logic of *competing interests* can create antagonism and ill-feeling between groups who could otherwise find common cause in their experiences of discrimination and violence. In decades past, the Black Panther Party were more than happy for Vietnamese organisations involved in the struggle against the war to adopt the name the Yellow Panthers. They were even happy for a group of white radicals to organise themselves under the banner of the White Panthers. The White Panthers worked with the BPP and others in the Rainbow Coalition, and issued a ten-point manifesto which stated 'We take as our heroes, those that we have been told to hate and to fear [...] The Red Guard are our Brothers, the Black Panthers are our Brothers, we join with them in the liberation of the planet.'[15] It's unimaginable that a similar attitude to sharing names or political slogans would be taken today.

In 2023, in the wake of the brutal murder in the UK of Brianna Ghey, a sixteen-year-old transgender girl, there was an intense online debate over whether trans people and their allies should use the slogan 'Say Her Name'. In this context, the slogan had been used because British media outlets had referred to Ghey by her 'deadname' (i.e. the one she used before transitioning). But some felt that using the slogan was a form of appropriation – the phrase 'Say Her Name' had been popularised by Kimberlé Crenshaw, a law professor and scholar of critical race theory, following the 2015 death of Sandra Bland (an African American woman) in police custody.[16] Since then, 'Say Her Name' had become a powerful rallying cry for justice and visibility in cases where black women had been killed at the hands of the state. Using it to mark the death of Brianna Ghey, a white teenager, was condemned by some as an expression of a 'desire to co-opt, diminish, and rebrand around movements and slogans specifically built around Black people [...]'.[17] It's strange to apply the language of 'rebranding' to a slogan which is about confronting the elites with the humanity of those whose lives are considered disposable – as though the logic of marketing creeps into even radical causes. In my view, it speaks to a trend in identity politics where people are more concerned with protecting intellectual property rights than, say, marginalised communities articulating shared interests and organising together in pursuit of justice. It seems frankly nuts that when a child has been murdered and misgendered in the press, anyone's priority would be haggling over who should use which slogan.

To be clear, I'm certainly not arguing that you shouldn't challenge bigotry or harmful behaviour when you encounter it. But it's a highly limited strategy, where anti-racism is seen less as a movement to participate in or a project of building collective power and more as a form of social policing that we all ought to do as individuals. And if we don't think that this social policing is happening enough, the thinking becomes that I, as a Muslim, can't work with the LGBTQ community until they demonstrate they're aggressively dealing with Islamophobia within their own ranks, or I refuse to align with striking workers until I'm confident that they're examining their own racism. This becomes particularly heated on social media, where you don't even need evidence that there is racism, ableism, sexism or bigotry prevalent in the thing you're critiquing. You can simply say that you, or even just a hypothetical person, hasn't been sufficiently taken into account – and that this is evidence of being systemically excluded, erased or oppressed.

A Little Less Conversation

If you want to know how far the concept of identity politics has come since its anti-capitalist origins, just look at how eagerly it's been adopted by corporations looking to beef up their Diversity, Equity and Inclusion credentials. Take, for instance, Robin DiAngelo's 2018 bestseller *White Fragility: Why It's So Hard for White People to Talk About Racism*. This book, particularly after the Black Lives Matter protests of 2020, was a smash hit with well-intentioned white liberals (and with one persistent man in my Instagram DMs who alternated between sending updates about his progress through the book and asking me to sell him images of my feet). DiAngelo's ability to anatomise the

everyday ways in which white people ignore, erase and mini-
mise the impact of racism on people of colour made her book a
runaway success, and her examination of race relations skewers
the myriad ways in which white people consciously and unwittingly uphold racism by being unwilling to challenge it when
they see it, or become defensive and brittle if challenged on it.
DiAngelo gives some examples of racial inequalities in wealth
and life chances in the United States, and in interviews, she has
observed that the racial makeup of a community is a powerful
determinant when it comes to things like pollution, nutrition
and access to clean water.[18] But in *White Fragility*, her focus
largely relates to interactions between individuals. 'Many of
us can relate to the big family dinner at which Uncle Bob says
something racially offensive,' she writes, 'or the party where
someone tells a racist joke but we keep silent because we don't
want to be accused of being too politically correct and be told to
lighten up.'[19] This ignores the systemic nature of racism – who
cares what Uncle Bob is saying when asylum seekers are being
locked up, or black people harassed by police? If I could live in
a world where people of colour didn't have to fear state persecution, Uncle Bob could say whatever he likes.

After the book became a hit, DiAngelo's clients came to
include the likes of Unilever and Amazon. She even addressed
over 184 Democratic members of Congress, less than a fort-
night after George Floyd was killed, for a "Democratic Caucus
Family Discussion on Race." ('For all the white people listening right now, thinking I am not talking to you,' she said, 'I
am looking directly in your eyes and saying, "It *is* you."')[20] In
2021, a micro-controversy was spawned after it emerged that
one of her training sessions had been given at a Coca-Cola
corporate event. One slide, which instructed attendees to 'be
less white' was the subject of particular ire.[21] Leaving aside
whether or not 'be less white' is meaningful advice to anybody,

the very fact that a corporation like Coca-Cola would have an anti-racism training at all tells you something about whether or not such workshops challenge the interests of the wealthy and powerful. Indeed, there is a certain hideous irony in the fact that DiAngelo implores us to think of the water crisis in Flint, Michigan, when considering the impact of race on people's lives, but not San Cristóbal de las Casas in Mexico – a town in the impoverished region of Chiapas, where Coca-Cola's stranglehold on the water supply means that its residents have been left with little safe water to drink, and a reliance on soft drinks that means diabetes kills over 3,000 people in the state annually.[22,23]

Robin DiAngelo, however, is not alone. This disconnect between corporations embracing identity politics and the actual impact of their profit-generating activities has become a feature of the modern-day diversity and inclusion industrial complex. Indeed in 2020, Lockheed Martin – *an actual fucking arms manufacturer* – sent three of its white male executives on an anti-racism training day. Lockheed were optimistic about the changes in their company culture. One programme director, reflecting on his own personal awakening, had a lightbulb moment when he realised that it was problematic to ask a black employee to bring 'a little swagger and attitude' to a client pitch.[24] Though the Combahee River Collective were unambiguous in their opposition to both capitalism and militarism, the inclusion efforts of the likes of Coca-Cola and Lockheed have been praised by a collection of diversity experts. By tackling internalised sexism and racism in the boardroom, gushed a collection of sociologists and workplace experts in the *Harvard Business Review*, corporations could retain talent and 'reduce risk to shareholders'. 'Members of underrepresented groups need powerful white male allies too,' they argued.[25] I wonder whether making billions of dollars selling the bombs which rained down over civilians in Iraq and Afghanistan constitutes a workplace microaggression.

Though mere decades separate the identity politics of the Combahee River Collective and the identity politics of corporate anti-racism training, they might as well be on different planets. But it's not just the identity politics of race which have been co-opted by the kinds of institutions that were considered the political enemy by the liberation movements of the 1960s and 1970s. In 2021, the CIA (yes, that CIA) released a series of adverts called 'Humans of CIA' as part of a recruitment drive. In one video, an agency librarian talks about how, growing up as a gay man in a small Southern town, he had been concerned that he might not be able to be open about his personal life at work. 'Imagine my surprise when I was taking my oath at CIA and I noticed a rainbow on then-Director Brennan's lanyard,' he intones earnestly. 'I remember being stunned.'[26] Inclusion is, apparently, 'a core value' at the CIA. In another upload, a Latina woman cites Zora Neale Hurston, refusing to be bound by 'the misguided patriarchal ideas of what a woman can, or should, be', and proudly proclaims herself to be 'a cisgender millennial who has been diagnosed with generalized anxiety disorder'.[27] These ads were so heavy-handed in their use of woke buzzwords, so toe-curlingly earnest, so violently cringe, that it's entirely reasonable to consider whether they were actually part of an elaborate psy-op intended to turn millennials and Zoomers against identity politics altogether. But a world in which the CIA – an organisation responsible for coups, assassinations, tortures and death squads – can celebrate 'intersectionality' is no more absurd than one in which Coca-Cola and Lockheed Martin attempt to brand themselves as allies in the fight against injustice.

What explains the shift in identity politics from the Combahee River Collective's unshakeable anti-capitalism and anti-imperialism of a half-century ago to corporations and human-rights abusers delivering diversity training today? America in the 1960s and 1970s had witnessed the emergence of a radical and culturally powerful anti-war movement. Activists such as Kwame Ture (then known as Stokely Carmichael), Huey Newton and Bobby Seale – leaders of the revolutionary Black Panther Party – were passionate opponents of the Vietnam War, and organised efforts to resist young black men being drafted into the military. They argued that America had no right to wage war on another nation in the name of democracy, especially when it denied basic rights to its black population at home. Proclaimed Ture, in one speech to students at Berkeley: 'If I were to believe [the President's] lies that we're fighting to give democracy to the people in Vietnam, as a black man living in this country I wouldn't fight to give this to anybody.'[28]

The Panthers drew on their Marxist class analysis to make connections between the conditions of black people in the US, and the conditions of non-black people of colour across the world. Naturally, they weren't too keen on corporate giants, weapons manufacturers or the CIA. They saw similarities between police brutality against blacks in American ghettos, and the occupation of Vietnam by the American military – and what's more, this empathetic identification was reciprocated by the Vietnamese.[29] At one conference in 1968, named the 'Hemispheric Conference to Defeat American Imperialism', American delegates handed their draft cards to Vietnamese representatives, who burned the papers on a stage. Hoàng Minh Giám – North Vietnam's Minister of Culture – then turned to a leading Panther and announced 'You are Black Panthers, we are Yellow Panthers!' When identity politics was originally being conceptualised, it was at a time when activists were thinking about how their struggle was connected to people who *weren't* like them, but who faced a common enemy – American capitalism.

It's not as if America has had a shortage of wars since the last US helicopter scrambled out of Saigon, and yet opposition to militarism has been noticeably decentred in modern identity politics. While there are certainly moments of reciprocal solidarity (in 2014, following the police killing of Michael Brown, activists across the States chanted 'from Ferguson to Palestine, occupation is a crime', and Palestinians shared advice on social media about how to deal with being tear-gassed), the language of anti-imperialism is now seen as almost a Cold War throwback. There has been a retreat from thinking about the interconnectedness of racism, sexism, the exploitation of labour, ableism and homophobia beyond how they intersect at the level of the individual. As identity politics became untethered from Marxist thinking and more bound up in liberal individualism it became less concerned with transforming society, and more focused on being represented in it.

Today's identity politics isn't so interested in the material injustices of food, jobs, bombs and money. Instead, we find ourselves endlessly debating the terms of the debate. Language, though important, has taken on an absurdly elevated status. We use language to signal that we're enlightened, virtuous and morally pure. There's an element of class dominance here – university-educated people imposing on others how to talk, and scolding them when they get it wrong. For those outside of this self-selecting subculture, there can be a sense of exasperation. How am I meant to know what to say? How can I keep up with all the new terms? Why does it matter anyway when wages are low, foreign wars are being waged and the planet is being burned? Though it's undeniable that the declining use of slurs in public space is a good thing, and that trying to shift cultural norms so that trans people are always called by their chosen names and pronouns would make their navigation of the social world a hell of a lot easier, we've become obsessed

44

with policing what people say, beyond a reasonable threshold for mutual respect. Communication is shot through with suspicion, as we maintain a constant lookout for words, phrases and frameworks which might betray a relationship to oppression. This has resulted in a crueller, more socially precarious culture in left-wing movements and spaces. We've forgotten that being a human is messy – it involves negotiating social interactions, and searching out what we have in common through experimentation, trial and error.

As adrienne maree brown writes in *We Will Not Cancel Us*, 'every kind of dissonance in movements is understood through a lens of violence, abuse, and victimisation.'[30] Though we identify ourselves with the victim status of hunted prey, brown writes, we behave en masse like predators in a 'feeding frenzy'. The stakes of disagreement, or divergent language, are ratcheted up to the point where they're seen as an assault on someone's personhood. And so, the consequences for such wrongdoing are no less extreme. A social ostracism machine kicks into gear, following the same script on social media. 'The callouts generally share one side of what's happened and then call for immediate consequences,' she writes. 'And within a day, the callout is everywhere, the cycle of blame and shame activated [...] Sometimes there are consequences – loss of job, community, reputation, platform. Sometimes there is just derision, and calls for disappearance. The details of the offence blur or compound as others add their own opinions and experiences to the story.'[31] This process of activating an invisible tripwire, leading to someone purporting to have been harmed, followed by a chorus of public shaming, has cultivated an atmosphere of frightened conformity.

Why are we actively seeking out reasons to throw each other away? Barbara Smith, one of the original members of the Combahee River Collective, blamed the decoupling of identity politics from its radical origins on people being introduced to the concept primarily at university, rather than in organising spaces. 'They don't have familiarity with how people mobilise and come together in order to make actual material change,' she said in a 2022 interview with *Moya Magazine*. 'It's like they embrace identity, but they leave the politics on the floor.'[32]

That's a nicer way of saying that identity politics has become a largely middle-class preoccupation, due to its spread in elite universities. The ideology isn't being shared in a context where the goal is to get people to work together towards the goal of social transformation; it's in the competitive yakkety-yak of arts and humanities seminars. That's the same incubation tank that I sprang from – one where the stakes were no higher than your own personal academic status, and the goal was to prove how much smarter you were than everybody else. The over-educated and insecure probably aren't the best people for creating a healthy political culture. It's not exactly the most useful approach to take if you're trying to organise people to work collectively.

Ideas like symbolic violence (a sociological concept which refers to how societal inequalities are enforced by norms, communication and social power) get picked up in the seminar room and applied willy-nilly to the real world. It's not that these ideas are bad; it's that students take a concept from the academy, plaster it over the world outside, and warp their perceptions of reality to fit an abstract definition. That is, after all, what you're meant to do when you're young. The problem comes when progressives have created a political culture where you can't question whether an idea is being deployed in an appropriate or accurate way, because of the fear of social ostracism.

This operates as a powerful disincentive to making ideas more useful and refined – and the threshold for identifying something as harmful gets dropped to a comically low level. In an article for the *Guardian* published in 2022, one yoga practitioner spoke earnestly about how classes run by white people 'who'd just come back from an ashram in India [...] wearing Indian clothes, and all the accoutrements, in a class full of white people' were 'traumatising' for people of colour.[33] Look, I get how Katie from Harpenden coming back from Goa as Chaitanya might seem like a trivialisation of Indian culture. I understand how contorting your body in a room full of Lycra-clad women who look nothing like you can trigger feelings of anxiety. But 'traumatising'? Come off it. If being in an all-white yoga class is 'traumatising', then there are no suitable words to describe the experience of racialised police harassment, stop and search, or targeted abuse. The emotional reaction to an event – and the political meaning assigned to it – becomes completely unmoored from how materially severe it actually is. To someone who isn't part of these very narrow subcultures, it comes across as hysterical. That's not great if you're looking to persuade people that anti-racism is capable of changing their lives, and society, for the better. For that, you need a sense of priorities.

Without a clear sense of material priorities, the cult of victimhood and competitive oppression takes over. Everything becomes a dystopian version of John Rawls' 'original position', a thought experiment which argues that if you didn't know how powerful you'd be in any given social system, you'd design that system to be as equitable as possible. Instead, when it comes to internet identity politics, the thought experiment is that if any action can be imagined to be harmful to a marginalised person, then it's automatically deemed oppressive, wrong and deserving of denunciation. In one particularly wild instance, a woman who took over a pot of chilli con carne to her neighbours (who'd recently moved in, and had been subsisting on takeaway pizza) was accused of having a 'white saviour' complex, of failing to take into account religious or disability-related dietary requirements, and potentially driving the chilli recipients towards

'autistic burnout' because of the mental toll exacted by an unin-
vited act of gift giving.[34]

In another viral incident, a woman shared on Twitter that
she and her husband drink coffee in their garden together every
morning and talk for hours. Some of the responses included a
man replying dismissively because he wakes up every day with
tarsal tunnel syndrome and has to wash down his OCD medi-
cation with an oat milk latte and another person chastising them
for not thinking 'of all the people who wake up to work gruel-
ling hours, wake up on the streets, alone, or with chronic pain'.
'You should be mindful next time before bragging about your
picture perfect life,' they continued. 'You might upset someone.'[35] Specific people, talking about specific contexts, suddenly
become the vehicles for experiences, grievances and societal
injustices which have little or nothing to do with the initial post.
This is, of course, part of the nature of social media: it's designed
to generate conversations unmoored from context. And it can
interact with a hyper-individualised form of identity politics
to create lines of antagonism (translation: online beef) where
you're encouraged to think of the warring parties as stand-ins
for a political position, or an identity group.

This is exactly what happened in the autumn of 2022, when
Jorts the Cat (a Twitter account where someone uses the persona
of a ginger cat called Jorts to support trade union disputes and
labour struggles in the United States) was accused of ableism.[36]
In reply to a Twitter user who had become so infuriated with a
worker on a groceries delivery app that she drove down to the
store and saw him idling on an aisle, Jorts tweeted, 'Idea: Go
get your own groceries'. But even though there was no indication that the original post was written by a disabled person,
Jorts the Cat was accused of ableism because grocery delivery
services can be an important lifeline to disabled people. 'Telling
people to just get their own groceries during a pandemic where

disabled people *cannot safely leave their homes without risk-ing death or serious illness* is callous at best' wrote one Twitter user;[37] another posted that 'Jorts account doubling down on ableism isn't what I had on my eugenics bingo card for today.'[38] For weeks, arguments raged about whether there was a tension between being pro-worker and advocating for the interests of disabled people. The idea that these aren't mutually exclu-sive categories was hardly entertained; that the Instacart lady might represent no other constituency than dissatisfied custom-ers with too much time on their hands, hardly spoken of. All this, I remind you, in the name of a guy pretending to be a cat named Jorts.

Such brief and niche controversies are characterised by an out-of-whack sense of proportion. Very little has happened to justify the outside amount of commentary that's generated, and the intensity of the argument feels wholly inappropriate to the real-life impact of the event. But there is also the psychological phenomenon of projection: our own experiences, trauma, neg-ative thought patterns and emotions are draped over other peo-ple or events. Projection is the dark twin of empathy – rather than extending our own humanity to something outside of our-selves, we force others into becoming totems of our pain. It's no surprise that social media, which presents us with vast quanti-ties of information from diverse sources in an individually tai-lored feed, tacitly encourages us to inject our own vulnerability into situations which have nothing to do with us. But this is an impossible standard to hold people to politically. No one can be represented in everything, or taken into account everywhere. And while it's certainly important to think about how move-ments which are supposed to be dedicated to the pursuit of social justice end up reproducing the boundaries which marginalise whole communities of people in society at large, that's not actu-ally what's happening here. The demand isn't 'include me in this movement', it's 'make me visible in this conversation'. It's all chitter-chatter, and absolutely no mobilising.

Arguments over language are used to enforce the notion that different identity groups are separate political constituencies and have competing interests. That idea of simultaneity that the Combahee River Collective wrote about gets lost in the insist-ence of reaching a goal before you even begin to work towards it. At best, we're weakened and atomised. And at worst, we see people who are also working towards the goal of social justice as opponents as opposed to allies. This reframing has made liberal identity politics an unwitting accomplice in the right's backlash against progressive politics.

Minority Games

Written at a time when antisemitism in the Labour Party was the subject of constant discussion in British media, David Baddiel's *Jews Don't Count* was an examination of what he calls a failure of the progressive consensus on anti-Jewish hatred. In Baddiel's view, there is an awareness and sensitivity to every other minority cause, from movements against Islamophobia to the advocacy of Black Lives Matter and LGBTQ rights, that is denied to Jewish people. The book, in many ways, is more autobiography than it is dissertation, and is informed largely by Baddiel's observations and experiences of social media debates. Not that it's a bad thing to take what happens on the internet seriously – indeed, a lot of us spend an unconscionable amount of our time there – but that what's *actually* being said online is frequently dwarfed by the amount of subtext, implication, imputation and history that Baddiel assigns to it. Take this incident, which the *Fantasy Football* host spends a couple of pages ruminating on: in 2020, an Arab-Australian poet called Omar Sakr tweeted a photographic recon-struction of Jesus of Nazareth's face, and said 'damn, what can

I say, he looks like family'. It went viral, perhaps indicating that a lot of people approved of the sentiment that Sakr was expressing. Now, to me, all that Omar Sakr meant was exactly what he said: he felt a moment of identification, a recognition of shared humanity, as an Arab Muslim looking at an AI-generated image of Jesus Christ. But according to David Baddiel, 'it reclaims Jesus. It says, Jesus was stolen by white people, and now we're setting the record straight and bringing him home.'

He continues:

> I think that's a positive thing to do. However, Sakr is a Muslim, who says that Jesus, like this, looks like family. He's not just claiming Jesus as a brown person: he's claiming him. Which, however you look at it – and however correct it is that Jesus was Middle Eastern – tramples on his Jewishness. As it happens, I look at that picture, and damn, he looks like family to me, too. But I know I would only be trolled on Twitter for saying so.[39]

This is, by anyone's standards, an enormous amount of meaning to hang on a single tweet, and a particularly brief one at that. I can't help but feel a bit sorry for Sakr: through no fault of his own, he's been accused of trampling a historical figure's Jewishness in a bestselling polemic about antisemitism. An awful lot is being assigned to his words, few though they were. Not only does Baddiel place Sakr within a debate about which race 'owns' Jesus, that Sakr himself has given no indication that he's actually participating in; his own race and religion are highlighted as reasons to view what he's saying in the harshest possible light. To reiterate, all Omar Sakr said is that this particular image of Jesus looks like family to him.

There's nothing to imply that Sakr wouldn't consider a Jewish person of Middle Eastern origin to look like family, or that it would be wrong for somebody who isn't Arab and Muslim to feel a similar sense of identification. Omar Sakr neither said nor implied any of the things that David Baddiel assigned to him, but – for no other reason than that he is Muslim – he is cast by Baddiel as someone whose interests are at odds with those of Jewish people. Indeed, this is a recurring theme of David Baddiel's contributions to the field of race relations. When a member of the Scottish Parliament said that Winston Churchill was a 'white supremacist mass murderer' for his role in the 1943 Bengal Famine, which killed between 2.1 and 3.8 million Bengalis, David Baddiel argued that this 'leaves no room to describe, say, Hitler'.[40] He added that he thinks 'there's an unconscious anti-Semitic effect here' – though it might be correct to highlight the historical suffering of people of colour, doing so has 'an unspoken critique of the conventional sense of the singular evil of The Holocaust'.[41]

Baddiel's reasoning here, to put it kindly, is sloppy at best. There's no reason why calling one person a 'white supremacist mass murderer' would undermine, prevent or obscure the proper condemnation of Adolf Hitler. Calling the Nazi Party racist, for instance, doesn't stop anybody from saying the same of the Ku Klux Klan. And just as nobody thinks that Stalin's victory over Nazi Germany somehow balances the scales of the Holodomor or the purges, Winston Churchill's racist complacency towards the suffering of Indians doesn't cancel out the fact that his role in winning the Second World War helped bring about the end of the Holocaust. It seems either that David Baddiel is astonishingly bad at grasping the idea of simultaneity – that bad things can happen at the same time, or that historical figures were capable of laudable achievements and grotesque injustices – or that there's something else at play. In projecting what he calls 'unconscious antisemitism' onto instances where the subjective or historical experiences of people of colour are being hoisted into visibility, Baddiel is effectively claiming that the proper status of antisemitism – of Jewish visibility – is being undermined and erased.

The preoccupation for Baddiel isn't 'what are the social and material conditions of Jews compared to people who don't experience racism?' – it's 'what is the cultural capital of antisemitism compared to other forms of racism?' There's a desire to be recognised as a victim – to be recognised as *the* victim – as opposed to a longing for liberation from racism. It's about the visibility value that's attached to suffering, rather than an attempt to actually organise against its source.

Indeed, playing minority victim-statuses off against one another is a particularly British political tactic. In the United States, trans-hostile sentiment is largely associated with the Christian right. But in the United Kingdom, there is a spectrum of political opinion – ranging from the 'old' left, through the centre, to the 'new' right – taking up the banner of feminism in order to oppose, or roll back, trans rights.

In February 2021, for example, the Brighton and Sussex University Hospitals NHS Trust updated their guidance for midwives and maternity staff on how to treat trans and non-binary patients in their care. It suggested that pronoun stickers be made available to patients to avoid staff misgendering them, and that staff could record patients' preferred terminology for gendered anatomy like breasts and vaginas.[42]

But this was presented in news commentary as women being erased. Rather than this guidance solely applying to a self-selecting group of patients, a misleading impression was created to suggest that women couldn't refer to their own body parts in the way that they were used to. 'Gender critical' feminists, therefore, claimed that this was an example of trans minority rights being incompatible with women's rights. Piers Morgan, king of the teacup-storm, tweeted furiously about it.

There was a lot of anger for a bureaucratic change which affected nobody but the handful of trans and non-binary patients accessing maternity services, and the clinicians treating them.

When you dig down into the story, you can only come to one conclusion – it blew up because Piers Morgan and gender critical feminists are hostile to trans people. But saying 'I want to make healthcare settings less welcoming for trans people' out loud doesn't sound all that morally righteous. In order to make attacking trans people palatable, principled even, you have to claim the mantle of victimhood. Despite there being zero material impact on the experience of women in healthcare settings, updated guidance on how to treat transgender people was presented as nothing less than an assault on womanhood.

This stuff isn't just a silly waste of time. It has a real impact on politics. In later chapters, I'll look at how trans-hostile feminism has hijacked the language of oppression to justify implementing discriminatory and dehumanising policy. But for now, I'm going to focus on how all the characteristics of liberal identity politics – the weaponisation of lived experience, obsessional focus on language and competing victimhood – have been mobilised against the cause of Palestinian solidarity.

You're already familiar with this story. On 7 October 2023, Hamas militants broke out of the Palestinian territory of Gaza (it's penned in by an Israeli-constructed barrier to the north and east, a border with Egypt to the south and the Mediterranean Sea to the west). Dubbed Operation Al-Aqsa Flood, the attacks killed some 1,200 people, and involved roughly 250 individuals being taken hostage.[43] In a swift and indiscriminate response, electricity, food, medicine and fuel were cut off by Israel to all two million people living in Gaza. Schools, universities, hospitals, homes and infrastructure were destroyed. At the time of writing, the death toll in Gaza has surpassed 40,000 Palestinians.[44] Thousands more lie buried under the rubble, as yet uncounted. Since 7 October, an average of ten Palestinian children a day have lost one or both legs in Gaza, with amputations often taking place without anaesthetic.[45] Holocaust scholars,[46] human rights experts[47] and the states of South Africa and Spain have argued that the ongoing war in Gaza meets the legal definition of genocide. I agree with them.[48]

The immense loss of life in Gaza does not come in a vacuum: since the establishment of the state of Israel in 1948, and before the 7 October attacks, hundreds of thousands of Palestinians were forcibly displaced, millions subject to Israeli military occupation and tens of thousands killed. Between 2000 and 2014, according to Israeli human rights group B'Tselem, Palestinians have accounted for thirteen out of every fifteen deaths in the conflict.[49]

But in the West, a funny thing has happened. Despite obvious war crimes being committed during Israel's military offensive in Gaza, media in the US and the UK became relentlessly focused on whether protests against these atrocities were antisemitic. Hours of airtime, and endless newspaper columns, were dedicated to the question of whether the slogan 'From the river to the sea, Palestine will be free' was a call for the extermination of Jewish people living in Israel. The American Jewish Committee has condemned the phrase as 'a rallying cry for terrorist groups and their sympathizers' in their 'Translate Hate' glossary;[50] in the UK, the Board of Deputies, the Jewish Leadership Council and the Community Security Trust slammed the slogan for 'its insinuation of acts of murder against Jewish people'.[51] Even when explicitly framed as a call for a two-state solution, the mere use of the words 'from the river to the sea' was condemned as antisemitic: a Labour MP, Andy McDonald, had the parliamentary whip suspended for saying 'We won't rest until we have justice, until all people, Israelis and Palestinians, between the river and the sea can live in peaceful liberty.'[52]

Does the slogan 'from the river to the sea' inherently call for the elimination of Jewish people in Israel, or threats to the wider diaspora? In a protest context, the slogan 'from the river to the sea, Palestine will be free' is generally meant as a call for Palestinians in the Occupied West Bank, Israel and Gaza to have their full political rights. It's incredibly common on pro-Palestinian demonstrations to see a Jewish bloc, where Jewish protesters chant the words along with their fellow marchers. Even interpreting it to mean, as the AJC does, that it symbolises 'Palestinian control over the entire territory of Israel's borders' doesn't mean that it's a call to genocide – unless you believe Jewish people and Palestinians can't exist as equals in the same country. Neither does it condone acts of murder against Jewish people in the diaspora. As Noah Zatz, Professor of Law and Labor Studies at the UCLA School of Law argues, it's 'bizarre to read a call to overthrow state-sanctioned Jewish supremacy in Israel/Palestine as an endorsement of genocide against Israeli Jews; a yet further leap is required to reach Jews like me living in the US, more than an ocean away in an entirely different geopolitical context.'[53] Indeed, in August 2023, a Dutch court ruled that the slogan 'relate[s] to the state of Israel and possibly to people with Israeli citizenship, [but not] to Jews because of their race or religion'.[54] In short, it's not antisemitic, or a call for violence of any kind.

But the truth doesn't matter when 'lived experience' rears its head. The Board of Deputies, the Jewish Leadership Council and the Community Security Trust blamed the slogan for con-tributing to 'our communities' current sense of fear and intimida-tion', and demanded that the police and the Crown Prosecution Service look into whether 'this chant meets the threshold for any criminal offence'.[55] By the time that these organisations were claiming that 'from the river to the sea' had created a climate of fear and intimidation in the UK, 3,785 Palestinians had been killed in Gaza since 7 October[56] – more than three times the death toll of Hamas' war crimes earlier that month, and a toll that has since increased tenfold. I have absolutely no doubt that some people – in particular, those who view Israel as a guarantee of Jewish safety in the diaspora – are made uncomfortable by the chant. They may even feel threatened, and such emotions are sincere. But that doesn't mean that they should get the final say on whether such speech is criminalised. What's more, the prominence of this debate during a time of indiscriminate military bombardment of one of the most densely populated territories in the world tells us something disquieting: that the lived experience of a minoritised community can be weaponised by political actors to obscure brutal and bloody injustices.

Sometimes, the claims of being threatened are so out of proportion that it's difficult to take them seriously. Take, for instance, what happened at a prestigious scientific research institute in London. In March 2024, staff at the Francis Crick Institute organised a bake sale in order to raise money for the charity Medical Aid for Palestinians. What ensued was warfare by the means of HR: management received a slew of complaints from people claiming that the 'alleged peaceful bake sale' had made them feel unsafe.[57] No specific threats on the day of the sale were reported. And unless you suffer from a particularly aggressive form of diabetes, no right-thinking person should feel intimidated by a slice of lemon drizzle. But while the substance of the complaints were silly, the consequences were far more serious. Francis Crick staff were initially banned from raising money for Gaza, and told that sharing information about Gaza was in breach of the employee code of conduct.

This isn't the first time that Israel's advocates have borrowed from the liberal identity politics handbook to clamp down on expressions of solidarity with Palestinians. Indeed, presenting Palestinian victimhood as a threat or insult to Jewish victimhood is a core tactic in the advancement of the cause. In February 2023, complaints lodged by UK Lawyers for Israel (UKLFI) resulted in Chelsea and Westminster Hospital removing a display of artwork created by Palestinian children.[58] UKLFI claimed that the exhibition of decorative plates – which included depictions of olive branches, fishermen and daily life in Gaza – made Jewish patients feel 'vulnerable, harassed and victimised'. I don't know about you, but I don't know what's more depressing: that people genuinely felt 'victimised' by children's artwork, or that a lobbyist organisation would cynically leverage antisemitism in order to erase the public display of a project that humanises Palestinians. In either instance, it's a move made possible by dropping what we consider harmful from material impact to a sense of being a victim.

There are some who'd say that I've got no right to say any of this, that it's up to marginalised groups to define their own oppression. But as Israel's advocates have demonstrated, oppression can be defined in politically advantageous ways. The International Holocaust Remembrance Alliance's definition of antisemitism (which has been adopted by the Labour Party in the UK, several cities in the US, and according to the IHRA itself, thirty states internationally) is one such example.[59] Nearly half of the examples of antisemitism given in the working definition relate to criticism of the state of Israel. Under the definition, it's unacceptable to say that 'the existence of a state of Israel is a racist endeavour' – even if you broadly object to the ideology of ethnostates. More than twenty Palestinian civil-society organisations condemned the definition as an attempt 'to erase Palestinian history, demonise solidarity with the Palestinian struggle for freedom, justice and equality, suppress freedom of expression, and shield Israel's far-right regime of occupation, settler-colonialism and apartheid from effective measures of accountability'.[60] Which minority, then, gets to define the parameters of acceptable criticism of Israel? At some point, we've got to admit that identity is a worse form of authority than truth.

How people feel is important. But it's not as important as a genocide,[61] ethnic cleansing or ongoing war crimes. It's not as important as what's *actually happening*. The problem for the left is that, by absorbing so much of liberalism's obsession with subjectivity and the individual, we've made it difficult to argue that there's a hierarchy of harm – and that the material reality outside of our own experience matters more than how we interpret it.

Identity politics has become the master-frame through which political conflict is understood. The central questions in politics aren't to do with power and material reality, but antagonistic identity claims. *Who am I? Who are you? And who really belongs here?* The reactionary right presents this as solely a political phenomenon which belongs to liberals and the left. When they talk about identity politics, they mean things like Black Lives Matter, transgender rights or #MeToo – movements, symbols, slogans and values which seek to advance the cause of historically marginalised groups. Women, queer people, racial and gender minorities: these are the people who embody or wield what is (often disparagingly) referred to as identity politics. But this is only a very partial understanding of how conflicts over identity shape our political and media culture.

The counterpart to minority identity politics is majority identity politics. In this vision, there is a silent, censored, forgotten or abandoned majority who are under attack by minority causes. Men can't talk to women at work any more for fear of being accused of sexual harassment. White people, and indeed the foundational pillars of law and order, are besieged by the radicalised thugs of BLM. Accommodations for transgender and non-binary people, like preferred pronouns, are an erasure of biological sex. Immigrants at the border threaten the character and ethnic complexion of the nation. These narratives are reinforced by political rhetoric, news and current affairs coverage and social media propagandising, to create an overall impression that majority identity groups – far from occupying a dominant position in society – are uniquely forbidden to advocate for their own interests. Socially gagged and culturally marginalised, it is this 'forgotten' majority which maintains that it has a better claim than any black, brown or queer person to feel like a minority. Far from rejecting identity politics, the modern political right understands the power of weaponised grievance and becoming the victim.

This contest of victimhood and visibility – whose suffering gets elevated, recognised and politically validated – forms the bedrock of culture war. In part, this is a result of politics being collapsed into media: if everything is an extension of press and communications, then feeling seen becomes indistinguishable from being a political priority. The currency of attention supplants wealth, investment and redistribution as a measure of status. But what the reactionary right have realised is that it's possible to use the media to cartoonishly warp people's sense of what their status in the attention economy actually is. The paradox at the heart of majority identity politics is that the best way to drive up an issue's salience is to claim (loudly, incessantly and in the national media) that you're banned from talking about it. *You can't say anything about these minorities any more*, goes the claim. *Criticising certain groups has become taboo.*

There is a material basis for attention becoming such a sought-after commodity in politics. That's because it's a real commodity in the digital economy. The material attention economy is what's going on every time you scroll on your phone, attend to a push notification, or drift through autoplay. It's often thought that platforms like Instagram or TikTok provide a service, and we're the clients. But that's not true. Our attention is the commodity. The content is just the lure, so we sit there and get squeezed for it. We live in a world of digital mousetraps, where information (be it holiday photos or a fourteen-minute instructional video on how to put up floating shelves) sits temptingly like a morsel of cheese. What's captured is our attention. Eyeballs convert into ad revenue, and delicious data that can be harvested. This is the material attention economy: the system that sucks up our time and focus and sells it.

Everyone is in the business of selling themselves online now. White-collar salaried professionals have joined tradespeople in having to market themselves and their skills; personal social media, if publicly accessible, needs to be as sanitised as your LinkedIn if you don't want to fall foul of HR. Influencers have taken this a step further – leveraging their personas and self-produced content to operate as a honeytrap for brands. Human attention is a commodity, and we are worth more for being able to attract it. So if we live in an information-saturated environment, where attention is a limited resource, what does that do to how we think and feel? It means that we get the intense sense that we must compete for the attention of others, as if that's the only way to be valued. And perhaps there's some consolation in getting attention, when everything else feels so big, so intractable and so out of control. Even if you're watching living standards decline, and politicians insist that they can do nothing about it, you're at least being reassured that you're important. The real economy of wages, rents, tax avoidance and crumbling public infrastructure is a basket case – but perhaps you might be acknowledged in the attention economy.

How we brand ourselves is a powerful determinant of earning potential. And presenting yourself as a victim is a potent personal brand. But there is a difference between vulnerability and victimhood. Vulnerabilities are real. They are measurable. They are material, and political, economic or social in their origins. A disabled person having their benefits cut, a trans school student being barred from competitive sport, a woman unable to report sexual harassment for fear of getting fired, a young black man being stopped and searched by police: their feelings of vulnerability tally with their social realities. They are made vulnerable in their interactions with the state, the economy, institutions of civil society and in interpersonal dynamics. The inequalities which lead to people of colour being more likely to be stopped and searched than their white counterparts, and on weaker grounds, don't solely exist within the minds of ethnic minorities.

The same goes for sexual harassment, racial abuse, bathroom laws, access to healthcare, incarceration rates, homelessness, employment discrimination, hate crimes and state violence. These things target, or disproportionately impact, particular identity groups. But the experience of structural vulnerability is not the same as identity. There is a recognition that our own vulnerabilities intensify, or diminish, according to context. We can accept that the vulnerabilities of others may be more acute, urgent or debilitating than our own. We understand that vulnerabilities can change through struggle. And perhaps, by understanding that our vulnerabilities are relational rather than inherent, there can be a gap between our sense of who we are, and the forces which conspire to make our lives worse.

Victimhood, however, is a perception of vulnerability that becomes a defining characteristic of somebody's identity. And being a matter of identity, a question of how we feel about ourselves and how others feel about us, it is much more open to being manipulated. It's static and closes down the possibility for positive change. Unlike vulnerability, which is fundamentally about how context determines experience, victimhood is static regardless of context. It is who you are, at all times, and in all spaces. It doesn't encourage us to think of experiences, or political interests, that we share with others. Instead, recognition of victim status is a zero-sum game: if *you're* being seen, it means that *I* am being pushed out of the frame. Being online all the time turns every political conversation into a competition for attention – indeed, that's the material basis for social media companies turning a profit.

Rather than thinking of oppression as a set of conditions and vulnerabilities that you share with others, victimhood elevates your voice and 'lived experience' above that of other people. There's a kind of perverse attachment to victimhood, to the condition of victimhood which isn't just one of suffering, but one where your suffering is acknowledged and validated by others. It is a status which confers authority, and when socially, politically and culturally recognised, compels those in power to act on your behalf. Victimhood, therefore, can be used as a pretext to exclude, police and even enact violence on other vulnerable people.

There's an incentive, then, for those in power to co-opt the victim status of others – or conjure it up entirely – in order to justify their role in upholding a deeply unequal society. Journalists, celebs and politicians claim they're being cancelled – i.e. silence and victimised – when more often than not they're just being criticised. Grievance gets exaggerated and manufactured, persecution complexes are nourished, in order to draw boundaries between legitimate, decent folk who are being unfairly treated, and the nefarious wrong 'uns who need to be drummed out of political life for the protection of society. The cult of victimhood is corrosive to the project of solidarity. It poisons the bonds of human connection and turns us against one another.

What is the point of the left? Why are we bothering to create political movements, participate in public conversations and
commit our precious and limited time to changing the world
around us? Is it just to be heard, feel seen and validated as an
individual? Those things are nice – indeed, no human being can
live without them – but that's not the purpose of a social movement. Feeling seen never changed the world.

You can fault Karl Marx and Friedrich Engels for many things,
but a lack of ambition isn't one of them. In *The Communist
Manifesto*, the two Germans defined the political mission that
lay before millions of workers:

> All previous historical movements were movements of
> minorities, or in the interest of minorities. The proletarian
> movement is the self-conscious, independent movement of
> the immense majority, in the interest of the immense majority.

What they meant was that, up until they were writing, all the
great upheavals of the world had been driven by one section
of the elite toppling another. The French Revolution was
about the city rich overthrowing the landed aristocracy, and
the American War of Independence was more about keeping
tasty colony revenues for themselves rather than any lofty
Enlightenment ideals (just ask the slaves whether they felt like
George Washington was on the side of liberty for all). These
were not revolutions by the majority, nor in the interests of the
majority: it was about replacing one class of exploiters with
another, more efficient one.

But the development of capitalism meant that the next revolution, a real revolution, would be of the majority class, the
working-class proletarians, rising up against the minority bourgeoisie ownership class. A movement of the immense majority, in the interests of the immense majority, is very different

from a cult of victimhood. By its nature, a movement of the immense majority against those who hold power and wealth will have internal contradictions. It will involve bringing together people who have viewed each other as others, rivals, and even enemies. Creating social capital out of suffering means that we have a perverse incentive to hold onto our victimhood, rather than work together to change the conditions that created it. It's an inherently minority endeavour, breaking us down into the most powerless political unit of all: the lonely, frightened and untrusting individual. And as we'll see in the next chapter, we're immersed in a media culture which primes us for being reactive and suspicious.

2

Talk Is Cheap

'And this morning, we're asking the question "Is Apu from
The Simpsons racist?"' The camera pans over, and there
I am, ready to debate this idiocy like I'm at the Oxford Union.
Looking at the footage now, a few years later, I cringe so hard
that I'm genuinely concerned that I've ruptured my appendix.

It's important, in this life, to be sceptical of your own moti-
vations for doing things. So what is it that has driven me to
repeatedly put myself on television to debate the most inane,
low-stakes, objectively stupid topics that current affairs producers have to offer? I try to say no to these kinds of debates
now, but if you had asked me at the time, I'd have said something about thinking that it was important for left-wing voices
to take up space on the airwaves, after decades of being shut
out from mainstream discussions. I was also in my mid-twenties,
broke, and scared that if I didn't play ball, opportunities to talk
about the urgent and material injustices which plagued society
would disappear. But as I watch back the Sky News clip, I can
only conclude that participating in such an undignified spectacle must actually indicate some deep psychological damage.
Because why on earth would any normal person think this was
important enough to talk about on television?

I attempted to inject a bit of nuance into the discussion, talking about my love of The Simpsons and discussing the history
of desi representation in comedy. But that was as doomed an

effort as trying to rescue the *Titanic* by swimming under the hull and pushing upwards. News channels are designed for viewers whose attention is split between the screen, their phone and a pile of ironing. It's about painting in primary colours and establishing a polarised argument in as simple terms as possible. The story is written before anyone opens their mouths. And there was my big Bengali face, yammering away as the Sky News chyron established the parameters of discussion in all caps: SIMPSONS RACE ROW | #TalkingPoint | IS APU RACIST? I could have been reciting the St Crispin's Day speech, and all anyone would have heard is another turbo-woke harridan holding forth on what you're not allowed to like any more. The content didn't matter nearly as much as the form.

These kinds of debate – trifling, polarised, with low informational content – have become a mainstay of news and current affairs programming. 'Can straight actors play gay characters?' asks *Good Morning Britain*.[1] Over on LBC, Nick Ferrari excoriates the Paris Olympics for having a 'transgender model, drag queens, and a mostly naked singer painted blue' at their opening ceremony.[2] And ahead of the 2024 Euros, where England would eventually be defeated once again by a Mediterranean nation with a superior midfield, the media had conniptions over whether a stylised version of the St George's cross on the kit was a covert nod to the Pride flag.[3] It wasn't, but that didn't stop then-Prime Minister Rishi Sunak, and his soon-to-be-successor Keir Starmer, from weighing in and demanding that Nike reconsider the design. I can feel myself losing braincells just typing this.

The spread of trivial shit across the media landscape is having a profound effect on how we perceive each other and our politics. What I'm going to show you over the course of this chapter is what being prodded into a state of reflexive reaction is doing to our sense of reality, and how the media's presentation of minority identities (hyper-sensitive, scolding and aggressive) breaks down our ability to find common cause with one another. In creating a false impression of Minority Rule, the media forms a ring of defence around actual inequalities.

But if I was going to understand outrage-driven TV, there was only one person I really wanted to speak to: the undisputed King of Clickbait, Piers Morgan. Though I'd been doing media for a while before ever encountering him in person, I was eventually part of a televised argument on his *Good Morning Britain* show where he accused me of idolising Barack Obama and I was forced to correct him on the nature of my political orientation, a clip which ended up being viewed millions of times online. If you know, you know.

It changed my life irreversibly. People would come up to me in London, New York and Barcelona to congratulate me on calling Piers Morgan an idiot to his face. I found myself treated to unsolicited rounds of shots at the pub. Long after the brouhaha subsided, I bumped into an ex I hadn't seen for years — he wordlessly unzipped his jacket, revealing an 'I'm Literally a Communist' T-shirt underneath. I wish seventeen-year-old me could've foreseen this when she got dumped.

I've been a first-hand witness to how Piers Morgan's ability to curate and drive explosive debates seeps through into the real world. And the style of debate favoured by Morgan, where an individual pundit stands in for a broader set of values or ideological positions, has dominated UK news media for the last few years. If I wanted to understand what it's doing to our political culture, I'd have to talk to the man who's built his television career on getting people addicted to feeling irate.

Though neither of us acknowledged it directly, this interview with Morgan was a quid pro quo: he spoke to me for this book, and I went on *Piers Morgan Uncensored* to create another viral moment. I intentionally disappointed on the latter front, by being so boring that nobody even noticed that I'd gone on the show (I also didn't accept the appearance fee). But Piers Morgan proved to be a candid interviewee, and not at all reluctant to reflect on his own professional practices – even if he couldn't help trying to start arguments with me about the culture war issues of the day.

'There are people who think that the culture wars are a confected thing,' Morgan said, gnawing on a chocolate bar in his studio green room when I interviewed him in the summer of 2022. 'I actually think that some of it is. For example, me ranting about vegan sausage rolls is confected entertainment. Obviously it's not going to make any difference to people's lives [...] I fire off a tweet about Greggs' vegan sausage rolls, they capitalise on it, and sell about a billion vegan sausage rolls and everyone's happy.'

But there's a big difference between 'fun, confected rows', and the issues that Piers Morgan holds dear to his heart. At the time of our conversation, that's the ongoing debate around transgender rights, and specifically the claim from some quarters that trans people being accepted as their chosen gender undermines women's rights. 'My issue comes where I believe there are elements of the [trans rights] movement, which create a new unfairness and inequality, like sport [...] And I think a lot of people care about it.' Morgan sees himself as the tribune of public opinion. 'When I did *Good Morning Britain*, for example, Susanna [Reid, his co-host] would probably be where you would be on a lot of things. But 90 per cent of the viewers were with me.'

That night's show would centre around a question that's dominated the news cycle for the past week. 'I genuinely think this whole thing at the moment, of "what is a woman?" is a fascinating debate,' said Morgan, shuffling forward on the green room sofa. 'It seems to tie world leaders in knots. It seems to be something no one can really address without getting toxic hell rained on them.' This particular discussion, and the way it generates social media backlash, and the backlash to the backlash, is something which engrosses Piers Morgan. And he's got a nose for issues which make politicians squirm. This exact question, of what defines womanhood, would be put to MPs and candidates repeatedly throughout 2023 and 2024. When we spoke, Morgan insisted that his views are in tune with those of the public at large. 'In almost all the cases that you might say are culture wars,' he said, adding the proviso that he's gleaned this opinion from *Good Morning Britain* polls and social media reaction, 'I reflect, probably, the majority of people's views.' So, is he right?

Research shows that people don't tend to have a blanket view on transgender issues (according to polling from YouGov, the percentage of people who'll always choose the most or least permissive option from a set of twenty-three questions about trans issues – the percentage of people, therefore, who are totally at one or another extreme on the issue – is statistically zero).[4] Most people will take pro-trans positions some of the time, and more trans-hostile positions at other times. On the specific issue currently agitating Piers Morgan – transgender women participating in women's sports – his view *is* in line with public opinion. But that very same public opinion has been profoundly impacted by the tenor and intensity of how the media has covered that issue.

As Piers Morgan himself acknowledged, there's a 'caveat of responsibility' when a media giant claims to merely reflect what others think, without any consideration of the possibility that they have a role in shaping the opinions of others. As polling from YouGov shows, support for trans rights has eroded amongst the general public just as these issues have become more fiercely contested in newspapers, broadcast and social media. Though the trend between 2018 and 2020 was that increasing numbers of Brits considered transgender women to be women, this actually went backwards again between 2020 and 2022.[5] There've been similar reverse-ferrets on issues like trans women being able to use female changing rooms, or whether allowing them to use spaces reserved for women poses a genuine risk to women's safety: attitudes were more accepting of trans people between 2018 and 2020, and then hardened during the following two years. The question of trans women participating in women's sports has undergone the most dramatic shift. The polling shows in 2018 Britons said participation should not be allowed by 48 per cent to 27 per cent. That sentiment 'is even more negative now', according to YouGov: '61 per cent now say trans women should not be allowed to take part in women's sport, with just 16 per cent believing they should.'

What's responsible for this regression in public opinion? In the intervening years, the visibility of transgender sportswomen has snowballed. Athletes such as Fallon Fox, Lia Thomas, Laurel Hubbard and Emily Bridges have been trailblazers in fields that had previously excluded or otherwise stymied transgender participation. But their breakthroughs into elite sport have been subject to markedly hostile media coverage, with the bulk of discussion focused on whether trans participation in sports was bad for women (rather than, say, good for social inclusion). *The Times* ran headlines such as 'Female athletes' views not listened to over transgender inclusion at Olympics, report says'; not to be outdone, the *Telegraph* published a story under the title 'Transgender players in Scottish rugby "putting females at risk"', though the number of trans women actively involved with Scottish rugby clubs at the time was just two. In debates helmed by Morgan himself on *Good Morning Britain*, the balance of opinion between two invited panellists was sharply skewed by Morgan's own interventions. In one debate, he accused two transgender sprinters in Connecticut of 'destroying women's rights';[6] in another, he asked a politician whether it was right for athletes born to male bodies 'to simply raise their hand'[7] and compete in the Olympics against women.[8]

How stories are framed really matters for what the audience will make of them. If nine times out of ten the discussion is about transgender inclusion in sports poses a threat to women, it's hardly surprising that the public will end up with more negative views of transgender participation. Nor does coverage of trans athletes exist in a vacuum. Language of 'risk', 'threat' and the 'destruction' of women's rights is reinforced by the vocabulary used to discuss transgender access to bathrooms, domestic violence services and the use of gender-neutral terms. The generally alarmist tone of coverage seeps through to frame transgender people, and in particular trans women, in a bad light. It might be that YouGov's stats simply show that Britons have spontaneously gone backwards on the progressive beliefs they held only a couple of years ago – or that, as hostility to transgender women has intensified in the media, people who previously didn't hold a strong opinion on trans rights now have negative ones. Piers Morgan is right when he says that his views are in line with public opinion. But as one of the most vocal (and voluble) mouthpieces in the media on this issue, he's got his thumb on the scale.

What's more notable is that people don't seem to *care* as much about this stuff as Piers Morgan, and many other prominent broadcasters and journalists, seem to. Despite the media obsession with litigating the boundaries of womanhood, transgender issues are remarkably low down on the public's list of political priorities. Research conducted by More In Common, based on polling of more than 5,000 people and twenty focus groups, found that just 2 per cent of Brits think that 'the debate about transgender people is one of the most important issues facing the country.'[9] YouGov's polling showed that two-thirds of people described themselves paying little or no attention to the trans rights debate at all.

You might think that actually existing public opinion, and how it's shifted over time, would make useful context for a debate show that purports to reflect the majority of people's views. But the low-information model of media is uninterested in examining its own practices. It doesn't matter whether or not people think the content you're producing is important – the key thing is that they keep consuming it. I asked Piers Morgan whether he felt like his coverage of trans issues – in prominence, frequency and tone – was proportionate to an issue only 2 per cent of people think is one of the most important issues in national politics. He sidestepped a straight answer. 'I mean, it's an interesting question, isn't it? I think that I try to find stuff to talk about on the show, as I will with you tonight, which is likely to create good debate.' A polarised debate? Sure. A good one, where people can listen empathetically to viewpoints other than their own? Not a chance.

The Yakkety-Yak Economy

There have been five main structural shifts in media that have led to this dominance of non-stories in current affairs media. The first was industry-wide changes which resulted in a decline of original newsgathering. Secondly, the doughnut ring of commentary has inflated around what news remains, filling the space left by the decline of old-style reporting. Thirdly, social media has completely upended how conventional media operates. Fourthly, the threshold for what constitutes news has lowered. And, lastly, reaction is no longer just useful context for a news story: it's how editors measure their impact – and it's often covered as news in its own right, feeding the loop of content that isn't really news but is treated as such.

Consider this: despite more people having access to news than at any other point in human history, and personal communications technology making us ever-hungrier for news content, the industry has gutted its own news-gathering capabilities. So, what's been going on in newsrooms? The 2008 financial crisis, declining advertising revenue, the emergence of online competitors and the coronavirus pandemic have pulverised the balance-books of legacy media organisations (that is, the big and venerable media organisations established before the internet). Between 2008 and 2020, employment in US newsrooms across print, TV and radio plummeted by 26 per cent, resulting in the loss of around 30,000 jobs.[10] Newspapers took the most punishing hit, with a 57 per cent drop in newsroom employment; digital-native employees, i.e. those involved in internet-first publishing like Buzzfeed or indeed Novara Media, increased by 144 per cent in the same time period. The growth of digital, however, was nowhere near enough to offset job losses across the industry as a whole.

In Britain, at least 245 newspapers have closed since 2005.[11] Those that remain have paid for their survival by sacrificing jobs at the altar of profitability. The *Guardian*'s return to the black, after a record pre-tax loss of £69 million, was helped along by 450 job losses (including 120 journalists).[12] In a single month, two newspaper groups (the *Mail* publisher DMG Media and the *Evening Standard*'s parent company) announced over 200 redundancies.[13] Even the invincible beasts of public service broadcast have jettisoned large portions of their staff. The Director General of the BBC, Tim Davie, warned that the crown jewel of UK media would face job cuts to compensate for a £285 million funding gap caused by the government freeze of the licence fee.[14] BBC News, despite being the dominant name in UK news (and one of the best-known and most trusted in the entire world), unveiled plans for 520 job losses in 2021.[15] And just in case you harboured hopes that the proliferation of digital outlets could stem the tide of media job losses, BuzzFeed, once a success story, has gone from cutesy curator of listicles to news-room carnivore. After a unionisation drive in BuzzFeed's UK newsroom failed in 2018, the company announced that it would be laying off 15 per cent of its staff worldwide (including seventeen editorial jobs in Britain) the following year.[16] Just weeks after buying HuffPost, BuzzFeed CEO Jonah Peretti announced that 47 US workers would be getting the sack, and the UK newsroom would be shuttered entirely.[17]

The general state of employment in the media has become much more precarious in the last decade and a half. The freelance pool of labour – people who make their money on a day rate, or get paid per appearance, article or photograph – has swelled. And the real-terms pay rate for freelancers has plummeted. Only a lucky few end up in a handsomely paid and secure staff job for a legacy media outlet, and in any case, many of those were well established in the media before the industry-wide bonfire of the payroll. The stubborn elitism of legacy media has endured while conditions for those without money or connections have worsened. BBC staff are twice as likely to have attended a private school than the average Brit.[18] Despite just 7 per cent of the population attending a fee-paying school for their secondary education, 43 per cent of the UK's hundred most influential editors and broadcasters are private school alumni. Nearly half of all newspaper columnists attended either Oxford or Cambridge universities,[19] and a disconcerting number of journalists have their parents' names in blue on Wikipedia. Decent jobs in media are a scarce resource, and disproportionately, they're earmarked for the sons and daughters of the already wealthy.

News is an expensive business, with high barriers to entry. But the yakkety-yak of commentary and opinion is very cheap indeed. All you have to do, as a producer or an editor, is pick a name out of your contacts list and set them up for a pennies-per-word article, or an eight-minute television debate segment.

This isn't necessarily a bad thing. Opinion and commentary can be well researched, beautifully composed and analytically valuable. But the golden nuggets of quality, information-rich opinion are not representative of the media industry overall. On television, fact-checking is basically non-existent; in print, it's patchy at best. It's not uncommon to find opinion and commentary riddled with accuracy errors, particularly when editors are burdened with commissioning and publishing large volumes of work on increasingly squeezed budgets.

Financial constraints are not, however, the only thing responsible for the ballooning of opinion-driven news content: ferocious debates make for compelling television. As explained in Robert Gordon and Morgan Neville's brilliant 2015 documentary *Best of Enemies*, left-wing intellectual Gore Vidal and conservative writer William F. Buckley pioneered an explosive and polarised form of news debate that would become a media mainstay decades later. In 1968, against the backdrop of brutal police violence outside the Democratic National Convention in Chicago, the pair were corralled by ABC News to discuss whether the cops were right to attack protesters carrying the Viet Cong flag. The two men famously loathed one another, with Buckley having previously insisted that he would never share a stage with the provocative author. On the night of the penultimate debate, tensions heated to a rolling boil. Vidal accused Buckley of being a 'crypto-Nazi'; Buckley, enraged, called Vidal a 'queer' and threatened to 'sock [him] in the goddamn face'. In later years, the two men sued and counter-sued one another for libel. And though many professed disgust at the tone and hostility of Vidal and Buckley's debates, it did not escape the attention of rival news channels that ABC's ratings ticked upwards every time the pair crossed swords.

Robert Gordon, the director of a documentary about Vidal and Buckley's fateful encounter, argues that this episode changed the face of television for ever. Debate moderators sought heat over light, and modelled their interventions on the riling jabs of bear-baiters. Discussion segments grew shorter, and the intellectual muscle of invited participants atrophied. As Gordon writes, Gore Vidal and William F. Buckley had well-regarded careers outside of television debates. They were both, undoubtedly, highly intelligent men. But today's pundits 'rely on the national camera as a sales tool, a profile raiser. They'll yip and yap for whomever is writing the checks. They know their place is filler between commercials: pseudo-content, the mere appearance of conviction.'[20] I'll try not to take his observation too personally.

News-gathering is expensive; commentary is both cheap and popular. And along comes social media to make these tendencies worse. According to a 2024 report by Ofcom, marginally more adults access news by going online than by watching television.[21] The number of people watching at least fifteen continuous minutes of television a week is declining, particularly amongst the young (last year just 48 per cent of 16-24 year olds tuned in at least once a week, compared to 76 per cent in 2018).[22] Almost half of all adults use social media to access news, and a fifth use news aggregators. Within these statistics are pretty significant variations by age and ethnicity, with older people more likely to watch more television and younger people and ethnic minorities more reliant on social media for news. None of this is particularly shocking or revelatory stuff, but it is important for getting to grips with how social media incentivises editorial and production decisions which value virality and search engine optimisation. It's simply a matter of making news content which will find an online audience, as any A Level Media Studies textbook might tell you.

What these statistics are unable to capture is that social media has a very different *feel*: as Richard Seymour describes in his book, *The Twittering Machine*, it's a disorientating mix of techno-utopianism and utter cynicism. The promise of unfettered access to the sum total of codified human knowledge versus the reality of the infinite scroll. The problems of trolling, fake news, desensitisation, racism, misogyny and every other phobia you could care to name are well known. But as Seymour notes, print and broadcast news deferred to the imagined community of the nation-state; with the internet has come the proliferation of 'lifeworlds', nebulous clouds of individuals who experience things together, but aren't necessarily contained within the same national boundary. These communities are both expansive – spanning across borders to connect people with aligned values, interests or identities – and insular. And online lifeworlds, in Seymour's words, 'seem continuously primed for explosion'.[23]

Technology is a world of intense emotional attachments, and as Seymour observes, 'Whether or not we think we are addicts, the machine treats us as addicts.'[24] Piers Morgan admits to me that if he goes 'even half an hour' without tweeting, he 'gets twitchy'. I can't claim to be any different either. It's the only thing in my life, aside from Tottenham Hotspur, that I allow to take up my time despite making every measure of my mental health worse. It is hunger, loneliness and alienation which glues us to the smartphone in our hands; and as we are made more hungry, lonely and alienated by social technology, we are stimulated by the flood of online human contact. Feeding an audience of bored, thirsty maniacs takes a different editorial mindset from cranking out *The One Show* every evening. While Twitter might be used by fewer UK adults than Facebook or Instagram, it has a disproportionate impact on news and current affairs.[25] As Moya Lothian-McLean argued in a 2022 article, 'What matters is who is on there: which people are experiencing the white-hot anger of engaging daily with the timeline.'[26] Though the Muskovite takeover has seen many high-profile tweeters quit the platform in favour of micro-blogging competitors such as Threads and Bluesky, nothing has been able to replace the original bird app as the online public square. Politicians, journalists, 'comedians', pundits, producers, editors, guest-bookers, special advisors, comms officers, strategists, pollsters – they're all on Twitter, even if it goes by a different name now.

High-follower accounts may talk at length about the unmitigated poison of cancel culture, anonymous accounts and the generalised nastiness of internet opinion-sharing. But there's little reflection on how being constantly online has shaped the behaviour and beliefs of the people who have ended up in charge of monitoring and moulding public opinion. It is a truth universally acknowledged that a pundit in possession of a stage show on the vileness of trolls must be one of the most insufferable cry-bullies on the timeline. Even those who profess not to care about the online chatosphere can't escape its gravitational pull. In his 2021 stand-up special *The Closer*, Dave Chappelle stands on stage and insists 'I don't give a fuck, because Twitter's not a real place'. I would have been more inclined to believe him had this not been said in the middle of a Netflix special entirely about how people on social media have criticised him and his comedy. Twitter might not be a real place, and yet it's where the political and media classes spend an awful lot of their time.

Stories about tweets become fully fledged events in themselves. In January 2024, the sports broadcaster Gary Lineker reposted a tweet which called for Israel to be sanctioned by FIFA for its breaches of international law – prompting outrage from Conservative MPs, pro-Israel media outlets and the Campaign Against Antisemitism.[27] This wasn't Lineker's first brush with controversy. After comparing the Tory government's asylum policy to '1930s Germany' in a 2023 tweet, he was suspended from the BBC while fury raged about the organisation's perceived impartiality (Lineker was reinstated after fellow pundits walked out in support).[28]

In 2022, a scant handful of tweets about Adele having said 'I love being a woman' at the BRIT Awards kicked off a round of ritual hooting in the media about how nobody can say anything these days without being considered transphobic. It didn't matter that there wasn't actually evidence of trans people finding what she said offensive, or indeed that Adele herself is a longstanding supporter of the LGBTQ community and has publicly backed the right to self-identify one's gender. If one or two tweets can be found which animate a pre-existing culture war framing, they can serve as the basis for reigniting identitarian conflict regardless of whether that's justified by the general complexion of opinion.

There tend to be fewer stories on television and radio which are based entirely on a tweet. But a network of incentives and professional practices means that Twitter ends up informing the content and framing of current affairs programming. Debates on TV and radio are produced with clipping for Twitter and Facebook in mind – indeed, legacy outlets like Sky News and the BBC have had to catch up with the speedy clipping and subtitling of their content by new media and dedicated Twitter users. So current affairs programming is produced with a view to reflect the kind of polarisation that exists on socials, because it's intended to drive polarised engagement ('Can you believe this prick?!' and 'I agree with them entirely' are equally powerful and compelling emotions, at least in this context).

Indeed, these priorities are baked into the workflow of current affairs programming. Before the broadcast comes the pre-interview, when a producer phones up a prospective guest to suss out what they're going to say on air. Quite often, they'll make their needs clear: 'We need someone to argue that supermarkets shouldn't put staff pronouns on name badges', or 'Do you think it's racist for pubs to run a curry night?' If you don't agree with the framing of the question, you think the discussion is ridiculous, or you have an opinion somewhere between the two extremes presented, you'll find yourself suddenly surplus to requirements. You might find it beneath your dignity to claim that we should look on the bright side of the British empire, but rest assured, there's another pundit out there whose sensibilities aren't quite so delicate. There have been multiple occasions where a producer from *Good Morning Britain* or TalkRadio has asked if I'll effectively denounce somebody when I've just told them in the pre-interview that I've never heard of them. If no authentic apoplexy can be dredged up, the synthetic stuff will do just fine.

In such a context, social media plays a critical role for the great unwashed of the freelance pool. You need to be visible if you want to make a living. A presence on Twitter means a greater chance of catching the eye of a commissioning editor or a guest-booker and provides an obvious way for them to get in touch. If you have a Patreon or a Substack of your own, social media is where you acquire an audience. What's more, there are far fewer barriers to entry on Twitter and YouTube than there are in legacy media. The impermeability of the class ceiling in British media doesn't exist in quite the same way on social media: you don't have to have gone to a pricey private school, attended one of only two universities or have famous parents to amass a following on social media. It's possible to take this point too far, however. As Symeon Brown illustrates in his 2022 book, *Get Rich or Lie Trying: Ambition or Deceit in the Influencer Economy*, hierarchy is literally encoded into social media platforms. The language of online networks shifted from the superficial egalitarianism of Facebook 'friends', to the more submissive 'followers' (and worse still, the cringingly abject 'simps' or 'reply guys'). The logic of the pyramid scheme is found everywhere on social media, argues Brown, from would-be influencers flogging Brazilian Butt Lifts just so they can get a free one, to Premier League footballers marketing NFTs on Twitter. But, exploitative as the online influencer economy is, it has made fame a lot more accessible. The same is true of news and current affairs commentary.

Social media has partially, but dramatically, democratised the public sphere. And, just as the invention of the guitar led to both the existence of Jimi Hendrix and dudes warbling Ed Sheeran at parties, its effects have been both wondrous and deeply depressing. The expansion of commentary infrastructure to include potentially anyone who is active on Twitter has meant that there is a better reflection in the world of professional opinion-sharing of the nation's diversity of ages, ethnic backgrounds, genders and socio-economic classes. The cost of entry for starting a video channel, podcast or blog is lower than attaining an equivalent platform in legacy media. With academic journals and an increasing number of newspapers locked behind paywalls, social media makes expertise accessible to those without institutional or financial access. And, for better or worse, there is greater pluralism of political opinion on YouTube as a platform than there is across the bulk of newspapers published in both Britain and America. That legacy media has been forced to accommodate voices and perspectives lifted from a sliver of those who'd otherwise be unfairly excluded from participating in public conversation is a good thing.

But with the widening of participation comes a problem of quality control. As Brown observes, 'fake it till you make it' is the unofficial slogan of the influencer economy. If you're not a fast-fashion model now, simply post photos of yourself wearing a perilously cut dress (and tagging the brand) until you're offered free merchandise, or better yet, a contract. Don't have experience in business or investment? No problem. With the right online branding, you can market yourself as a 'finfluencer', encouraging your followers to invest their money in risky day-trading, or charging exorbitant sums for financial advice that's as flimsy as a Fashion Nova garment. Appearance is everything: if you can *look* like a success on social media, the platform promises to make that aspiration a reality.

That logic extends to news and current affairs commentary. Technology reporter Chris Stokel-Walker has documented the rise of the niche Twitter expert: someone on social media who seems to know more about a particular event, topic or region than your average journo-generalist. The Russian invasion of Ukraine in 2022 was a boom year for the niche Twitter expert. Viral Twitter threads purporting to be from aviation, international relations and Eastern European experts popped up, and circulated to the tune of tens of thousands of retweets. Follower counts exploded 'off the back of effortlessly expressed expertise, often starting a thread with a brief nod to their prior experience in the field' writes Stokel-Walker, 'before weaving a compelling narrative about why a little-known doctrine adopted in 1986 by a Soviet general, for instance, might mean ruin for Vladimir Putin's invading army today.'[29] In their hunger for informed opinion, Twitter users — both your common-or-garden followers, and blue-tick accounts with large reach — blasted niche Twitter experts into the stratosphere, without either the ability or the inclination to work out whether what they were amplifying was particularly accurate. This isn't a snipe, as I'm sure I've done the same thing more times than I'd be able to count. Twitter is designed for frictionless sharing, and even the most conscientious users use signifiers of legitimacy (like an academic institution or think-tank in bio, or a tweet being shared by a reputable journalist) as a substitute for independent verification. The right Twitter gimmick, at the right point in the news cycle, can end up wielding influence that's wholly disproportionate to its informational value.

Twitter has become a neurotic fixation — it has melted our brains and warped our behaviour. But it has also transformed how people working across politics and media do their jobs. Social media has combined with the economic pressures on newsrooms to lower the threshold on what enters print and broadcast media. If you're a reporter that's chained to a

computer eight hours a day, expected to churn out multiple stories a shift, combing social media for controversies is a pretty
cost-effective way to meet your word count. To feed the rav-
enous appetites of the content economy, somebody tweeting
something – regardless of how many followers they have, or
how representative their post is of a broader social phenomenon – is a decent enough pretext to publish a news story claiming that there's a 'Twitterstorm' afoot.

The job of a producer isn't to think about how you might
put together a panel of speakers and a line of questioning which
can illuminate various facets of a particular topic: it's to theatri-
cally stage an argument that's already taking place online, which
itself has been fuelled by media coverage, which has been driven
by social media engagement, on and on forever in a feedback
loop of content and outrage. The result of all this is that the
threshold for what constitutes news has dramatically lowered,
and reaction to that 'news'– the arousal of angry, impassioned
attention at a speed that bypasses audience awareness – plays an
outsize role in shaping the news cycle instead.

Some poor soul at the *Daily Express* is tasked with knocking
out a story every time I tweet a joke involving politics, football
or the royal family. 'Corbynista uses England's Euro 2020 success for shameless dig at Churchill' ran one headline,[30] though
my favourite will always be when the beleaguered Oliver
Pritchard-Jones was forced to produce 500 words about a tweet
of mine which argued (correctly) that 'DMX could cut a ribbon
but Prince Philip couldn't make *Flesh of My Flesh, Blood of My
Blood*.'[31] The elevation of something trivial, like someone saying something contentious, doesn't only apply to public figures.
When it serves particular political or narrative purposes, which
I'll explain later on, this scrutiny is extended to private citizens
too. Placards at protests, random interactions on the street, viral
TikTok trends all become the subject of news.

This is where the power of reaction comes in. Much of what I've described already, from combative television debates to Twitter beefs, is about a reactive model of media. Reaction to news has, of course, always formed a part of the way a story is contextualised. A typical news story structure will have both new information and an overview of how different political constituencies respond to that information, as a way to help make sense of it. But modern media values reaction in a very different way. Reaction is both how news outlets assess the impact of a story and becomes an engine driving the production of even more stories. And as George Saunders argues in *The Braindead Megaphone*, this heightening of our attentional environments moulds and warps our very sense of self. We're primed for outsize reactions catalysed by trivial material prompts.

When it comes to how far something goes on social media (the number of shares or amount of times viewed: something which social media has, of course, made quantifiable in a way it never was before) reaction is vital. In May 2023, computer scientists at Cornell University and University of California, Berkeley found that Twitter users were being shown more emotionally provocative content.[32] The platform's algorithm was boosting content that was angry, antagonistic or expressed hostility towards opposing views. A media outlet's ability to tap into those human emotions had a better chance of getting its content seen widely than those that didn't. But what makes somebody feel animated by rage? It's not enough to convey that there's an injustice (after all, the world's full of them). It has to feel personal. People react to content that feels like it's about them, or better yet, is an attack on them.

As William Davies writes, 'Our public sphere is frequently dominated by events you could call "reaction chains", whereby reactions provoke reactions, which provoke further reactions, and so on.'[33] Pundit says something controversial on TV.

Outraged tweets pour in. The next day, a segment focuses on the content of those tweets. Perhaps the day after, the conversation is no longer about what Piers Morgan said, but about whether the backlash amounts to being cancelled. Marina Hyde pops up in the *Guardian* to say how fatuous this all is. The circus moves on. Impulsive emotional responses are both the measure of a story's worth, and the content of that story.

These five trends in media – less original news, more opinion, the explosion of social media, declining standards of newsworthiness and the primacy of reaction – have led to the rise of the microevent. A microevent is something you'll instinctively recognise if you've spent any time consuming news over the last decade. It's a story where the amount of reaction is inversely proportional to the scale of what's actually happened, like a Christmas cracker that generates a nuclear fallout. The defining feature of a microevent is that nothing much has happened, not many people are directly impacted, and yet we're somehow all talking about it.

On Sunday 27 March 2022, at the 94th Academy Awards, Will Smith slapped the comedian Chris Rock across the face. Chris Rock had made a *GI Jane* crack about Jada Pinkett-Smith, widely presumed to be a reference to her public struggle with alopecia which resulted in the loss of her hair. Pinkett-Smith was visibly uncomfortable as the audience, including her husband, laughed at the joke. Seconds later, Will Smith rose from his seat and slapped the comedian, before he sat back down and shouted 'keep my wife's name out your fucking mouth'. Chris Rock reacted the way many of us would have, exclaiming 'Wow, Will Smith just smacked the shit out of me!' He then added, 'That was the greatest night in the history of television.' A little later in the ceremony, Will Smith won the Oscar for Best Actor, an accolade he had openly coveted for decades. But it was the smack people would remember in pub quizzes for years to come.

As the afterparties in Los Angeles wound down, UK Twitter woke up. Memes, banter and hot takes fizzed around the chatosphere at dizzying speeds. A picture of an unimpressed Jada did the rounds, captioned 'Tupac would've shot him down.'[34] But there were others who were taking the whole thing Much More Seriously. BBC *Woman's Hour* invited Nimco Ali, the Independent Government Adviser for Tackling Violence Against Women and Girls (and close friend of Boris and Carrie Johnson), to discuss what was rapidly recast as a 'punch'. Judd Apatow, producer of every movie that's been critically acclaimed by *LadBible*, went further. 'He could have killed him,' he tweeted, seemingly with total sincerity. 'That's pure out of control rage and violence.'

Right-wing talking heads on American cable news made hay of the opportunity to cram as many racist innuendos as they could into eight-minute segments. Jeanine Pirro, when asked for her take on the brouhaha, answered primly, 'I think the Oscars are not the hood.' Helping to turn anti-black subtext into 20 pt Times New Roman, Fox News host Jesse Watters claimed that the slap 'explains why there's such a huge crime problem in this country', alleging that 'it's the first time I've seen the media cover Black-on-Black crime.'

But it wasn't only Smith's detractors who saw the Oscars fisticuffs through an explicitly racial lens. In contrast to the likes of Judd Apatow, Jameela Jamil insisted that Smith only 'slapped him softly enough that Chris barely moved'. 'Don't say #protectBlackwomen for two years and then only condemn Will here,' Jamil tweeted, adding a photo of Will Smith beside a quote taken from Malcolm X's 1962 speech to women in Los Angeles: 'The most disrespected person in America is the Black woman. The most unprotected person in America is the Black woman. The most neglected person in America is the Black woman.'[35]

The slap was the commentary equivalent of a cluster-bomb, polarising on multiple culture-wars lines at once. It was a liberal hero doing something bad. It touched on feminist themes about male violence, libertarian talking points regarding freedom of speech and the myriad ways in which black woman have their humanity degraded. Pundits leveraged the hook of the Oscars to confer a soupçon of newsy spice to what they wanted to say anyway, with one journalist naming Putin's invasion of Ukraine 'the Will Smith Doctrine'. Political leaders and A-listers were expected not only to have an opinion, but to have the *right* opinion. Though no one chose to address it, Will Smith slapping Chris Rock presented a much more urgent question than whether it was right or wrong to smack a comedian for mocking your wife's medical condition: *have we all taken leave of our senses?*

Considering the dominant role of Hollywood in the world's culture industry, it's not wholly surprising that someone getting slapped when presenting an award at the Oscars was big news. But mountains may be made of molehills. There appeared to be a slippage, where the event being widely televised became itself indistinguishable from political significance. Nobody stopped to ask whether there was something faintly absurd about asking the Prime Minister whether they approved of the guy from *Shark Tale* smacking the dude from *Madagascar*. As Will Smith himself might have said, it was one little fight. While the events at the 94th Academy Awards certainly wouldn't have felt trivial to those involved – the slap was a career-defining moment for Jada Pinkett-Smith, Chris Rock and Will Smith – it most certainly is trivial in the grand scheme of things.

Placing events in a wider context is what the media is supposed to do. But the right context doesn't always make for good telly, unlike framing that heightens the stakes and positions trivial things within a larger narrative of cultural conflict. The dissolved boundary between social media chatter, online content production and legacy media output means that contextual histrionics have become a distinctive attribute of current affairs commentary. The most trifling of conflicts is framed within much weightier battles of values, ideologies or identity positions. This isn't necessarily always inappropriate, but it is often overblown. Just because you *can* make various thematic, political, social and cultural connections doesn't mean you always *should*. Yes, something can be contorted so it touches on some wider theme. But that doesn't mean that it's accurate, proportionate or has any great informational value to do so. I've got no real interest in debating the morality of the slap – really, I'm a woman of simple pleasures and find myself agreeing with Chris Rock that it was the greatest night in the history of television. What's actually important isn't the fracas itself but rather its unimportance, and how that shows us the way that microevents like these play such an outsize role in the landscape of media, politics and social commentary.

The defining characteristic of a microevent is that *the number of people impacted by an event, or its severity, is disproportionately small when compared to the volume of commentary that it generates*. A small change in hospital policy regarding how radiographers approach gender identity becomes a staple of morning telly debates and radio phone-in shows. A furore about 'Rule Britannia' being played (but not sung) at the BBC Proms gets brought up in Parliament.[36] And a millionaire entertainer smacking another millionaire entertainer becomes a global headline for days, with leading politicians in Britain and America tasked with coming up with a line which can appease both the pro- and anti-slap lobbies. As T.S. Eliot wrote of *Hamlet*, there is a lack of *objective correlative*: a situation doesn't quite justify the powerful emotions it subsequently unleashes.[37] Or, to put it colloquially, someone's doing too much. If you can wrench yourself from the tumult of the drama, you clock that the script is more than a little overwrought.

To understand the pathology of microevents, let's take a look at a random selection of stories from our old friend Piers Morgan's 2020 book, *Wake Up: Why the world has gone nuts.* An impassioned broadside against cancel culture, wokeness and hypersensitivity, *Wake Up* lists all the ways the world has – in Morgan's view – gone totally gaga. He rattles off a litany of newspaper stories which wound him up: a transgender woman being named 'Female Athlete of the Year', PETA banning the word 'pet',[38] Oxford University students issuing a prohibition on clapping, Canadian Prime Minister Justin Trudeau calling for the word 'mankind' to be outlawed. Just as individual snowflakes make up an avalanche, each one of these microevents piled up to suffocate freedom of speech (in Morgan's view). The world, he writes, has become 'a place where common sense was ignored [and] dissenting views instantly crushed by a howling self-righteous mob'.[39] There's just one problem – all of these examples cited by Piers Morgan, which supposedly show that there's an international crisis of censorship, are wholly or significantly misrepresented by him.

Oxford students didn't ban clapping. Instead, a rather boring motion was passed at the student union allowing sabbatical officers 'to encourage the use of British Sign Language (BSL) clapping, otherwise known as "silent jazz hands" at Student Council meetings and other official SU events.'[40] PETA didn't want to ban the word 'pet',[41] as Morgan claims. What they did do, however, was recommend that animal-lovers update their vocabulary with terms like 'companion' (and generated a shedload of publicity off the back of outraged headlines).[42] Prime Minister Trudeau never suggested making it illegal to utter the phrase 'mankind': he light-heartedly suggested someone use the term 'peoplekind' instead, at an event in 2018. CeCé Telfer, a transgender runner, *was* granted the accolade 'Female Athlete of the Year' – but by *Outsports*, a sports news website that solely covers LGBTQ issues in sports and athletics. It's not surprising that they'd celebrate Telfer's achievements as the first out trans woman to become an NCAA track and field champion – it's literally their *raison d'être*!

In our conversation, Morgan claimed that he doesn't mind admitting when he's wrong ('If I'm spewing inaccurate assertions, which are simply untrue... I think that's irresponsible', though he can't help adding 'it doesn't happen very often'). But when I point out that Justin Trudeau never, as Morgan specifically alleges, 'called for the word mankind to be outlawed because it was sexist',[43] he becomes agitated. 'I didn't say that!' Morgan interjects hotly. After a bit, he softens his stance, insisting that just because he said that the Prime Minister of Canada wanted to outlaw a word, it didn't imply that he wanted to make it illegal. He accuses me of 'confecting a false argument, about a false interpretation', then demands I provide him with evidence of the text. A helpful producer supplies us with a copy of *Wake Up*, so I can remind Piers Morgan of what he actually wrote; that he'd invoked the alleged incident as 'the purest, maddest example of the world going stark raving bonkers, and it came from one of the most powerful men [...] on Planet Earth'.

Despite reluctantly acknowledging that perhaps he shouldn't have used the word 'outlawed', Morgan remains truculent and defensive. 'I think we're playing unnecessary semantics,' he huffs. And in all honesty, I don't like trying to catch people out on the basis of individual words either. But while haggling over precise phrasing is trivial, its implications are not. No one has tried to ban the things that Piers Morgan claims to be under threat. It's a fatal weakness in Morgan's argument that he professes to be disgusted, outraged, horrified and alarmed at the state of society on the basis of news headlines which are at best misleading, and at worst outright falsehoods. He's sacrificed accuracy at the altar of impact. Say what you like about the Oscars slap: at least it happened.

To be fair to Piers Morgan, he's not alone in doing this. Recent years have seen news and current affairs media dominated by frothing outrage at scandals which had only a passing relationship to reality. In 2020, during the height of the global Black Lives Matter protests, Britain's press was up in arms about an episode of *Fawlty Towers* (the 1970s sitcom starring John Cleese) that had supposedly been 'banned' because it repeatedly featured the N-word. Following a massive wave of protests ignited by the murder of George Floyd, a father of five, by cops in Minneapolis, the international movement against racism had broadened its scopes beyond the police to include the enduring legacies of slavery and colonialism. On 7 June 2020, protesters toppled a statue of Edward Colston, one of Britain's most wealthy slave traders, and chucked it in the very harbour where his ships used to dock. Winston Churchill's monument in Parliament Square was graffitied with text that stated (factually) that he 'was a racist'. Cultural artefacts were being fiercely contested on the grounds of race in the UK and the media was hungry for more tales of censorship and vandalism.

Enter UKTV, a BBC-owned streaming service watched only by the hungover, the poorly or the ancient. On 11 June 2020, they removed the *Fawlty Towers* episode pending a review of its content. It was reinstated a few days later, with updated guidance signposting the episode's inclusion of offensive racist language. When you consider that almost all film, television and radio programming comes with warnings for violence, nudity, language and the like, it's difficult to see how FawltyGate was an example of 'the wrath of the censors' coming down like a tonne of bricks on beloved British comedy.[44] But this microevent's low stakes and speedy resolution didn't stop it generating days of furious debate. Jonathan Swain, a *Good Morning Britain* correspondent, was sent to broadcast live from outside UKTV's offices like it was a ministerial resignation: 'Not just statues', he tweeted sombrely, 'but reporting on the removal of a #faultytowers [sic] episode from #UKTV.'[45]

LBC, a digital and FM radio station, covered the story across multiple shows – prompting one affronted woman to tweet that the removal of the episode was proof that the country 'is beyond decadent and gone to the dogs'. 'Our history, culture and way of life is under threat from militant racist groups', she thundered, adding that the government needs 'to reassert the rule of law while lockdown still has some force'.[46] Even after the episode was restored, I was invited to debate on BBC 5 Live whether the brouhaha showed there was a conflict between British values and the Black Lives Matter movement – in spite of the fact that not one protester placard had mentioned *Fawlty Towers*.

John Cleese himself weighed in on Twitter. He accused the BBC of being 'cowardly and gutless and contemptible'.[47] The purpose of Major Gowen's N-word rant, Cleese argued, was to discredit the character's racist views – although oddly enough, the former Monty Python man had approved of a 2013 decision by the BBC to broadcast the episode with the N-word edited out entirely.[48] Though Basil Fawlty's brush with censorship was brief, it birthed further opportunities for Cleese to fulminate against the dangers of oversensitivity. In 2021, it was announced that he would present a documentary for Channel 4, aired the following year, titled *John Cleese: Cancel Me*. The programme would examine 'why a new "woke" generation is trying to rewrite the rules on what can and can't be said':[49] because nothing screams 'I'm being silenced' like being commissioned to explore an experience of being censored that can barely be said to have happened in the first place.

There are too many more microevents which turned out to be less than the sum of their outcry to name them all: the condemnation from public intellectuals like Richard Dawkins and Tom Holland because Stirling University removed Jane Austen from its syllabus to 'decolonise the curriculum'[50] (they didn't, it was a special module which changed author every year), fury in the *Daily Express* that Brighton schools banned staff using the terms 'Mum' and 'Dad' because of 'woke cancel culture'[51] (didn't happen – four schools simply suggested teachers say 'grown-ups' to children who aren't being raised by their mother or father) and so on.[52] How are we to explain this epidemic of misleading coverage, and disproportionately scandalised commentary, that's poisoning our information environment?

Perhaps journalists have spontaneously all become rubbish at their jobs, and each inaccurate report is simply the result of honest mistakes in fact-checking. But there's a shared theme amongst all these stories: an illegitimate, but powerful, minority has somehow hijacked the levers which dictate the boundaries of what's considered socially acceptable. And they're using that power to crack down on the speech and opinions of a silenced majority. The problem isn't isolated instances of erroneous reportage: it's that the incentives of journalism have changed. You're rewarded for producing content which contributes to a narrative that certain minority identity groups are oppressing the public at large. Each misleading microevent stacks up to create a deceptive overall impression. And our modern media culture, obsessed with making big splashes out of small-time stories, is particularly advantageous for the political right.

Why is this the case? First and foremost, individualised, identity-driven stories tend to perform better, and generate more online reaction, than news stories about systems and structures.

Foreign affairs, climate change, housing, corporate activities and long-term social trends often don't get clicks: because they're impersonal, and often lack individual villains, they're not rewarded by social media feeds that prioritise polarising, or personalised, content. Though the government's failures on constructing social housing, or backsliding on climate commitments, certainly impact people's lives, it's not articulated in a way that cuts particularly close to the bone. These stories can be stats- and jargon-heavy. They don't stimulate impulsive emotions.

Even for outlets which have unusually politically aware audiences, this is challenging. Whenever my colleagues and I peek under the bonnet at Novara Media, a consistent finding is that it's difficult to get our audience to engage with the content they tell us they want more of in reader surveys. We're constantly asked to make more content about big, macroeconomic and geopolitical matters – but it's consistently less popular than Westminster commentary, or culture war interventions. This is very good news if you're a right-wing political strategist. Every media incentive is aligned to make slow-moving societal disintegration slide down the reaction agenda. Anger is directed away from elite interests, and towards matters of identity, especially those joyless snowflakes who tote their own moral purity like it's a Birkin bag. I suppose there's something simpler and more satisfying about getting annoyed by self-righteous vegans, rather than a climate crisis that's making every food item you buy more expensive.

You'd be forgiven for thinking that this might mean that 'social justice' causes – feminism, anti-racism, LGBTQ rights, etc. – would stand to benefit from the heightened visibility of identity-driven media stories. It's certainly the case that there is far greater awareness, and pop cultural representation, of minority identities. This is something I'll explore in detail in a couple of chapters' time. But there's a reason why you don't tend to see these identity groups, and their political advocates, getting a favourable hearing on shows like Piers Morgan's. It's because the framing is stacked against them from the start, and the nature of political discussion online makes it easier to present such causes in a favourable light. Social media, for all of its virtues, is an infinity pool of people posting nuts things. So if you're the editor or producer on a debate show, and you want to have a big hoo-ha over whether trans rights have gone too far, it's remarkably straightforward to pluck a tweet out of context where a trans person appears to be saying something unreasonable and get pundits to react to it on telly.

Indeed, it doesn't even have to be a real tweet, from a real trans person, to make this shtick work. In January 2023, Morgan found himself infuriated that an online trans rights group had accused Aretha Franklin of perpetuating harmful gender stereotypes with her 1968 hit 'Natural Woman', and called for Spotify to remove the track from its streaming platform. He tweeted a news story about the demand, lodged by 'The Trans Cultural Mindfulness Alliance', writing 'It's time to tell these woke wastrels to f*ck off and end this nonsense.'[53] This particular story fitted with a generalised narrative that trans rights were in conflict with majority values, and that trans people were prone to making hysterical and unreasonable demands in order to protect their sensitive constitutions. But like so many of the micro events cited in *Wake Up*, there appears to be no evidence that any trans rights group had sincerely called for 'Natural Woman' to be censored. In fact, 'The Trans Cultural Mindfulness Alliance' admits to being a parody account, and does not appear to have any trans individuals involved at all. It was an anti-woke satire, taken with utmost seriousness by one of the most famous and well-paid journalists in the world, who in theory was aligned with its own anti-woke stance. I'd suggest that certain media operators have selectively lowered their threshold of scepticism when it proves politically expedient to do so. Social media has proved helpful to the left in disseminating progressive ideas. It's also been a godsend to our political opponents, to make us look ridiculous.

But as I mentioned earlier, it's not just public figures and political organisations (both real and fictional) who get held up as objects of derision. It happens to private citizens as well. In June 2019, a young woman was filmed shouting 'Nazi scum' at a male Donald Trump supporter in London and laughing when the man had a milkshake thrown at him. Though she later apologised for her actions, that didn't stop the UK press from publishing her name and trawling through her social media accounts. The sorry episode was used as a pretext to cast aspersions on the left in general. On BBC Two's *Politics Live*, I was asked to debate whether the 'hard left' had a nastiness problem with two Conservative MPs, Tony Blair's former speechwriter and a journalist from the right-wing *Sunday Telegraph* – not exactly what you'd call a fair fight. The framing of the discussion made it clear there was only one answer that would be considered acceptable. Yes, the left are all bastards. We're mean, angry and violent. No, we're not a legitimate voice in politics. Sure, I can see myself out. Ironically, after the cameras stopped rolling, one of my fellow panellists got themselves into such a fluster that they ended up screaming and swearing at one of the Tory MPs. Weirdly though, *Politics Live* didn't then see fit to programme a whole show about whether pundits are uniquely nasty or unable to emotionally self-regulate. What happened is that one woman's unfortunate outburst was used to disparage a political movement of hundreds of thousands of people. And if you queried whether it was reasonable to hold a private citizen to the same level of accountability as journalists might a politician, you were cast out of the circle of respectable opinion-holders. This technique, as with how the

'Libs of TikTok' account has singled out individuals to demonise LGBTQ people in the United States, has a powerful effect on shaping the political and media agenda.

The media's distorted portrayal of social justice causes, with its emphasis on hysteria, absurdity and antagonism, is a core component of the Minority Rule moral panic. The impression you get from news and current affairs programming is that left-wing and identity-based movements are teeming with people who want to scream at you. The left, despite its claims to represent the majority of people's political and economic interests, is obsessed with transforming social norms in order to meet the needs of fundamentally unreasonable people. But one of the reasons that it's not so easy to dismiss this relentlessly negative depiction of the left in the media is that many people have direct experience of getting drawn into hostile debates on social media.

Whether it's relatively closed networks like Facebook, or open ones like Twitter and TikTok, social media makes finding people who vehemently disagree with us, and vice versa, totally frictionless. Angry interactions are boosted algorithmically, but they also appeal to a foundational human desire: the need to be right. On scales both small and vast, being on the receiving end of an online backlash is a modern-day rite of passage. It sucks to be told that you're ignorant, reprehensible, offensive or wrong-headed (even if we are all capable of being those things). And it's easy for feelings of defensiveness to curdle into a sense of persecution. Broadcasters like Piers Morgan, who have their own yarns to spin about being unfairly maligned by the woke mob, are able to tap into more ordinary experiences of being done wrong by the internet. This structure of feeling, where the media colludes with tech platforms to make us more suspicious of one another, and more pitying of ourselves, is once again advantageous for the right. It's inherently alienating, and corrosive to the project of solidarity between strangers. Left-wing movements require people who don't know each other to work together. But despite the internet's promise to connect us with near-infinite numbers of human beings, we've ended up with fathomless petty conflict. Social media generates ever more reasons for us to mistrust and resent one another, by pulling us into low-stakes beefing and calling it a leisure activity.

Social media and legacy media haven't simply turned our attention into a commodity: they've done the same with our identities. It's useful for producers and guest bookers to treat Twitter and YouTube as a pool of prospective pundits. Here are a load of people already sharing their opinions for an engaged audience, who have an intuitive sense of what kind of content goes far on social media. The Twitter-to-TalkRadio pipeline makes perfect sense when broadcast media has experienced a profound shift, thinking of itself more as 'content' than programming. But there's something else going on here too: the leveraging of identity. Race, gender and class identification are stand-ins for all kinds of political and cultural positioning. If you're young, BAME, a woman or part of the LGBTQ community, you become the personification of a broader cloud of beliefs and political outlooks. You're the voice of BLM, trans rights, climate activism, i.e. views associated with identity-based liberation movements or progressive-left politics. This kind of typecasting, however, has also generated the emergence of a pundit whose job is to play *against* type.

There's an old saying in journalism: when a dog bites a man, that's not news because it happens so often. But man bites dog? That's a different story entirely. A black person who rails against the evils of critical race theory; a woman who decries feminism; a millennial who adores conservatism; a gay person who deplores the transgender community. Leaving aside the question of whether these individuals are always wholly sincere in their beliefs, their function in the hot take-industrial complex is to convey a misleading impression of the distribution of opinion amongst any given demographic. You can, of course, find people of colour who are hostile to the aims of anti-racist movements, or women who look sceptically at claims of being disadvantaged on the basis of their gender, but that's not an accurate representation of what most of those who share the same identity characteristics think.

No identity bracket is a monolith, but you can find a majority or plurality consensus on particular issues. The media actively seek out brown people who decry woke culture, or women who are transphobic, precisely because it makes movements against racism and transphobia seem a lot more controversial within communities than they are. These individuals are the linchpins of the Minority Game. They're minorities themselves who tell audiences that minority causes are a threat to majority interests and should be variously mocked, dismissed or crushed.

And there's reason to believe that this is a deliberate and manipulative strategy on the part of editors and producers. The use of people of colour as a mouthpiece for racist, reactionary or so-called 'anti-woke' opinions isn't just a case of thoughtful pundit casting. It's been alleged that the process is a lot more underhand than even I'd assumed. In September 2023, Dominique Samuels, then a broadly conservative black British writer, alleged that the *Daily Mail* had published ghostwritten articles under her name, without indicating that they had been written by somebody else.[54] One was an article in which she argued that Meghan Markle's break with the British royal family had been because of her 'woke views' and not, as Markle alleges, racism. Samuels said that the paper had asked her 'to be the face of a ghost-written, negative, verging on racist piece' about Notting Hill Carnival,[55] in order to whip up an 'outrage fest' directed at Caribbean culture.

Neither Samuels nor the *Daily Mail* responded to my requests for comment, but one newspaper reported that an internal investigation has been launched at the tabloid in light of her allegations.[56] Though Dominique Samuels insisted that 'it's pretty much standard' for newspapers to ghostwrite guest columns, this is absolutely not true. Politicians and celebrities regularly get someone else to write op-eds for them, but pundits and commentators are generally expected to pen their own pieces. After all, it's their opinions that the readers are interested in. And no newspaper wants to pay twice for the same article. If it's true that Dominique Samuels' articles were ghostwritten, the reason why is obvious: the *Daily Mail* wanted to lend credibility to its anti-black editorial position by attaching reactionary opinions to the face of a young black woman. It's the opposite of authentic, serious politics. It's playing a game with people's identities, to undermine the cause of anti-racism.

There has always been a ring of commentary around news media – but social media has profoundly shifted the balance between the two. Commentary infrastructure has blossomed, while news-gathering has shrunk. The searing dysfunction of online opinion culture is, to a significant extent, a result of chronic malaise in the world of legacy media. The trivial, identity-driven controversies that dominate current affairs media present an essentially misleading picture of what's important. The level of outrage provoked by canny broadcasters, columnists, editors and producers is totally out of kilter with actual harm. The world of reaction, debate, accusation and condemnation created by the likes of Piers Morgan is a carnival hall of mirrors. Big issues look small, and trivial ones are grotesquely inflated. We're jabbed into impulsive states of emotional arousal, our critical faculties are dulled. While we're debating whether Apu is racist or whatever, the Mr Burnses of the world are robbing us blind. Wages and living standards fall while we're locked into trivial outrage cycles. We can't think before we react; we can't stop to wonder whether the thing that's making us so mad is actually true.

The media machine that drives Minority Rule works by turning citizen against citizen: we're more inclined to mistrust someone who shares our material conditions, than those who are in charge of shaping them. Reality manipulation is key to any power grab – and as we'll see in the next chapter, elite political media is both unable and unwilling to put up much of a fight. Our paranoid fantasies about Minority Rule allow the real elites to wriggle off the hook.

3

The Lobby

An MP, on the day of her much-publicised defection from the Labour Party over antisemitism, gestured at me on the BBC's *Politics Live* programme while saying that 'the recent history of the party I've just left suggested it's not just about being black or a funny tinge'. And it was then that I had a mini-epiphany: the average politician is a lot stupider than the average member of the public.

I wouldn't say that I ever had a particularly high opinion of politicians. But there were certain assumptions that I took for granted. I thought that even those who actively made this country and planet a worse place to live were at least clever, purposeful and coherent. This belief didn't survive contact with meeting them in real life. For every MP or advisor I came across who was shrewd, strategic and formidable, there were three more who had a runny egg where a brain should be. There was the ex-speechwriter to a Prime Minister who turned the air blue screaming invective at one of his political opponents as soon as the cameras stopped rolling. There was the Shadow Leader of the House of Commons who complained to the radio host about being asked a question on rent caps rather than answering whether her party supported them or not. Time and again I came across political operators who were thin-skinned, thick-witted and oddly bad at emotionally self-regulating. They weren't people you'd trust to make a salad dressing, let alone dictate the fate of a nation.

People are the products of systems. As a friend of mine likes to say, if aliens came down tomorrow and tried to work out what was really important to the citizens of Earth, they'd be forced to conclude that our species is dedicated to identifying individuals who are really good at football. Most young males, at some point in their lives, will come into contact with a teacher or coach who will assess them for speed, agility, ball retention and reflexes. If you've got the skills and the desire, you'll ascend upwards through a pyramid which culminates with the Jules Rimet, the Ballon d'Or and the Carabao Cup (all right, some of these are more prestigious than others). It's as close to a meritocracy as we've been able to create: even nepo babies like Erling Haaland are undeniably good at what they do. And when you, the punter, see Lionel Messi carving up a defence, or Kylian Mbappé going sicko mode, you can reasonably infer that this guy is probably the best guy in the world who could do his job. Now look at your Prime Minister, or President, and ask yourself the same question: is this the best person for the job, out of all the people who could possibly do it? Are they the most intelligent, dedicated and empathetic individual out there? The answer is no – and it's because a system of filters and incentives made it that way.

This chapter lays out how the system works to keep producing a political class whose primary functions are to chase headlines, protect capital and divert public anger towards convenient targets. Key to this is understanding how the distinction between politics and political media has collapsed, and what that's done to our sense of what's important. Politicians have become little more than glorified podcasters – and podcasters have gone through the revolving door into the halls of power. Rather than setting the agenda through their impact on the material conditions of the country, our leaders are caught up reacting to press prompts about the outrage of the day. This has happened because, instead of holding MPs' feet to the fire on substantive issues, the lobby's news agenda is an extension of social media and tabloid culture wars. They lend legitimacy to moral panics and incentivise politicians to take up increasingly reactionary positions in the hope of ventriloquising the values framed as those of the silent majority. Politicians become pundits, rather than decision-makers, acting as though they're an extension of the commentariat. This has been fertile ground for those looking to breed paranoia about there being a malign agenda on the part of progressive movements to establish a form of Minority Rule. What this is all designed to conceal is the fact that the political class has gladly ceded its power to corporations, oligarchs and the ownership class. The state has become ever more subservient to the bloated god of market forces. Politicians have become petty and diminished figures in a reflection of what capitalism has done to their domain.

What do politicians dream of?

One nondescript autumn day in October 2022, in an unlovely meeting room in Birmingham, a woman dressed in cerulean blue shares her most cherished ambition with a rapt audience. Suella Braverman, daughter of Indian migrants from Kenya and Mauritius, is the Home Secretary. Though she'll later resign in disgrace, she's currently the third Home Secretary in a row to come from a minority ethnic background, and, at this moment, three of the four great offices of state are held by people of colour. If a time-traveller from forty years ago (a time when nearly every MP in the House of Commons was white, and most were men) had the fortune to wander into this Conservative Party conference event, they would have thought that they'd stumbled upon a progressive's paradise. The colour bar has been smashed. So what does Suella Braverman, high-flying tribune of post-racial utopia, aspire to? 'I would love to be having, [on] the front page of *The Telegraph*, a plane taking off to Rwanda,' she says, flinging a grin at the associate Politics Editor of that very newspaper. She turns to beam at the audience. 'That's my dream, that's my obsession.'[1] Not slaying the five giants of poverty, eliminating serious youth violence, or even putting your name to a suspension bridge. No, the most a minister could hope for was being patted on the head by a right-wing newspaper for deporting asylum seekers fleeing war or persecution, just as her own father did in the 1960s.

Later we'll look in detail at the history of immigration policy in UK politics. But right now, I want to explore the system of incentives which produced a Home Secretary who dreamt of nothing more ambitious than being the dog who was wagged by its tail. We've seen how the talking-head industrial complex rewards pundits who play against type, such as women arguing against feminism, or black people condemning BLM. But this wasn't just any old pundit. She was one of the most powerful MPs in the country. What's significant isn't simply that the Home Secretary was gung-ho about a particularly nasty, inhumane policy. It's not even that, as a South Asian woman, some might expect her to have been more sympathetic towards migrants and people of colour. Suella Braverman, like any government minister, was supposed to have a mandate that comes from the electorate, not the *Telegraph*. But the way in which politicians and the press work together has landed us with politicians whose one lever of power (to paraphrase one of the greatest political analysts of our age) is turning a big dial that says 'Racism' on it, and looking back at the audience for approval like a contestant on *The Price Is Right*.[2]

This exchange, between Suella Braverman and *Telegraph* writer Christopher Hope, suggests something troubling: the distinction between politics and media has collapsed. Politicians behave more like pundits, signalling their stance on social issues to be cheered by sections of the media, rather than people who actually have the power to transform conditions in the country at large. Meanwhile, political journalism (in particular, the work of correspondents whose job it is to stalk the corridors of power) has failed to fish crap out of the information pool. Indeed, all too often, these custodians of quality news are responsible for pumping rubbish into it in the first place.

To be fair to Ms Braverman, she's not alone in twirling for the applause of newspaper editors. She's merely the only person willing to admit the truth about the incentives that determine how politicians behave. There has been a shift in the balance of power between the place where politics happens, i.e. the Houses of Parliament, and the means by which those politics are disseminated to the public, i.e. political media. The press and communications portion of a politician's job has ballooned with the expansion of mass media. Once upon a time, parliamentarians could rely on newspapers printing their speeches in full – Harold Wilson, when he was Prime Minister in 1966, objected to the BBC being allowed to film inside the House of Commons in case they 'cut the videotape up' and took 'a little bit of speech and introduce[d] it into a magazine programme.'[3] It didn't take long, however, for MPs to adapt to the era of soundbites. From Margaret Thatcher's insistence that 'the lady's not for turning' to Tony Blair feeling 'the hand of history' on his shoulder, the art of speechwriting focused less on grand argumentation and more on snippets that would sound good out of context. These days, if you can bring yourself to watch the entirety of a politician's interview, you'll notice how weirdly repetitive they are: it's not uncommon to see an MP parrot the exact same sentence in response to two or three different questions. This isn't because they've been kicked in the head by a mule; MPs simply speak that way because they know that the tape will invariably be cut up, with little bits put online. No one sees a politician offer their full line of reasoning any more. They're all just disembodied heads, floating around on the internet, hoping to get a focus-grouped talking point out into the atmosphere.

But I don't think that the unedifying spectacle of admitting, out loud and on camera, that you dream of making the *Telegraph*'s front page can simply be explained by the emergence of soundbite politics. It speaks to a deeper transformation in how elected representatives view their roles. There are two traditional modes that usually get cited when people discuss representative politics: the delegate model, where MPs are sent forth by their electorates as delegates from the constituency, to reflect the views of the voters who elected them, and the trustee model, where they're instead imbued with the autonomy to speak and act as they see fit, even if it means going against the desires of their constituents. Both of these models are predicated, however, on MPs doing things that have the power to really change the social, political and economic circumstances of the people who vote them into office. Recent years, however, have seen the emergence of a third model of parliamentarian: the pundit.

The pundit politician behaves much like the talking heads discussed in the previous chapter. Their job, like mine (except not, because it's not their real job), is to pop up on telly (or in print) and say things which purportedly reflect a wide body of opinion out there in society. Their purpose is to contest media space, with matters of policy secondary to signalling positions on the airwaves. It's a curious combination of heightened visibility, coupled with declarations about how powerless the political system is to do anything about the problems of the day.

And perhaps no one has been able to leverage this contradiction better than Nigel Farage. More than any other single public figure in the UK, Farage has been able to catapult fringe issues into the mainstream. Though Euroscepticism was a prevalent sentiment, it wasn't a big electoral motivator in the early 1990s and 2000s. UKIP, in 1997, only managed to get 0.34 per cent of the total vote share. And well, now look.[4] In 2020, Farage went to the English coast on a near-daily basis, sharing self-shot video of asylum seekers arriving by small boats, until the mainstream media followed suit. 'The invasion is on,' he declared on Twitter.[5] Just a few days later, the BBC was running stories with headlines like 'Channel migrants: Small boats "major threat to UK"'.[6] During the COVID-19 lockdowns, Farage ran a similar one-man campaign against housing asylum seekers in hotels – and once more, where Nigel's Twitter videos led, legacy media followed. Both stopping small boats arrivals and shifting asylum seekers away from hotels and towards barges and barracks would become mainstream Conversative policies.

In July 2024, three young girls were stabbed to death, and ten more people, eight of them children, were hospitalised when a Taylor Swift dance class was attacked in Southport. At the time of writing, this is breaking news. A seventeen-year-old male named Axel Rudakubana, born in Wales to Rwandan parents, has been arrested and charged. As rumours swirled online that the assailant was a Muslim, or a small boats asylum seeker, the far right began to gather in Southport the next day. They rioted, attacking a mosque, looting a shop, hurling bricks at police and singing racist football chants. The following night, further rioting broke out in Hartlepool, where videos emerged online of a non-white man being punched for no obvious reason while walking down the street. And among the horror, trauma, grief and shock, Nigel Farage has once more spotted an opportunity for political advancement. He posted a self-shot video on social media, asking why the brutal murders weren't being treated as terror-related, speculating that 'truth is being withheld from us'.[7] Of course, as a sitting MP, Farage could've used his parliamentary position to get more answers out of the government. At the very least, he could have attended the statement on the Southport stabbings in the House of Commons.[8] He did neither; being a pundit, whipping up fear and speculation, served his purposes better. Farage derives his power from being an anti-politician, and not from behaving like one.

The pundit-politician loves nothing more than a gesture. In 2020, when thousands of people took to the streets in support of Black Lives Matter, the Labour Party were under pressure to come up with a response to the sight of the nation's youth demanding action on institutional racism. Their answer was to stage a photoshoot, in which Keir Starmer and Angela Rayner took the knee in an empty conference room, gazing into nothing. The image was shared on Twitter, bearing the caption 'We kneel with all those opposing anti-Black racism. #BlackLivesMatter.'[9] The Labour Party leader's solidarity with BLM protesters, however, didn't last long. Later that month, he denounced the movement's call to defund the police as 'nonsense', adding that 'nobody should be saying anything about defunding the police, and I would have no truck with that – I was the Director of Public Prosecutions for five years.'[10] While it would come as no surprise that Keir Starmer isn't an abolitionist in the mould of Angela Y. Davis, what was remarkable was how easily Starmer dismissed the complaints of protesters alleging widespread and institutional racial discrimination in UK policing. Keir Starmer claimed instead that the protests were solely concerned with the murder of George Floyd, and were 'about reflecting something completely different... what happened dreadfully in America just a few weeks ago'. The symbolism of taking the knee was completely decoupled from any meaningful policy stance. It was just about signalling where he stood on a news story, rather than suggesting any particular political change he would enact were he to form a government. Keir Starmer wasn't just hollow behind the eyes when he took the knee against anti-black racism: it was a completely empty gesture.

Keir Starmer certainly isn't the only politician to have taken a side in a BLM-flavoured culture war. Priti Patel, then Home Secretary, joined the esteemed ranks of Dominique Samuels and Calvin Robinson, all of them people of colour, in declaring that football fans had the right to boo their national team taking the knee in protest against racism.[11] 'I just don't support people participating in that type of gesture politics,' she told GB News.[12] There's a certain irony here. On the one hand, the erstwhile Home Secretary was professing that she couldn't stand gesture politics. And yet, on the other, here she was participating in the exact same kind of values-signalling that she decried: the entire purpose of that comment was to demonstrate to a certain section of the media, and the audience that it serves, that she's not on the same side as all those wokies and protesters.

Patel's comments came hot on the heels of Lee Anderson, at the time a Conservative MP, vowing to boycott England's games in the Euros while they continued taking the knee. He wrote on Facebook that 'For the first time in my life I will not be watching my beloved England team whilst they are supporting a political movement whose core principles aim to undermine our very way of life.'[13]

Leaving aside whether it's telling on yourself to call anti-racism a principle that undermines your very way of life, the kind of hyperbolic parping here from Anderson is more like something you'd see from a *Good Morning Britain* guest than an elected Member of Parliament. These cycles of shrieking, denunciation and condemnation are the very definition of pundit behaviour. It's unedifying. And while you might expect a right-wing populist like Lee Anderson to dive head-first into culture wars issues, even snoozefest technocrats find themselves compelled to weigh in. Why? Because it's what's demanded of them by the country's top political journalists.

It's often said that 'there are decades where nothing happens; and there are weeks where decades happen'. While I was writing this book, the British Conservative Party toppled one Prime Minister (Boris Johnson), appointed another (Liz Truss), and then ditched her just over a month into her premiership. Her replacement, Rishi Sunak, ended up leading his party into a bruising general election loss against Keir Starmer's Labour Party. I'll count my lucky stars if he's still in Downing Street by the time this gets to print. It's been a good long while since nothing happened – volatility has become the new normal.

But if there's one constant, it's the lobby: a chosen coterie of journalists with access to Parliament who function as a kind of Greek chorus to the grand tragedy of British politics. While most people in the country aren't that engaged in politics, these guys (and they are mostly guys) are obsessives. It's their job to communicate to the rest of the country what's going on in the halls of power, and what the most important political stories of the day are. The lobby are meant to hold politicians to account. Political reporters even have their own offices inside the House of Commons. Known as 'Burma Road', for reasons which have been lost to the mists of history, this third-floor hallway is the 'throbbing heart of the parliamentary lobby system',[14] in the words of veteran political reporter Andrew Marr. Journalists who've been bestowed a lobby pass – a mark of favour that elevates you above the humdrum scum working the crime or culture beats – are fond of emphasising the Burma Road's distinct lack of glamour: stained carpets, stale air and mouse droppings. But despite the affected protestations of 'what, this old thing?', a lobby pass is highly coveted by those working in news and current affairs. It's a passport to insider status, a sign that you've made it. The lobby comes wreathed in a cloud of importance and authority, dictating headlines and shaping the political agenda of the day. Sir Alan Duncan, a former Conservative minister, described them as 'the media's elite commandos', who have a 'critical place in the informed reporting of our politics'.[15]

In times of instability (i.e. pretty much continuously from 2016 to at least this very day), the lobby truly come into their own: buzzing around Westminster like wasps at a picnic, cornering special advisors, spokespeople and MPs, churning out hastily compiled insider analyses of what's supposedly going on in the literal corridors of power. 'At a time when the questions are bigger, our responsibilities are bigger and we take it very seriously' explained then-BBC Political Editor Laura Kuenssberg in an interview with *Press Gazette*. 'As hacks we love stories that are crashing all around you rather than taking a long time to develop and eventually emerge.'[16]

But the lobby's love for stories which fall into their laps, as opposed to the ones they have to find for themselves, isn't always the best guarantee of producing good journalism. Not that I'm one to talk, but lobby journalists are glued to their phones. The 2019 general election was a moment where we really got to see how much of the lobby's work involves simply repeating whatever somebody has texted them. A few days before the country went to the polls, Kuenssberg, along with ITV News editors Robert Peston and Paul Brand, and the *Telegraph*'s Associate Editor Camilla Tominey all tweeted within the same five-minute period that a Labour activist had punched a Conservative special advisor outside a hospital in Leeds. Tominey went further, claiming that the activist had been arrested for assault. The only problem? It never happened. A video emerged on Twitter not much later showing that a protester had been pointing at something and the distracted advisor had walked into him, lightly tapping his head against the back of the activist's hand.

Not to be deterred, Kuenssberg branded the video evidence a 'pretty grim encounter'. If this counts as a grim encounter, I can only imagine what Kuenssberg would call a stubbed toe. Perhaps a war crime?

Though she and Robert Peston apologised for the 'confusion' of saying someone was punched, they both stressed the authority of their sources. The BBC Political Editor insisted the story had come from no fewer than two sources, while Peston said that he had been told by 'senior Tories'. Journalists made a magnanimous show of being 'happy' to correct false information; none seemed particularly interested in how they themselves ended up being conveyor belts for that false information. It didn't cross their minds that the problem might have been tweeting, as cast-iron fact, something that had come to them from highly partisan sources, without first making sure that it was actually true. As the columnist Gary Younge wrote earlier that year, senior political journalists had clearly begun to think of themselves as mere conduits for whatever fraff has been WhatsApped to them by powerful people. It is 'conveyed neat – uncritiqued, unfiltered and unprocessed', and then 'injected into the conversational bloodstream caffeinated by social media'. In Younge's words, 'the act of journalism is limited to getting the quote and distributing, and does not extend to verifying it, contextualising it and making sense of it.'[17]

Often, social media's effect on traditional journalism is likened to internet vandals ransacking the marble palaces of Rome. In fact, it's often the opposite: people with staff jobs at venerable broadcasters and print publications use Twitter in a way which is wholly at odds with the journalistic standards they're meant to uphold. To be blunt, it's standard practice amongst the pantheon of elite political journalists to simply tweet out whatever they've been texted by a source and present it as gospel. Though it's common to find journalists decrying the real problem of online misinformation, they're less interested in examining their own industry's role in perpetuating it. Twitter, the great equaliser, turns everyone into a dumbass.

The incentive for journalists to sacrifice accuracy for speed was, of course, sharpened by social media accelerating the speed at which information circulates. But this did not create the problem of journalists being used as the personal mouthpieces of powerful people who wish to manipulate public perception. Indeed, that is encoded in the DNA of British political reporting.

Since the nineteenth century, the lobby has acted as both ferryman and gatekeeper of political news. The creation of the journalistic lobby came at the same time that the public were barred, in the 1870s, from entering the Members' lobby and 'inconveniencing' politicians. Literally, the public were kicked out, and the trusted journos took their place. This is the central contradiction of the lobby. Whatever their role in imparting critical political information from Westminster to the nation at large, the lobby was set up to protect those in power from the public. Twitter makes it easier to detect symptoms of journalistic dysfunction, but it is not the underlying cause of malaise itself.

Lobby journalism is built on the foundation of access in return for anonymity. Though attribution practices have changed over the years (in the lobby's infancy, briefings were so secret that no one was even allowed to admit that they existed), lobby rules still dictate that journalists don't name their sources in dealings with MPs. The justification for this shadowy network of anonymous sources is that it enables lobby journalists to convey advance information about government policy, trends of opinion amongst MPs or divisions amongst ministers, and shed light on the various plots, schemes and factional eye-gouging that make up the business of Westminster.[18] At its best, the lobby operates as a kind of TMZ for unattractive people. Sources in the know drip-feed information to journalists deeply embedded within the system, and the public gets to see at least some events unfold in the real time of the Westminster working day.

But this alignment of professional interest has a deeply personal dimension, one which is less easy to immediately detect. Though they compete with each other for plum positions and sources, the members of the lobby are very much a tribe. There's a reason why Westminster is only half-jokingly referred to as a 'village'. The working environment in and around Parliament is cloistered, bordering on claustrophobic. So when I find a lobby journalist who's willing to lift the lid on how their enclave operates, it's on the condition of anonymity. They'd lose their job if they went on the record. 'The incentive [in lobby journalism]', he tells me, 'is for there *not* to be a predator-prey relationship' between reporters and the politicians they're supposed to be holding to account. 'So much of it is about access. How you rise – how you become successful as a lobby journalist – is getting access to politicians, and government ministers.' And the best way to get access? 'Go for coffee, get drinks, get to know them, be friends with them!' Chumminess is the lubricant of lobby journalism.

There's a price to pay for not playing the game of chums. 'If you do have a go at them,' says the anonymous lobby hack, 'advisors and MPs won't speak to you. You don't get invited to certain things.' If you're seen as too critical or too bolshy, and people in cannily positioned political jobs stop wanting to be your mate, then your worth as a lobby correspondent plummets. 'It makes it hard to get a promotion, it makes it hard to get picked up by publications.' And this, I'm told, plays a crucial role in 'narrowing the range of people that get to the top'.

Revolving Door Goes 'Whoosh'
This culture of collegial camaraderie between political journalists and politicians blurs the lines that would otherwise make

their roles distinct. 'There's a kind of revolving door between the two,' explains my lobby source. 'There are so many members of the lobby who've got partners that are Conservative MPs. Or they were previously Conservative advisors, or they've gone back and forth between the two.' It's not difficult to decipher who he's got in mind. As we were chatting in London Bridge, the 'Partygate' scandal rumbled on just a hop, skip and a tube ride away in Westminster. Prime Minister Boris Johnson (who'd be toppled from his post just a couple of months later when disgruntled Tory backbenchers decide that his non-monogamous relationship with personal integrity posed too much of a danger to their own political ambitions) was scrapping for his premiership's survival, after reports emerged that parties raged in Downing Street while the rest of the country was locked down to prevent coronavirus transmission. And how did the story reach the public sphere? Because Allegra Stratton – ex-*Newsnight* editor-turned-government spokesperson – had joked about such a gathering in leaked footage. After the recording emerged in December 2021, Stratton resigned in disgrace. 'I will regret those remarks for the rest of my days,' she said tearfully, reading from a piece of paper outside her Islington home.[19]

In politics, anyone is expendable – and Allegra Stratton learned that particular lesson in an especially brutal fashion. But in case you were in danger of feeling too sorry for her, recall that Ms Stratton was familiar with some of the crueller practices of the trade. In 2012, when she was editor of *Newsnight*, Allegra Stratton interviewed council employee and mother-of-one Shanene Thorpe. Thorpe had been approached by the BBC to share her experiences as a working mum, forced to claim benefits in order to cover the cost of living. Instead, she was subject to aggressive and humiliating questioning, including being asked why she chose to keep her child. Stratton asked why Thorpe didn't simply share a small flat with her mum rather than claiming housing benefit. 'It's a choice you're making,' she argued, 'and it's a choice that comes with a price tag attached.'[20]

The BBC were later forced to apologise on air (after Shanene Thorpe circulated a petition) for wrongly characterising Shanene Thorpe as unemployed and wholly dependent on benefits. But rather than being an honest mistake, allegations surfaced suggesting that Allegra Stratton had been hell-bent on finding someone to interview who fitted the mould of work-shy scrounger. According to *Private Eye*, Stratton had rejected interviewees put forward by Tower Hamlets council whose stories were unsuitably sympathetic: the magazine reported that she shouted, 'You must have got people living on benefits as a lifestyle choice!'[21]

And with that media background, Allegra Stratton certainly did not lack for friends in high places. Her days as a journalist for the BBC and ITV News meant there was a chorus of sympathetic voices from across punditland to soften the blow of a forced resignation. By resigning, she showed 'a sense of responsibility' absent from those in charge of designing and enforcing lockdown rules, said Fraser Nelson, editor of the *Spectator* and the boss of James Forsyth, Stratton's husband and political editor of the same magazine.[22] In an article about the furore, Nelson framed himself as 'a friend of Allegra Stratton'.[23] Her only crime, he wrote, was to 'mock [the] absurdity' of lockdown rules (an odd way of describing what actually happened: the people she worked for made the rules and then broke them, and she was filmed having a good old giggle about it). The *i*'s Jane Merrick praised her for having the decency to proffer a speedy resignation.[24] And ITV's Robert Peston, never one to damn a fellow insider with faint praise, tweeted: 'I've known [Allegra Stratton] for years. She was a brilliant colleague on the show. As I would expect, she has done the honourable thing, and swiftly resigned. Whatever you think of what she said in the clip obtained by @

itvnews, she is a model for many in modern politics … in that she has taken responsibility and quit without prevarication.'[25] To openly subordinate objectivity to personal relationships – indeed, to effectively nominate oneself to do PR for a disgraced political operator – might be considered too embarrassing for most other journalists. But not the fearless Peston.

Fortunately for Stratton, she could rely on more than just warm words from former colleagues. It wasn't long before the industry she had left for a government job brought her back in from the cold. Little more than six months after her tearful resignation, it was announced that Allegra Stratton would return to political journalism, joining *Bloomberg* as UK contributing editor. Nor did she have to worry that her ignominious exit from politics would damage her Westminster connections. Rishi Sunak, the former Chancellor of the Exchequer under Boris Johnson and a schoolyard chum of Stratton's husband James Forsyth (they both attended Winchester College, whose fees today cost more than the UK median annual salary[26]), could be counted on as a close friend. They reportedly stand as godparents to each other's children. Promoting her 8 July 2022 newsletter for *Bloomberg* about Sunak's bid to replace Johnson as Conservative Party leader, Stratton neglected to mention these details while praising his 'slick' candidate video and support from key Tory MPs.[27]

I asked her if it's weird writing about the guy who was best man at your wedding as if you don't know him, but never got a reply. On reflection, perhaps Robert Peston was right when he called Allegra Stratton a model for modern politics: a privately educated journalist who bullied benefits claimants, became the official mouthpiece for a Conservative government, fell on her sword to protect a notoriously dishonest Prime Minister, and then was admitted back into the media fold with nary a squeak from her colleagues about conflicts of interest.

Allegra Stratton is a particularly egregious example of how close interpersonal relationships and the professional hokey-cokey blur the distinction between political operators and the journalists assigned to hold them to account. But she's certainly not alone. Sebastian Payne, after serving as the *Financial Times*' Whitehall editor, left journalism to become the head of a right-wing thinktank and repeatedly (though unsuccessfully) put himself forward for consideration as a Tory parliamentary candidate. Ross Kempsell had been Political Editor at TalkRadio – but a month after conducting a bizarre interview with Boris Johnson, in which he nailed the then-leadership candidate on tough questions like 'What do you do to relax?'[28] – it was announced that he'd be taking a job as Boris Johnson's advisor.[29] After a year working for the government, he returned to broadcast as a Times Radio special correspondent. Kempsell then whirled through the revolving door one more time and took up a post as political director of Conservative campaign headquarters.[30] At the grand old age of thirty-one, he was appointed to the House of Lords by Boris Johnson. I'm not suggesting that Kempsell deliberately soft-served (maybe he's just genuinely shit at interviewing people), but had he been the kind of journalist to strike fear in the hearts of trembling politicians, it's unlikely he'd have been given a job by the new Prime Minister, or ended up as Baron Kempsell of Letchworth. No wonder we end up with low-calibre politicians, when journalists who give them an easy ride are actively rewarded.

But it's perhaps more damning that, after a soft-serve interview and a year's spell in government, the news industry welcomed him back with open arms, only for him to desert journalism again in order to work for the Tories. At no point did anyone seem to ask whether a man who has clear professional interests in supporting a Conservative government should be trusted to hold the powerful to account as a journalist. Nor does it seem that the lobby has troubled themselves over whether Kempsell's return to politics, after a brief rebound fling with Times Radio, raises any difficult questions about the nature of the revolving door. In 2024 Kempsell made a return to media, as Contributing Editor at right-wing politics blog *Guido Fawkes*.[31] The revolving door turned once more, and he's come out sitting on both sides of it.

Then there's the Labour Party to consider. Ayesha Hazarika worked for Labour leaders Gordon Brown and Ed Miliband before becoming a comment writer – she's now in the House of Lords. Ed Balls (married, as it happens, to the current Home Secretary Yvette Cooper) was Shadow Chancellor until he lost his seat in 2015. Via a stint on *Strictly Come Dancing*, he ended up presenting *Good Morning Britain* – and in August 2024 even jointly interviewed his own wife, Home Secretary Yvette Cooper, about the government's response to racist rioting that had broken out. No conflict of interest there, I'm sure. Paul Waugh was a high-flying political editor for *HuffPost* and *PoliticsHome* before representing Rochdale in the Commons. What does it say about the integrity of political media that someone can go from holding politicians to account to actually being one and then going back again? It's about as hostile a relationship as the one I have with a box of Lindor.

'Alex Wickham, whether or not he is actually the godfather of Wilfred...' begins my lobby source, referencing allegations that Boris Johnson's child with Carrie Symonds is the godson of the *Bloomberg* reporter. 'He's certainly a close friend of [Boris Johnson's] wife. And he's never denied it.' Wickham's ascent to being 'one of the main gatekeepers' of the lobby isn't a path that could ever be replicated by someone from the left. A former contributor to Breitbart, the far-right news platform then managed by Steve Bannon, Wickham penned articles about political scandals with sensitive opening lines like 'Who cares about chinky-gate?'[32] While at *Breitbart*, Wickham also began writing for right-wing blog *Guido Fawkes*, then *Buzzfeed News*, *POLITICO* and *Bloomberg*.

'He's been laundered straight into the mainstream,' says the anonymous journalist. 'And it could never happen on the other side of the coin. You would never have someone who wrote for *Skwawkbox*, and was friends with Jeremy Corbyn or whatever, being taken up by the *Mirror* and the *Guardian*. It just wouldn't happen.' Different rules apply to socialists and to centrists and the right. Owen Jones can write comment pieces for the *Guardian*, but there's no way they're letting him near the news desk.

The general view within the lobby is that there's balance, because there's Tory papers and Labour papers. 'But actually, there's a lot of Conservative papers, and there's one or two nominally Labour-supporting papers. And the range of opinion is quite narrow within those. I've had discussions with people in the lobby, and some of them aren't Conservatives. But the one thing that the lobby could always agree on was that Corbyn is useless, and his supporters are idiots.' There's a 'herd mentality', but the consensus isn't equally hostile to the far right and the socialist left. In practice the supposedly progressive papers and outlets have a firewall that keeps out left-wing journalists – but the right is able to ferry journalists from more extremist outlets right into the heart of power and influence. These aren't things that journalists are socially permitted to discuss openly. There's an unspoken rule that insiders don't go after one of their own: so, reports that one journalist employed by the Murdoch media empire 'was bullying staff in the canteen', or that a particular Political Editor is a 'really nasty piece of work' are consigned to the shadow realm of things known, but never uttered. 'They're friends, close mates with *Guardian* journalists,' explains my source. 'Because you're all part of the same club, you all work together, you all turn up together. And if you've ever criticised it … then you're very much excluded.' And social ostracism can mean career suicide: 'there's only a few publications, and people don't want to piss people off.' Lobby journalism is governed by the law of *omertà*: a code of silence that sets boundaries on what's permissible to talk about, and who's considered fair game, according to what's professionally and politically expedient.

And these unwritten, unspoken norms shape what gets covered, and what doesn't. The lobby is not neutral: they tell some stories and muffle others, depending on what's politically advantageous. In one case, Sebastian Payne – a lobby journalist-turned-right-wing think-tank director – admitted on LBC that one of Keir Starmer's closest advisors had openly boasted during the leadership campaign of his boss's intention to break his left-wing policy promises when he became party leader ('Look at those pledges … Not one of them is going to tie our hands').[33] Now, you'd think that would've made a cracking story at the time (after all, it's tantamount to an insider confessing to running a deceptive campaign). But he didn't write it up as a story at the time. Indeed, it seems that the first time the information was made public was in a passing comment on the radio two years after the leadership campaign. It's difficult to imagine why any journo would pass up a scoop – unless, perhaps, they agreed that lying to a left-wing membership in order to impose a more right-leaning programme was a good thing to do.

In February 2022, it was reported that a Labour MP had been banned for six months from all bars on the parliamentary estate after making racist comments to a British-Chinese journalist. Neil Coyle had told Henry Dyer, a reporter for *Business Insider*, that he 'looked like he'd been giving renminbi' to an MP who'd been accused of accepting donations from a Chinese agent. When Dyer went public with his experience, publishing an account of what happened in an article and a statement on social media, many Westminster journalists were rightly supportive of the politics reporter, and condemned the loutish behaviour of the Bermondsey and Old Southwark MP. Coyle had the Labour whip removed, meaning that he was forced to sit out the rest of the parliamentary term as an independent MP (though still, by and large, voting along with his former party). What was telling, however, was that reporters didn't seem exactly surprised by what happened.

'Coyle should have been out of Westminster years ago and everybody knows it,' tweeted Alex Wickham, who was then at *POLITICO*. Gabriel Pogrund, from the *Sunday Times*, noted that Coyle's conduct was 'nothing new in SW1'. In *Left Out*, Pogrund and his colleague Patrick Maguire's account of the downfall of Jeremy Corbyn, it had been revealed that Neil Coyle had repeatedly sent abusive late-night texts to the former Labour leader.[34] An anonymous Labour MP told journalist Eleni Courea that 'Coyle has form at being abusive and obnoxious' in Parliament bars.[35] Neil Coyle's track record of aggressive and inappropriate behaviour was in the public domain, and supposedly, there was a consensus amongst Westminster insiders that he wasn't fit to sit in the House of Commons. So, why had it taken so long for this pattern of conduct to be a problem for his political career?

The truth is that, before the lobby turned on him, Neil Coyle was useful to them. He was a key generator of the anti-Corbyn news stories they were all desperate to publish after the latter was elected Labour leader in 2015. Despite having been one of the MPs who initially nominated Jeremy Corbyn to the leadership ballot, Neil Coyle rapidly and dramatically turned against the Islington North MP and his supporters amongst the party's left flank. A few days before the 2019 general election, Neil Coyle took Toby Helm (Political Editor of the *Observer*, a paper which had taken a distinctly anti-Corbyn line from the moment of his accession) out with him door-knocking. The journalist and the MP between them spoke of voters being 'repelled' by the Labour leader, and the piece quoted liberally from individuals who branded him a 'terrorist sympathiser' and a 'twat'.[36] Helm claimed that Labour MPs had kept schtum on their own personal reservations about Jeremy Corbyn as a politician, writing that the Labour leader's detractors had been observing a 'vow of silence about Corbyn for more than three years' – which strains the bounds of credulity, seeing as the very MP who had invited him on this walking tour of electoral discontent had been open with the press about his antipathy towards the party leadership.

For Helm to claim that Corbyn's critics had been united in dignified silence for the past three years in an article *about Neil flippin' Coyle* speaks to either a profound ignorance of his own journalistic beat, or a willingness to ignore the truth in order to produce an article that served his political agenda. Political journalists collectively turned a blind eye to Neil Coyle's shortcomings (despite, in Alex Wickham's words, everyone knowing that he should have been out of Westminster 'years ago') because he was a useful mouthpiece for an opinion they all held and wanted to write: that Corbyn 'is useless, and his supporters are idiots', as my lobby source put it. Once Corbyn was gone, and Coyle's value depreciated as a source for Labour stories, it became convenient to notice a pattern of aggressive behaviour that had long been common knowledge. In short, he became expendable to journalists (though not, apparently, to the Labour party itself under Keir Starmer: he's since had the party whip restored and been laundered back into respectability, winning re-election in 2024).

What the Coyle episode demonstrates is that there are stories that the lobby want to tell, for ideological reasons. That ideology is shrouded in the language of impartiality: the supposed ironclad law of journalistic objectivity. But that impartiality is a mask for a variety of biased practices: indulging unreliable sources when it suits and jettisoning them when it no longer does; cosying up to politicians, and even going to work for them, after defensively snapping at anyone who suggested that their coverage might have a partisan political bent; happily parroting right-wing ideas around economics like they're immutable laws of physics (the country's credit card is maxed out, we've spent all the money, there is no alternative to austerity, and so on). But of course, there were alternatives. It just wasn't the done thing to give them serious consideration.

There are, of course, journalists who work within this system but who are capable of producing genuinely insightful and newsworthy journalism. But these individuals are sadly rare, and I'd wager that their work is worth reading in spite of the incentives that govern lobby journalism rather than because of them. And there'll be members of the lobby reading this, scoffing to the high heavens at the suggestion that their job is little more than to serve as a glorified ventriloquist's dummy for establishment interests. 'No one tells us what to write!' is the familiar defensive bark of the hack in response to criticism of their trade. But as Noam Chomsky pointed out to Andrew Marr in 1996, you don't need force to silence politically inconvenient opinions – the entire education system, as well as the system of promotion and demotion within journalism, 'gets you to understand that there are certain things you just don't say'.[37] Journalists like to think of themselves as difficult, dogged and disputatious people. But this self-image is a sham. After my Novara Media colleague Rivkah Brown published an article in July 2024 exposing how the *Guardian*'s politics team had lobbied hard for the paper to endorse Keir Starmer in the general election,[38] lobby hacks didn't give her a pat on the back for getting a scoop. A journalist, who for obvious reasons would prefer to remain anonymous, overheard hacks complaining about Brown's story in the lobby cafe ('it's very uncollegiate!' one reportedly whined). The lobby, drawn to Westminster by a fascination with power are, as a class, obedient in the face of it.

Through prompting, framing, scoffing and haranguing, journalists prod politicians into taking more reactionary positions. There's a very low threshold for writing off, dismissing, maligning and demonising movements associated with the left. When hundreds of thousands of Britons took to the streets in October 2023 in opposition to Israel's indiscriminate bombardment of Gaza, they found themselves being presented as terrorist sympathisers by the country's press. Veteran broadcaster Andrew Neil described young people occupying their university campuses as 'posh pro-Hamas student protestors',[39] and even BBC News had to correct itself after characterising a demonstration in London as being 'in support of Hamas'.[40] One journalist for the influential *Playbook* newsletter wondered aloud: 'Do the police have the powers they need to stop scenes such as those in central London on Saturday (which Playbook witnessed first-hand after getting caught up in the crowd while on a trip to, checks notes, the Lego store, and can confirm were pretty unedifying).'[41] I also happened to be at the protest, covering it for Novara Media. I didn't witness anything that could plausibly be described as 'unedifying', unless you're just uncomfortable with pro-Palestinian protests in general. At least 100,000 people were in attendance; only ten arrests were made, according to the Metropolitan Police.[42] For comparison, this year's Glastonbury had thirty arrests for 210,000 attendees. I've yet to see a journo argue that police need more powers to crack down on Dua Lipa fans. But they have their own biases, and views on the world, which leak out into what they pressure politicians to do.

There's something deeply embarrassing about seeing politicians behave like pundits. Whether it's Kemi Badenoch getting into a slanging match with Doctor Who, or Suella Braverman complaining that she couldn't get the Pride flag taken down from the Home Office, it's hard not to view their demonisation of vulnerable groups as evidence that their own status as statesmen has been woefully diminished. As we've seen, it's partly down to the outsize role that the media plays in terms of incentivising the behaviour of politicians. I think, however, that there's something deeper at play too. Later in the book, I'll examine in detail how rentierism – basically, the massive expansion of corporate landlords in the economy – has sucked the wealth out of society and poisoned the planet. But you only have to look at Keir Starmer's election-winning manifesto and early announcements to see something written clear: the Westminster consensus is that corporations should be more powerful than democratically controlled institutions.

Riding high on a stonking parliamentary majority of over 150 seats, you'd perhaps have expected PM Starmer and his Chancellor Rachel Reeves to go big. Without any political obstacles to passing legislation, it would be the perfect opportunity to shake things up. But timid numbers belied the splashy headlines. The size of Labour's fiscal package (that is, tax rises and spending pledges) was minuscule. According to the BBC's Ben Chu, it amounted to just 0.2 per cent of GDP – a quarter of that pledged by the supposedly more right-wing Liberal Democrats.[43] Starmer and Reeves promised not to implement income tax rises on high earners or raise corporation tax, and repeatedly ruled out wealth taxes. That's even though the 350 richest people in the UK control more wealth than the GDP of Poland,[44] and even Tory voters would like to see a wealth tax on multi-millionaires implemented in the UK.[45]

This small-c conservatism was music to the ears of the UK's elites. The billionaire property developer John Caudwell took to the *Newsnight* sofa to praise Keir Starmer for taking 'all the left out of the Labour party'. And just in case grouchy leftists like myself might miss it, he hammered the point home further. This Labour leadership has 'come out with a set of values and principles in complete alignment with my views as a commercial capitalist'.[46] Indeed, one of Labour's first promises was to host a 'global investment summit' in its first 100 days in office, and even before entering government, their top team held meetings with BlackRock, Lloyds Banking Group, Santander and HSBC.[47] Starmernomics means that the role of the state is to create new assets to sell off to private interests, rather than keeping them in public hands. You can see why billionaires like him: his greatest dream is to operate as the interface between capital and the public. It's puppet work. And in the next chapter, we'll see how the dominance of capitalism hasn't only poisoned our politics – it's corroded class solidarity too.

4

Economics Are the Method

At 5.30 a.m. on Friday 5 July 2024, I was on the first tube of the morning and finally on my way home. I used to see this side of the city – the early-bird commuters, office cleaners and tourists trying to make an early flight – after kicking-out time at the club. Now, because I'm in my thirties and scared of young people music, it's because I've watched the general election results roll in. My head buzzed from ten hours of non-stop coffee ingestion, and from the effort of trying to make sense of what had unfolded. The Conservatives, who had been in power for the entirety of my adult life, had just suffered a crushing defeat. Keir Starmer, leader of the Labour Party, had cruised into Downing Street on the kind of majority that would give psephologists heart palpitations.

But although the Conservatives were out of office, the far-right had made it into the House of Commons. Nigel Farage (alongside four of his fellow Reform UK compatriots) had become a sitting MP for the first time in his political career (on his eighth try). Keir Starmer's Labour had got elected after abandoning nearly every progressive policy he had run on to become leader, including the abolition of tuition fees. Though I wasn't able to fall asleep, it wasn't because I felt excited. As I lay awake, willing the caffeine to leave my system, I found myself thinking about that moment in 2017 when I was twenty-five and the general election exit poll showed that the Conservative Prime

Minister had gambled away her parliamentary majority in a snap election against the socialist Labour leader Jeremy Corbyn. I'd celebrated in absolute elation with my friends and colleagues. Lager arced through the air like England had just scored an equaliser in the ninetieth minute, and by morning, our voices were hoarse from cheering.

It wasn't that we supported the red team against the blue team – it was that our bloc of young renters, trade unionists, peace activists and ethnic minorities had defied all the odds. We were told that our candidate was electoral kryptonite, that Theresa May would steamroll us, that she'd waltz back into No. 10 on a stonking majority. But we'd taken her to the edge of defeat. An anti-imperialist, socialist backbencher had managed to attract 40 per cent of the national vote share on a platform which promised to tax the rich and fund public services. Next time, for sure, we'd finish the job. I was twenty-five, and certain that the left was on the brink of making history.

In hindsight, I was self-deluding and hubristic. I got swept up in the fantasy of what a socialist government could be like. It could end austerity, renationalise rail and water and end adventurist warfare in the Middle East. And if journalists, commentators, activists and unions applied pressure, it could do so much more to make society fairer. It could abolish fee-paying schools, implement a four-day working week, impose a wage ratio so bosses could no longer earn hundreds of times more than their office cleaner. But what I should have been paying attention to was what it would take to win the next election, rather than what Labour would do if they won. Concealed by the headline figures of constituencies being won and lost were ominous electoral trends. The Conservatives had actually managed to increase their vote share by 5.5 percentage points since the last general election two years previously. Though nearly thirty seats switched from Tory to Labour, the six which went the other way were all geographically located in the Midlands and the North of England – traditional Labour heartlands. This was a sign of things to come.

Just two years later, in the 2019 election, I learned my lesson the hard way, much the same way falling flat on your face teaches you something valuable about looking where you're going. It was painful and embarrassing. Boris Johnson, having successfully taken over the Conservative Party, ruthlessly exploited the country's polarisation on Brexit to secure an eighty-seat majority. Sure, the circumstances were in his favour (anti-Corbyn MPs split and formed their own party, Nigel Farage's Brexit Party made a deal not to stand in Tory-held seats and much of the press were fairly open in their hatred of the left) – but Johnson's team had pursued the right strategy, while the left had pursued the wrong one. And despite the fact that I wasn't a policymaker, a strategist, an MP or an advisor, I felt a horrible sense of personal responsibility. I wrote articles arguing that Labour should take more of a pro-EU stance than a pro-Brexit one. I lobbied hard on things like more ambitious climate commitments, ending immigration detention and adopting universal basic income. I forgot the number one rule in politics: learn how to count. Because there were far more people in the country who weren't like me than those who were. As I trudged around news studios after the exit poll came out, looking for all the world like someone who'd just been told that they'd have to pass a kidney stone, I could feel a narrative emerging around me. Metropolitan elites like me had lost the working class. We didn't understand the country and were despised for it. It was the fault of us young, left-wing graduates that the country had taken such a sharp lurch to the right. The next few months of doing media felt like a one-woman self-flagellation roadshow. The 2020 COVID lockdown ended up feeling like a reprieve. I was quite relieved not to show my face for a while.

I watched as my bit of the left – the graduates without a future, the ethnic minorities, the progressives – got politically sidelined. Keir Starmer, elected to the leadership in the wake of the 2019 debacle, purged his party of any hint of socialist or radical tendencies, expelling members, MPs and parliamentary candidates. A part of me, still tender and bruised from the humiliation of 2019, wondered whether this was actually what we deserved. Perhaps by giving the left a kicking the working class would come back. But then the 2024 general election result turned all my assumptions on their head again. Yes, Keir Starmer won a parliamentary majority of more than 150 seats. But he did so on a mere 1.6 percentage point increase from Jeremy Corbyn's 2019 drubbing, which actually translated to half a million fewer votes. Undoubtedly, the Labour Party under Keir Starmer had delivered a masterclass in 'voter efficiency', meaning that they were able to hone in on winning over exactly the right people to flip seats. But it was also a sign that the electorate didn't have much faith in the ballot box.

Turnout overall had dropped, meaning that fewer people participated in the 2024 election than five years previously. No one was talking in jubilant terms about the return of the working class to the Labour fold. In fact, turnout was lowest in the constituencies with fewer homeowners and a greater population of ethnic minorities. Working-class voters weren't being pursued by political parties; indeed the Liberal Democrats targeted voters wherever a Gail's bakery could be found.[1] After a combination of global trends and Liz Truss's disastrous mini-budget saw interest rates soar, mortgage-payers had their revenge at the ballot box. As one report stated baldly, 'Put simply, the "haves" speak much louder than the "have-nots" in British democracy.'[2]

In recent years, between a third and two-fifths of voters can be expected to switch parties between elections.[3] What the upshot of all this means is that elections are decided by particular kinds of people, in particular kinds of seats. Politicians are obsessed with finding out who those people are and tailoring their pitch to them precisely.

These swing voters always get ridiculous names: Mondeo Man, Stevenage Woman, Joe the Plumber. They're probably not *rich* rich, but they're certainly not the poor, who don't tend to vote, and therefore in electoral terms, may as well be dead. They're not students, they are either in work or are retired, and they aren't massively ideological. They might not identify as middle class, or have gone to university, but owning their own homes puts their interests at odds with the hordes of renters being crushed by rising house prices. Their worldviews are, like most people's, drawn from all over the map (case in point: a woman I met in Milton Keynes who wanted the government to ban animal testing, and experiment on prisoners instead).

Human experimentation aside, there's nothing wrong with any of these things. But a political system where parties and politicians are incentivised to chase after a geographically dispersed cohort of homeowners, and can safely ignore tenants, benefits claimants, students, non-voters and people who live in densely populated urban constituencies isn't a good one. If politicians can write off millions of voters, we don't have democracy. We've got a dictatorship of the focus group.

But do swing voters end up getting a good deal? The short answer is no. Whatever funding bungs a constituency might receive in the short term are nowhere near enough to tackle regional inequalities, or the long-term devastation of losing the factories and mines with nothing to replace them. Public sector cuts impacting schools, hospitals and local authorities have hacked the social safety net to pieces. And swing voter or not, you're still living as part of an ageing population on a heating planet. What elites are offering is the chance to feel seen. But being told that you're good, hard-working and decent isn't the same thing as getting a fair deal in material terms.

But the persistence of groups like this reminds us that class remains central to the way politics is conducted. What this chapter looks at is the role that class, and class identity, plays in politics. The right has been successful in defining who the working class are in a way which suits the right's political interests, and the centre-left has been forced to follow in their footsteps. In the UK, working-class interests have been pitted against those of immigrants and asylum seekers. But as migrants have been shunted into low-wage, low-security jobs with fewer protections, conditions for British-born workers haven't improved. Instead, bad pay and crap contracts have been generalised outwards after being first imposed on the migrant workforce. Identitarian conflict has obscured this reality. Rather than shaping a sense of class identity around shared material and economic conditions, like widening inequality, unaffordable housing, real-terms decline in wages or crumbling public services, it's instead defined by political and cultural outlooks. Got a regional accent? You're working class. Know what an avocado is? You're middle class. The working class are not a monolith, being geographically dispersed, ethnically diverse and occupying a mix of housing tenures. But these differences have been ruthlessly exploited to divide them further and to turn democracy into a means of preserving class inequalities rather than eliminating them.

I've used the word class a lot so far, without ever really defining what I mean by it. And that's because it's difficult, contested and replete with contradictions. But if we're going to look at how elites view, deploy and manipulate social class, I've probably hit the end of the road where hoping we all mean the same thing is concerned. So I'm going to jump headfirst into a debate which sociologists have wrangled over for as long as the discipline has existed, and get specific about what we're saying when we talk about class.

When I say 'working class', 'middle class' or 'upper class', chances are that you have a pretty clear image in your mind of the kind of person who occupies each category. When you hear 'working class', it's likely that you'll think of a man who didn't go to university. They probably work in construction or manufacturing. You'd never hear their accent reading the ten o'clock news. A middle-class person, by contrast, almost certainly went to university. They live somewhere you'd either describe as 'metropolitan' or 'leafy' – and they don't have a job, but a *profession*. If they've got a regional accent, it's been disciplined by higher education and office jobs to resemble that of a BBC or CNN anchor. And unless you're upper class yourself, you probably don't have a particularly high-def picture of what being part of the landowning aristocracy involves other than horses, boarding schools and mysterious activities like fives or lacrosse. This colloquial, informal understanding of class might not be the product of in-depth peer-reviewed research, but it's got a vibes-based power of its own. It's widely intuited, even if it's not comprehensive or richly detailed.

There are different models for defining class that sociologists, pollsters and policy makers rely on. One that's particularly dominant in the UK is the NRS social grade, which uses ABC1 and C2DE. You might have heard of it being talked about in the context of voter behaviour during post-election autopsies: the categories establish social grade based on the occupation of the head of household. ABC1s are basically white-collar workers, ranging from top management to junior clerical staff. C2DE includes all manual workers, from skilled to unskilled,[4] unemployed people and recipients of the state pension. Though it was never intended to be a marker of class identity (it was developed as a marketing tool in the 1950s) it's been used as

a shorthand for social class by journalists and political operators, with ABC1 standing in for 'middle class' and C2DE for
'working class'. But there's a lot missing from it. In the ABC1
C2DE format, there are no distinctions on the basis of income,
asset wealth or home ownership. So someone who works in a
call centre for £24,000 a year, while renting a room or living
with parents, would count amongst the ABC1s, while a skilled
manual worker on 50 or 60 grand a year, who owns their own
home, or a pensioner who tops up their income by renting out
properties, are both in the C2DEs. Clearly, someone working
on or just above the minimum wage isn't 'middle class', even if
they've got to wear a button-up shirt every day.

What about a definition that just looks at income and wealth?
For Marx and Engels, what class you are depends on your relationship to the means of production. Do you own the stuff which
enables goods and services to be made, like natural resources,
technology platforms, factories or a property portfolio? Then
you're part of the bourgeoisie, or the capitalist class. If you have
to sell your labour power for a wage – work in a job where you're
not the boss, basically – then you're a part of the proletariat, or
working class. For Marxists, what constitutes a class is those who
have common interests (for instance, wages going up or down),
are conscious of those interests and work collectively in some
way to advance those interests. In my own political life, I tend to
use a version of this as my working definition of class in a modern context. If you sold all your worldly possessions, added your
savings and the value of any investments, and then deducted the
sum total of all your personal debt (whether that's credit cards,
Klarna, a mortgage or uni fees) would you have enough to live
on? If the answer is yes, then congratulations: you're part of the
bourgeoisie. If the answer is no, then welcome to the struggle.
It's how I work out who's part of the big 'us', and who makes
up the smaller 'them', to draw a nice bright line of opposing

interests. I'll go into this in more detail in Chapter 7. But there are significant omissions and limitations to this model of thinking about class. Taken by itself, it's reductive. It doesn't take into account how people live. And it doesn't look at how those differences in lifestyle, habits and values are themselves a product of economic forces.

Dan Evans' brilliant 2023 book *A Nation of Shopkeepers: The Unstoppable Rise of the Petty Bourgeoisie* tackles this particularly well. In it, he points out that the opposite of what Karl Marx and Friedrich Engels predicted ended up happening. Instead of shopkeepers, artisans and small landlords sinking to join the proletariat, the ranks of the petty bourgeoisie have swelled in recent decades. In 1975, one in twelve workers were self-employed – by 2019, this had increased to one in seven.[5] Rather than being forced into factories or dark Satanic mills, the petty bourgeoisie has thrived as a 'sprawling class'[6] of self-employed tradespeople – plumbers, beauticians, salespeople, electricians and mobs of graduate freelancers. They all own their means of production (like a laptop, workshop, tools or a van), but you wouldn't compare them to the capitalists of big corporations (hence the petty, or 'petit', in bourgeoisie). What Evans points out is that the petty bourgeoisie is deeply divided along the lines of politics and culture, despite being connected by the shared condition of economic precarity. The downwardly mobile graduate doing freelance copyediting or on a short-term academic contract and the doing-all-right-for-themselves self-employed trader both have to deal with a lack of pensions and paid sick leave. But how they live is totally different. The former is likely to be living in a rented house-share in a city, riding their bike or using public transport to get to work, and probably supported Jeremy Corbyn but now votes Green. But drawing on his own experience of going home to Porthcawl, Evans points out that his friends who didn't go off and get degrees seemed to be better off than him. 'Many of them were self-employed brickies, cops, soldiers, or salespeople in one of the many enormous call centres that have replaced heavy industry in my area' he writes. 'They were married to nurses, beauticians and hairdressers. They had nice cars and almost always owned their own houses.'[7] And when it came to politics, they could be tempted to vote for right-wing parties. I'll come back to this later in the chapter.

We're hardly ever only thinking about income and wealth when we're talking about class. When discussing the incoming ban on American Bully XLs in the UK, my friend and colleague Craig Gent complained that whenever his own angelic bully-mix Bella has been attacked, 'it was by a middle-class dog'. And though that's not a sentence that makes any kind of objective, logical sense, I knew exactly what he meant: some kind of spaniel, setter or Labradoodle. We think about class in terms of habits, consumer behaviour and objects. Certain coffee orders are middle class; a grey velvet sofa isn't. The qualities of people become transposed onto things – which is how you end up with a British politician pretending not to know what a latte is and squirming mid-interview when his 'frothy coffee' was served 'with little biscuits and a posh cup' rather than a mug.[8] Thank God it didn't come with oat milk. There's something faintly pejorative about being called middle class. It's soft, chi-chi, disconnected. Conversely, there's something authentic, resilient and in touch about being perceived as working class (particularly if you're actually middle class). There's a reason why Keir Starmer says 'my Dad was a toolmaker' rather than 'I live in a nice house in Kentish Town', despite both things being equally true.

Of course, who your parents are and how you're raised is profoundly important to shaping your sense of self. But an over-emphasis on this when defining class, at the expense of your present material circumstances, ends up presenting social class as something akin to an inherited genetic trait, never changing over the course of intervening generations. Helen Pidd, then the *Guardian*'s North of England editor, was Twitter's main character for the day after interviewing a businessman who owned a pizza restaurant in a piece about working-class voters who'd voted Conservative in Leigh,[9] and tweeted defensively that 'you can be working class and run a restaurant – or indeed be a property developer.'[10] The idea that there's such a thing as being a working-class property developer was torn to shreds; it's like saying you can have working-class oligarchs, or working-class monarchs. But this framing spoke to something that's pervasive in mainstream media and politics – that class identity is determined by accent, voting behaviour and vibes, rather than how much you own. To be fair, Helen Pidd is far from the most egregious example of this thinking. Ian King, a business presenter on Sky News, wrote an article in 2019 citing the examples of Chris Dawson, Michelle Mone and Alan Sugar. 'He left school at 16 and is a billionaire,' King points out of Sugar. 'Try telling him he isn't working class.'[11] OK, Ian King – as a billionaire, Alan Sugar is not working class.

How did we get to this point, where people are genuinely debating whether property developers and literal barons are working class? Part of it is down to the familiar story of media idiocy. Probing these questions would mean not taking rich and powerful people at their word, or sacrificing a narrative which suits your political purposes. But the weakening of class consciousness extends far beyond news and current affairs discourses. Over the past forty years, there has been a concerted effort to destroy and enfeeble the engines of class consciousness, which tied people's sense of social identity to their material conditions.

Here's the potted history. When people reminisce about things being better in the past, they're often thinking of a particular era between 1945 and 1979. This was the post-war period in which

Britain founded the NHS and massively expanded the welfare state. Trade union membership was high. It was the golden age of social democracy – job security, leaps and bounds in the standard of living, high union density, low inequality, council houses galore. Today, we struggle to build 250,000 homes a year – but by the late 1960s, more than 400,000 homes were being built in the UK annually because local councils were constructing hundreds of thousands of them.[12] There was a consensus among both Labour and the Tories that government policy should be geared towards bettering the living standards of the working class; as the Conservative Prime Minister Harold Macmillan put it, 'most of our people have never had it so good'.[13] People didn't have to move away from their families to find work, they could live in secure and affordable housing, and the kinds of jobs that were available – though backbreakingly strenuous – brought them in contact with others in their community. There was a virtuous circle between these institutions and class consciousness. Working-men's clubs, communities built around heavy industry, council housing and active trade union membership forged and deepened a collective working-class identity. This identity couldn't be reduced to consumer choices, such as liking the same music, activities, food and fashion: it was a political identity, defined by living together, working together and fighting together. Working-class people voted Labour as a bloc – the ties between the organised labour movement and the party were solid, if occasionally strained, and class consciousness was strong.

'Economics are the method,' said Margaret Thatcher in a particularly candid newspaper interview. 'The object is to change the heart and soul.'[14] And she did exactly that after coming to power in 1979. Even though she (and her neoliberal counterparts in the Americas) loathed communism with every fibre of her being, Thatcher understood better than anyone the old Marxist maxim that conditions shape consciousness. To ensure long-term democratic consent for an economic programme where public assets were handed over to corporations and oligarchs, the neoliberals would have to change how people thought of themselves. It would be the economy which would create Tory voters, and not the other way around – and she pursued policies which broke the back of the British working class. Her strategic objective was to dismantle the institutions that produced strong community ties, and thereby working-class consciousness – i.e. trade unions, council housing and the like. In practical terms, that meant defeating the most militant trade unions (especially the National Union of Mineworkers), introducing 'Right to Buy' (which both depleted council housing stock and created a new class of property owners and landlords),[15] and decimating the industrial base. Under Thatcher's rule, and that of the successor governments of her ideological offspring, New Labour, Britain's industrial output fell, and the size of the financial sector boomed. Social democracy was effectively replaced by home ownership – the state wouldn't look after people any more, but an asset which appreciated in value would. Subsequently, housing tenure became the most powerful determinant of voting behaviour. When politicos talk about swing voters, they're almost always talking about homeowners whose interests align with elites.

Class, and how people identify themselves within it, is complex, layered and occasionally contradictory. It would be tempting to just swing the bourgeoisie/proletariat binary like a broadsword and cut through the knot, saying that where you went to school, where you live, whether you have a university degree, what kind of accent you have just don't matter. But it's how these things interact with the broader context of widening inequality and a global theft of wealth that explains how democracies deliver electoral results which protect capital rather than redistributing it. What the right has been exceptionally skilled in doing – and what the centre-left has been forced to copy – is to wield a reductive and simplified idea of what it means to be working class in order to advance a reactionary political agenda. And to find out more about this, I went and talked to perhaps the most skilled strategist in the country at doing so: Dominic Cummings.

Constructing a Majority

There's north London, and then there's *north London*. In the summer of 2021, as I cycled to meet Dominic Cummings, Boris Johnson's former consigliere and the man credited with delivering both the Brexit referendum and the 2019 general election, I couldn't help but feel like I was pedalling to a different planet. Ocado delivery vans glided serenely through the streets, houses stood awash with the tasteful shades of Farrow & Ball, even the children were made of sourdough. A moment of eye contact with a chic young mum improved my credit rating. This leafy enclave, nestled between Islington and Hackney, is worlds apart from Tottenham, despite being only a few miles away. If Cummings' neighbourhood is alien to me, it is practically in an alternate dimension to the English 'Red Wall' constituencies in the North and Midlands that voted Leave in 2016, and for the Conservatives a few years later – Conservatives whose strategy was being directed by Cummings himself.

People vote, but it's places that decide elections. The Red Wall, as a term, was only coined in August 2019. But by the time of the election in December that year, it had been accepted as a part of the political nomenclature and deployed with easy familiarity by journalists as if it had been there for ever. The phrase first surfaced on Twitter when pollster James Kanagasooriam used it to describe an 'electoral roadblock'[16] of

Labour-voting constituencies that stretched from North Wales across Merseyside, Warrington, Wigan, Manchester, Oldham, Barnsley, Nottingham and Doncaster.

Many of these areas contained seats which, on the basis of age, home ownership and 2016 Brexit vote, shouldn't really have been Labour at all. The Tory share of the vote had been ticking up, or Labour's share declining, in these seats since 2001. But they hadn't yet been able to tip over from red to blue. According to Kanagasooriam, entrenched anti-Conservatism (a hangover from the days of a strong trade union movement, and the enduring pain of Margaret Thatcher's attacks on industrial labour) was a cultural barrier to the Tories doing as well as statistics indicated they should. Labour hasn't been banished entirely here: in 2024, most of these seats flipped back to their control. But Nigel Farage's Reform UK attracted an average of 22 per cent of the vote in Red Wall constituencies, splitting the right-wing vote.[17] Keir Starmer was the beneficiary of a collapsed Tory vote, rather than a reinvigorated Labour one.

As with any pithy shorthand, the phrase became unmoored from its original and specific meaning. A chunk of the constituencies newly won by Boris Johnson in his 2019 victory over Jeremy Corbyn's Labour had been in Kanagasooriam's Red Wall, including Workington, Blyth Valley, Bolsover, Crewe and Nantwich, and Barrow-in-Furness. As explanations cluttered the airwaves to shed light on how and why this happened, the term 'Red Wall' came to signify an awful lot more than the specific set of demographic indicators Kanagasooriam had outlined. The term encompassed a story about how the country is divided on socio-economic lines, reflecting the concentration of wealth and investment in the south-east. It became a kind of identity, synonymous with white, working class, socially conservative and non-urban. 'How will this play in the Red Wall?' has become the media's preferred way to ventriloquise reactionary political positions, whether that's opposition to transgender rights, green policies or a humane asylum system. The Red Wall isn't just a place; it's a political and cultural disposition. The Red Wall's Wario, therefore, was the London metropolitan elite: which brings us back to Dominic Cummings.

According to some people, Cummings is the cleverest man in Westminster. He's a visionary who could see things in a way that others couldn't and pulled off the most dramatic political realignment this country had seen for a generation. In the words of one journalist, he's either 'mad, bad, or brilliant'.[18] Or perhaps, as the *Observer*'s Carole Cadwalladr has said, Cummings is merely an 'amoral opportunist' with alleged links to Russia. His crowning glory, the 2016 referendum, was won on dodgy data practices and a £350 million lie plastered on the side of a bus. Between 2016 and 2020, Dominic Cummings was like Manchester United under Ferguson: hated, adored, never ignored. You get the sense that he enjoyed notoriety as much as admiration. In our interview, and despite his reputation as a master of media bullshit, Cummings answered my questions with refreshing candour, but had a marked preference for stories where he's right and everyone else is stupid.

The view from Vote Leave was that, across party political divides, there's a conservative social majority: enough people, if you stack up votes from Labour and the Tories, to deliver Brexit. Cummings recalled a focus group that took place in 2015, set up to get an idea of what Tory voters were thinking. They started off talking about immigration, because every group did that year. The horrors of the Syrian civil war, as well as terrorist insurgencies and human rights abuses in African and South Asian countries, had displaced millions of people. While most of them were hosted by countries neighbouring the ones they had just fled, over a million people arrived on European shores to claim asylum. Many had risked their lives in the perilous journey across the the Central and Eastern Mediterranean, or arriving in Italy or Greece: 3,692 people died in 2015 taking those two routes,[19] often in dangerously unseaworthy boats. These images, of desperate migrants crossing west and northwards across the waves, or being beaten by police in Eastern Europe, gathering at Calais or trying to reach England, did not always inspire sympathy amongst UK voters. The migrant at the border became a symbol for the nation under siege, and the failure of the ruling class to adequately defend it.

'Outside London,' explained Cummings, 'people [would talk all the time about] things like the fucking Channel tunnel.' Ventriloquising their exasperation, he became more animated. 'They see all these people walk through the tunnel. And then the politicians go "Well, there's nothing we can do." *It's a fucking tunnel*. It's as wide as a hotel – you can block the tunnel if you wanted to. These people don't want to. And you can see millions of people are looking at it, and concluding these wankers in charge are just completely out of line because they don't want to deal with the problem.' That was the mood amongst the voters corralled in Cummings' focus group: too many migrants were coming here, and the government needed to get tougher in repelling them. While the displacement of people was on a historic scale – in 2015, more people claimed asylum in Europe in a single year than at any other time since the Second World War – these talking points were fairly typical for Tory voters regardless of the circumstances. But as the conversation moved on, and the focus group started talking about the economy, he noticed something was amiss.

'I went, "Hang on a second... Who do you guys vote for?"' Dominic Cummings leant forward across the rickety café table, gearing up for the punchline. 'And it was Labour, Labour, Labour.'

Someone had mixed up the order of the focus groups, and it hadn't been a bunch of lifelong Tories talking at all. It was telling, he says, that for the half-hour when immigration was the sole topic of conversation, Labour voters were indistinguishable from Tories. It was only on things like taxation, spending and the NHS where the ideological difference was obvious. 'That was something which I don't think Labour people' – meaning party strategists and leadership – 'understood.' Another former senior Conservative strategist I spoke to agreed. 'The country, fundamentally, is conservative,' he said, taking a little bit of enjoyment from my grimace. 'They want more money into the NHS, and more money for public services. And they want Albanian [criminals] kicked out the country quick.' What the Vote Leave team did, both in the 2016 EU referendum and the 2019 general election, was play a tune which hit both those notes.

For Cummings, there were obvious overlaps between the traditionally right-wing terrain of immigration and the traditionally left-wing one of public services. 'Immigration creates fears in some parts of the country about public services,' he says. 'Things like "These people come here, a lot of them are poor, they're not gonna contribute, this is a big burden on the NHS." In some parts of the country it's a kind of feeling of "This area has just changed a lot over the past 20 years." If you're rich and you went to private school, and you've got lots of friends who are ethnic minorities and blah blah blah, you just don't think about the world in the same way. Like some Indians have moved in next door or whatever, it doesn't feel threatening.'

As I listen, I feel a little queasy. It's hard to live up to the expectations of being a perfectly neutral interlocutor when you're also one of the Indians who might be perceived as a threat when you and your family move house. I think about the neighbours we had, living in a working-class outer London suburb when I was a kid. They'd post lit cigarettes through the letterbox and piss all over our front door, just for the pleasure of seeing my mum stoop to clean it up. And I think about the elite university I attended years later, where a guy with a cut-glass English accent rhap-sodised about his admiration for Enoch Powell's racial politics. It's not like ethnic minorities only pop up in your social circle when you've reached a certain tax bracket, or that hostility to ethnic minorities is unique to any one social class. I didn't grow up rich, and I didn't go to private school. Dominic Cummings did. The simple fact is that I'm comfortable with immigration because the humanity of ethnic minorities is not alien to me, for the obvious reason that I am one. But it's impossible to get a read on whether my heritage feels as present to Cummings in this conversation as it does to me. Call it the melanin elephant in the room.

It's a different story in the Red Wall, he continued. Immi-gration, in this version of events, is the government's abandon-ment of former industrial communities made flesh. 'If you're in an environment [where] the whole area seems to have gone to shit materially, the factories are closed, the shops have gone. Everyone basically feels that the area's gone downhill. And then they go to school and think "everyone's talking a foreign lan-guage at the school gates and I can't speak that language. What's gonna happen to my kids at the school?" ' For Cummings, immi-gration is salt in the wound of managed decline. '[It's] the feel-ing of "I feel frightened, and I can also see on TV that people in charge don't seem to care." And then, you put on top of that very extreme things like terrorism.' Threat, neglect and vulner-ability: immigration is the embodiment of a loss of control over the world around you.

The way Dominic Cummings frames it, anti-immigration sentiment is a natural response to 'out of whack' immigration policy. It's inevitable and can be dealt with very mechanistically. If you fix the 'problem' of immigration policy, you neutralise anti-immigration feeling. The idea that anti-immigration views might be the product of something other than immigration policy doesn't really cross his mind. This isn't a criticism: Cummings is a strategist, and not a philosopher. It's his job to win with the tools that are available to him, not to ask questions about how they ended up in his hands in the first place. I get the point about how being in an environment which has been blighted by deindustrialisation, under-investment and decline can create a sense of fighting for scarce resources. But it's not simply a law of physics that 'deprivation + brown people = anti-immigration sentiment'.

There are lots of images which could stand as potent symbols of political abandonment, and loss of control of the world around you. Shuttered factories, decimated bus and rail services, inequalities in life expectancy between the rich and the poor: these are all symptoms of government indifference. Or perhaps more viscerally, in 2021 alone water companies pumped raw sewage into English waterways over 370,000 times.[20] Why should an Indian family moving in next door, or hearing a foreign language at the school gates, symbolise decline more than a literal river of shit? Imaginative connections between neglect and demographic change aren't natural features of human psychology. Wedge issues don't grow on trees; they're a product of rhetorical barrage from media, think-tanks and politicians. The public do not exist in a state of ideological purity, uncontaminated by the press and political infrastructure that surrounds them.

The influence of the media and political environment transforms people's attitudes, regardless of whether or not it's something they consciously engage with. When I was at primary school, in Year 5, there was one little girl who everyone liked to pick on. This girl – Yasmin – hadn't done anything to deserve the year of mockery, social isolation and under-the-table kicks to which she was subjected. She was just a kid who had somehow blundered over the invisible and unspoken boundary that children use to determine who's in, and who's out. The pupils were brutal, and the teacher not much better. She turned a blind eye for the most part, and made it quite obvious that she didn't much care for the sweet, shy girl who'd been assigned to her class. Amongst the humdrum cruelty and daily indignities, a particular insult was favoured by Yasmin's bullies: 'asylum seeker'.

So how did a term which just means a person seeking protection in another country because they've been forcibly displaced from their home end up in the mouths of Enfield's primary-aged children as a schoolyard insult? No one knew for certain whether Yasmin or her parents were actually asylum seekers. It's not as if nine-year-olds have a particularly solid grasp of immigration policy or status, and she'd been with us the whole time through Juniors anyway. But the label stuck. It seemed to suggest that there was something weird, dirty and suspicious about her ethnicity. Her foremost tormenter, a freckled redheaded boy who was preternaturally good at football, sang a song of his own composition to the tune of DJ Ötzi: 'Hey, hey Yasmin! I wanna know why you're such a Turk'. Granted, she wasn't Turkish either, but that was the nearest disparaging term for a kid with deep olive skin and dark hair that a table of nine-year-old boys could think of. Though the school (located as it was in the diverse, global city of London) was pretty mixed when it came to the racial composition of its pupils, the words 'asylum seeker' marked Yasmin out as uniquely Other. 'Asylum seeker' became a ubiquitous slur on the playground. It meant gross, dodgy, unclean and uncool. Of course, the kids at my school didn't know what or who an asylum seeker really was or have any insight into why they were saying it. But they knew it must be really bad.

How did a word which should otherwise invite feelings of sympathy, solidarity and welcome become a trigger for repulsion, hostility and suspicion? If you're aligned with the Dominic

Cummings model of thinking, you'd say the parents of those kids who are careening around the playground, disparaging their peers as asylum seekers, are simply experiencing cultural and economic anxieties. Demographic change, goes the argument, is in itself destabilising, which creates discomfort and animosity, and this filters down from parents to their children. And in this framing, we're all just objects in a Newtonian political universe. Every action has an equal and opposite reaction, and those in power, like the press, politicians and lobbying organisations, have little to do with public opinion.

In the mid-2000s, a variation on the asylum moral panic emerged, which managed to combine two of Middle England's pet peeves in one: migrants issuing parking tickets. The story made it into newspapers on the other side of the world: 'Out of Africa, the traffic wardens take revenge', parped *The Sydney Morning Herald* darkly. 'Nearly all London parking attendants are immigrants,' the writer claimed. 'Some are asylum seekers and most are African. No one else will do the job.'[21] The *Sunday People*, not content with smearing asylum seekers as 'cheats and criminals', spoke vividly in March 2000 of a 'decent English family' being forced to move house because their Romanian neighbours were 'too noisy and filthy to endure any longer'.[22] In the early 2000s, intensely negative framing of the asylum issue became so normalised that even the BBC began uncritically recycling tabloid tropes like 'bogus asylum seekers'.[23]

But no paper was as frenzied, nor as politically influential, in advancing its anti-asylum editorial line as Murdoch-owned tabloid the *Sun*. Its coverage conjured provocative images of Britain being assailed by floods of immigrants out to game the system. 'Swamped immigration officials are kicking out just TWELVE new bogus asylum seekers a month – out of 3,200 who should be sent packing' claimed a story published in February 2001.[24] But the appointment of Rebekah Wade as the *Sun*'s editor in 2003

turned the paper's anti-asylum disposition into a full-blown cru-
sade. Wade had a shrewd instinct for sensationalist tales which
were emotive, populist and unencumbered by journalistic integrity. Just one week after Wade's appointment, the *Sun* published
a satirical feature which presented an updated roster of Mr Men
cartoons which reflected the 'sad side of Britain today'. They
included 'Mr Yardie', a black Rastafarian equipped with a joint
and a gun; 'Mr Albanian Gangster', a knife-wielding pimp;
and 'Mr Asylum Seeker', a roaming scammer who wanted
everything for free.[25]

Later that year, the paper ran a front-page story declaring –
without evidence – that 'Callous asylum seekers are barbecu-
ing the queen's swans'.[26] The *Sun* later had to admit, in print,
that no arrests had been made for the crime of illicit swan consumption (despite its initial claim that the story had come from
'an official Metropolitan Police report'). But the paper didn't
restrict itself to pouring xenophobic untruths and outright
racism into the public's ear: Rebekah Wade made sure that
anti-asylum missives were also precision-targeted at the government of the day. Headlines clamoured for the New Labour
government to 'Halt the Asylum Tide Now', and stories were
published that were carefully calibrated to spook Labour's
strategists. The paper splashed a poll it commissioned from
YouGov which showed that 77 per cent of those questioned
'think some parts of our cities are no longer truly British'.[27]
The following day, it warned readers that Britain was threatened by a wave of HIV infections brought by African immigrants, reported a brawl between asylum seekers and Brits at a
Butlins holiday camp and blamed refugees for the deterioration
of hotels at an English seaside town. With coverage like that,
it doesn't take a sociologist to work out why the *Sun*'s readers
might have a negative view of asylum seekers and immigration
more generally.[28]

Though the *Sun*'s coverage of immigration and asylum issues
was consistently hysterical and often less than reliable, it was
powerful in shaping the policy agenda of Tony Blair's government. To aid his campaign in the 1997 general election, Tony
Blair had struck a deal with Rupert Murdoch: Labour would leave
the news mogul untroubled in pursuing his business interests if
he lent Blair the backing of his British media empire. The two
men had met repeatedly after Blair became leader of the Labour
Party, and the Australian billionaire was said to be impressed
by the Sedgefield MP's youth, dynamism and corporate-lawyer
image. In 1995, after Blair flew to Australia to address attendees
gathered at a News Corporation conference, Rupert Murdoch
joked that 'if the British press is to be believed, today is all part
of a Blair-Murdoch flirtation. If that flirtation is ever consum-
mated, Tony, I suspect we will end up making love like two por-
cupines – very carefully.'[29] But while there's nothing to suggest
carnal relations, prickly or otherwise, the pair ended up in bed
with one another politically. Following Blair's landslide victory
in 1997, Murdoch's tabloids took credit for Labour's return
to government with their 'It's the *Sun* Wot Won It' headline.
Over the years, Blair's mutually beneficial relationship with
the Murdoch empire deepened. In 2011, it emerged that Blair
had become godfather to one of Rupert Murdoch's younger
children with media executive Wendi Deng.[30] That same year,
Blair had offered his services to James Murdoch, Rupert's son,
and Rebekah Wade, now Brooks, as an 'unofficial adviser' when
Murdoch newspapers were engulfed in the phone-hacking
scandal, and just days before the latter was arrested for related
offences (she was later cleared in court).[31]

So when No. 10 got word that the newspaper was going to run
a week-long campaign on the 'immigration crisis', they collabo-
rated with the *Sun* in order to neutralise the allegation that they
were soft on immigration and present an image of themselves

as being tough on asylum seekers. An interview was scheduled with then-Home Secretary David Blunkett,[32] published at the end of the week, who promised to introduce 'tough measures to crack down on asylum cheats' and said that he didn't dispute the newspaper's coverage. The *Sun* ran its 'asylum madness' series as planned, publishing alarmist stories, opinion polls and pushing a reader petition. But the pre-agreed intervention from Blunkett meant that the Blair government could appear in touch with the common man, by pandering to the paper's howling xenophobia. Meanwhile, the *Sun* could crow about its success in shaping the political agenda. Everybody wins: that is, unless you're an asylum seeker, or someone who might be mistaken for one.

Between 1997 and 2007, Tony Blair's government passed five pieces of legislation which made life more difficult for immigrants, asylum seekers and refugees.[33] These included measures which meant the children of failed asylum seekers could be taken into care, removal of the entitlement of immigrants to means-tested benefits and stripping asylum seekers of cash benefits, instead replacing them with vouchers. In 2003 Blair announced his plans to slash the number of people applying for refugee status in the UK by half, despite warnings from NGOs that this would endanger the human rights of vulnerable people.[34] When Blair first came into power, asylum had barely featured in his policy platform; by 2002, he listed it as one of his top two domestic issues.[35] But if Labour strategists hoped that shifting to a more tabloid-friendly, hardline position on asylum would reward them in the polls, they were mistaken. By 2008, the proportion of Brits who thought that Labour had a better immigration policy than the Tories had actually declined.[36] Instead, it was the right who were the beneficiaries of public approval.

Defenders of the *Sun*'s editorial line would argue that the paper was simply reflecting the opinion of its readership: it might not be pretty, and it's certainly not politically correct, but it's how people were responding to the cultural and demographic changes they saw all around them. Indeed, the *Sun* often presented its asylum coverage as being a conduit for the voice of the people. A petition launched by Rebekah Wade, urging the government to stop 'bogus' asylum seekers 'flooding the country' attracted over half a million signatories by the weekend, representing a sixth of the paper's paying readership.[37] But people's sense of what's going on around them isn't always accurate: indeed, it can be warped to produce wholly deceptive perceptions if it coheres with narratives coming from the press and politicians. In the Hertfordshire commuter suburb of Broxbourne – home to a big Marks and Spencer, and very little else – voters in the 2003 local elections professed to be sick to the back teeth of asylum seekers. A reporter from the *Guardian* newspaper[38] roamed the suburban cul-de-sacs and found no shortage of fifty-somethings grumbling that asylum seekers were ruining the neighbourhood. 'Everybody has had enough of them,' said one Terry Harmone. 'You are better off being a foreigner in this country than being English.' Meanwhile, the aptly named Maureen Brownless complained of witnessing asylum seekers cashing their benefits cheques at the local post office.

There was just one problem. There weren't any asylum seekers in Broxbourne at the time. Despite Terry and Maureen's lurid tales of hotels chock full of asylum seekers, their families arriving by the busload, there was not even a single one in the Broxbourne area, according to some neat sleuthing by the *Guardian* into local council figures. The good people of Broxbourne, professing alarm at the influx of asylum seekers into their area, were 'chasing an urban myth'. But imaginary in origin or not, the anti-asylum grumbles of white suburban baby boomers in Broxbourne were enough to gift the BNP – an explicitly far-right, anti-immigration and ethno-nationalist party – their first ever council seat in England's relatively wealthy South in the 2003 elections. Despite the BNP's attempts to clean up their image in the early 2000s, distancing themselves from the vulgar racism and violence of far-right street movements, connections to its extremist roots endured. Their successful Broxbourne candidate had been a treasurer for the National Front, a white supremacist party with origins in the British Union of Fascists.[39] The unreconstructed nastiness of the British National Party even drew the condemnation of the *Sun*: in 2004, they ran a front-page headline slamming the 'vile racist party' of 'Bloody Nasty People'. But despite the *Sun*'s haughty reproofs, the BNP counted on the tabloids as a key political ally. 'There's that old saying that you need quite a bit of luck in politics,' said Simon Darby, a BNP council candidate who also stood in 2003's local elections. 'Well we've had quite a bit of luck in that newspapers have become obsessed with the asylum issue. I have not been able to believe the *Daily Express*. Issue after issue, day after day, asylum this, asylum that. So we now have the luxury of banging on people's doors with the mainstream issue of the day.'[40] The hardline anti-asylum editorial positions of the *Sun*, *Daily Mail* and *Daily Express* 'legitimised us', noted Darby. 'We are mainstream now.'

As asylum issues became more fiercely contested, reports of racist attacks on asylum seekers, or those perceived as asylum seekers, ticked up. The Crown Prosecution Service dealt with a 20 per cent increase in racially motivated crimes between 2001 and 2002[41]; what's more, the Institute of Race Relations found that places which had been the focus of alarmist 'tabloid exposés' about the asylum-seeking menace became particular hotspots for racist violence.[42] The English city of Peterborough had been the subject of such newspaper scaremongering, and had even come under extraordinary attack by its own mayor: in 2004, he accused asylum seekers of having turned it into a 'crime-ridden, rubbish-strewn hellhole', assailed by 'newcomers [who] have learned to milk the system'.[43] 'They receive benefits and comfortable housing, then take cash-in hand jobs,' he alleged, 'flaunting flashy cars, designer clothes and mobiles, they have infuriated locals.'

That same year, a fifteen-strong gang attacked an Asian dairy owner with a concrete block before viciously beating a Kurdish man with sticks. A nineteen-year-old Iraqi begged the local council to rehouse him after a petrol bomb was lobbed through his window: 'I am now scared to stay here,' he said, 'and am going crazy because I feel that I have no way to escape this violence.' In 2001, two Iraqi men were chased to their home by a gang who smashed up the windows, looted the property and beat one of the residents with a hammer and an iron bar; in 2003, flats which housed immigrants were targeted by arsonists.[44] The united efforts of anti-asylum narratives pushed by sections of the press and politicians created a paranoid vortex, swirling together the themes of asylum and crime, ethnicity and filth. And this climate of hysteria, disgust and hostility meant that lines pushed by politicians and the press ended up in the mouths of street thugs in Peterborough and playground bullies in Enfield. Wealth may not trickle down, but hatred certainly does.

At its core, the asylum moral panic was a product of press and political collusion – whipping up a frenzy of racist and indiscriminate loathing while simultaneously denouncing the inevitable nastiness which followed. But the populist packaging of anti-asylum narratives by the tabloids, and the validation of those narratives by the government of the day, had another profound impact on UK politics: it split the British working class along the lines of race and migration.

As we saw with the imaginary asylum seekers of Broxbourne, you didn't actually need people applying for refugee status in any given area for there to be a big to-do about how marauding gangs of Afghans/Iraqis/Somalis/whatever were snacking on swans and terrorising the neighbourhood. The public's perceptions of the number of asylum-seeking households were often completely out of whack with how many there actually were – instead, it tended to reflect the intensity and tone of media coverage. But that didn't mean that there weren't increases in people seeking asylum during the Blair years, or that they were evenly distributed around the country. Indeed, a core component of Tony Blair's asylum policy was enforcing the 'dispersal' of asylum seekers away from London. Instead of being able to shape a life for themselves in a diverse, multicultural city where they were more likely to be able to connect with their kinship networks and wider community, asylum seekers were instead forcibly distributed around the country, often in areas which had high levels of deprivation and low levels of opportunity (or, to quote Dominic Cummings once more, places that had 'gone to shit materially').

The message coming from the right-wing media, and reinforced by the centre-left government, was that these newcomers were out to game the system and get something for nothing. Many of the attack lines used against asylum seekers bear remarkable resemblance to those used to demonise benefits claimants under David Cameron's austerity government: these are undeserving graspers who claim benefits but have flashy phones, designer gear and are assigned prime council accommodation. In the next chapter, we'll look in detail at how these discourses of an ethnically diverse 'chavvy' underclass were eventually abandoned in favour of a narrative of the left-behind white working class.

Economics were the method – but what did it do to our souls? For all the flaws and limitations of mass council housing, industrial labour and the trade union movement, at least these institutions pulled people into contact with one another. In July 2024, as I watched the brass bands at a rainy Durham Miners' Gala, I got a powerful pang, feeling what had been taken from the country in the past forty years. Hand-painted and sewn banners were hoisted by union representatives marching down the high street. Some depicted pit villages, collieries or convalescent homes for coal miners. But others were totems of working-class political ambition. 'All men are brethren,' declared one. Another showed a worker, shirt sleeves rolled up, strangling a snake labelled 'capitalism'. As a nation, we've largely lost these parts of ourselves as the institutions which promoted connection, collectivism and solidarity were systematically undermined or destroyed. The nature of work has changed, atomising people even further. Where once different ethnic groups would have been forced into proximity by working at the same factory, now immigrants are funnelled towards lonely, invisibilised forms of labour. There's little opportunity to mix with people who aren't from your background when you're driving taxis, delivering food, cleaning empty offices or fruit and veg picking with dozens of others who've been brought over from the same country as you. The economic conditions have primed us for the politics of suspicion and hostility. Our souls, our social selves, have been transformed.

With asylum seekers and 'small boats' dominating the airwaves again, Nigel Farage's Reform Party with seats in the House of Commons and a centre-left government in power, we've now got all the ingredients of another powerful, xenophobic moral panic like that of the noughties. And this is concerning not just because migrants and asylum seekers are deserving of dignity, tolerance and a good standard of living, but because attacks on these groups inhibit the project of building class power. Migrant families are often in the worst accommodation our broken housing system has to offer, beset by problems of damp and overcrowding.[45] Migrants in the gig economy, fruit and vegetable picking, cleaning and industrial food production are overrepresented in the ranks of underpaid, exploited and mistreated workers. When these groups are viewed as being outside of the working class – indeed, as being opposed to the working class – it paves the way for crap conditions to be rolled out and extended to people who were born here. Migrant workers are still more likely than British-born to be employed on zero-hours contracts, but the imposition of such contracts has been expanded across the economy in general:[46] 1.1 million people in the UK are on zero-hours, with nearly three-quarters of them counted as being in 'extremely insecure' work.[47]

In July 2024, a few weeks before the subsequent wave of far-right riots set off by the Southport incident, unrest broke out in the Harehills neighbourhood of Leeds, in the north of England. In some ways, Harehills is the quintessential Northern urban neighbourhood, filled with back-to-back terraced housing, carved up by ginnels. It's pretty mixed: majority white British, but with a sizeable South Asian and Eastern European presence. In Harehills South, nearly three-quarters of all households meet the threshold of being deprived, according to the 2021 census.[48] On this occasion, police had been called at around 5 p.m. to assist social services with taking some Roma children into care – a crowd gathered, and videos quickly circulated on WhatsApp and social media of children in distress.[49,50] A cop car was smashed up and flipped onto its side. Then a bus was set alight, thousands of residents crowded the streets, and local councillors appealed for calm and restraint while teenagers attempted to throw wheelie bins and pallets into the conflagration.[51] Locals put out much of the blaze themselves. By the morning, the trouble had dispersed, with nothing on the streets but burnt plastic and hot takes.

My Novara Media colleague Craig Gent, who lives in Harehills and was on the scene (without Bella the bully-mix in tow), told me what it was like on the ground. 'People are desperately looking for a racial dimension,' he explained in a phone call the next day. 'But if you're looking for an ethnic breakdown of the rioters and riot-stoppers, as you can expect, it was just *fucking everyone*. It was a bit of everyone doing the chucking stuff onto the fire, and it was a bit of everyone trying to stop them doing that.' It wasn't a black or white, Muslim or non-Muslim, immigrant or British-born antagonism. There were some members of the community who wanted to set fire to a bus, and some who wanted to stop them. But on the far right, a narrative had already been set in motion. Nigel Farage blamed 'the politics of the subcontinent' for the unrest.[52] His colleague, Richard Tice, opined that 'Multiculturalism has more than failed – this is the consequence of people with no respect for Britain'.[53] And the ever-opportunistic Tommy Robinson, sharing footage on Twitter, pointed the finger at 'Muslims',[54] 'imported families'[55] and 'Punjab origin gypsies'.[56] None of these men were in Harehills at the time.

These comments make an interesting contrast to how the far right reacted in 2023, when a protest outside a hotel housing asylum seekers in Knowsley, in Merseyside, ended in violence. As in Harehills, a police van was set alight, and objects were thrown at the cops. Knowsley, again like Harehills, has a high level of deprivation, though it has a notably higher percentage of white British residents. All in all, there was a similar level of disorder as there would be in Leeds the next year. But Nigel Farage was quick to emphasise the legitimate concerns of those out on the streets: 'The migrant hotel protest in Knowsley happened because many local parents are concerned for the safety of young schoolgirls,' he wrote on Twitter. 'They are decent, honest people with genuine worry – and certainly not "far right".'[57] Tommy Robinson had actually encouraged people to protest at the hotel in Knowsley, describing the protesters as people 'who are aggrieved with ILLEGAL ECONOMIC MIGRANTS (from third world s***holes where kiddy diddling is fine)'.[58] Even *Telegraph* columnists, while being careful to condemn unlawful behaviour, characterised those present as 'mainly local mums and dads concerned about the safety of their kids after scores of undocumented young male migrants were billeted without consultation in their area'.[59] By virtue of being both white and anti-asylum seeker the Knowsley rioters were transformed into being tribunes of ordinary, common-sense, neglected, working-class Brits. The Harehills rioters, due to suspicious levels of melanin within the community, were nothing less than the barbarian hordes. What it means to be working class, then, has little to do with your material conditions. It's defined by political positioning in relation to immigration.

This contrast between the working-class Red Wall, and the rich elitism of London, then, doesn't stand up to a great deal of scrutiny. There are immense geographic imbalances in investment, infrastructure and average pay, but that doesn't mean that class and regional inequality are the same thing. As Owen Hatherley points out in *Red Metropolis*, Barrow-in-Furness has a home ownership rate of 74 per cent compared to Hackney's paltry 20 per cent.[60] Nearly half of Hackney's children are classed as living in poverty;[61] in Barrow, that figure is just over a fifth.[62] Hackney has a higher unemployment rate than Barrow; the spiralling cost of living in the city means that, on average, Hackney's citizens have much lower rates of disposable income. As Hatherley notes wryly, 'this is a strange elite'. Indeed, it is a strange economy where – depending on which indicators you're looking at – an inner London borough like Hackney is *both richer and poorer* than a Red Wall seat like Barrow-in-Furness. Framing one as somehow more authentically working class than the other is simply absurd.

We instinctively have trouble getting our heads around the fact that the working class are diverse, spread across the country, and live very differently from one another. And somehow, we're always falling into the trap that one group is more authentically representative of the working class than another. Deprivation has very different characteristics depending on which part of the country you're in. In big cities, like London, Manchester and Birmingham, extreme wealth and entrenched poverty rub up next to each other. The London constituency of Bethnal Green and Bow is one of the capital's poorest by income,[63] has the highest rate of child poverty in the country and sits in the cold shadows of the City of London's dizzying skyscrapers. Kensington and Chelsea, home of both the nouveau and aristocratic super-rich, is also where scores of working-class people died in the Grenfell Tower blaze. The poorest parts of the UK's big cities also tend to be the most ethnically diverse, have the largest immigrant populations and record the lowest levels of hostility towards migrants. This is a strange elite indeed.

These labels don't reflect income or wealth. They reflect the political geography of Britain, in an electoral system which disenfranchises large swathes of the working class. We've ended up with a definition of class that plays both sides of the minority game. Class is defined as a feeling of affinity with a reactionary conservative ideology, presented as majority values ('Everyone thinks this way, you're just a hard left extremist, you don't understand the country, etc.'). But at the same time, these so-called 'majority values' of hardline xenophobia cut the working class off from its actually existing demographic majority. Though geographically and culturally diverse, everyone who's excluded from the ownership classes is impacted by migrant workers being paid and treated like crap. Those precarious, impoverished conditions spread from being applied to an exceptional few, to larger sections of the workforce. If you view those whose conditions are connected to yours as cultural enemies, or rivals, what hope can there be of fighting for something better? A splintered working class is a weak working class. What we'll see in the next chapter, however, is the explosive power that can be unleashed when marginalised people see themselves reflected in each other's struggle and combine class conflict with demands for racial justice. It's precisely that unity which terrifies ruling-class elites. They pulled an absolute blinder by defining class on a cultural, rather than a material basis. Because in doing so, organising on the basis of class becomes a minority pursuit – and no matter who comes out on top at the ballot box, capital wins again.

5

One Big Gang

The first week of August 2011 was one of those London summers you spend a long, drizzly winter praying for: light until well past 9 p.m. and sunny enough for shorts, stunners and an ice lolly. I was nineteen years old. Having moved into a uni house-share a whole fifteen miles away from my mum, a couple of beers at a day festival were enough to set off the twinges of homesickness, so I decided to surprise her with a visit, but the trains, buses and tubes going to north London were all messed up. When I eventually emerged at Enfield Town station, just a few minutes' walk away from where I went to secondary school, I realised why.

Facing off against lines of riot cops, more than I'd ever seen in the neighbourhood, were scores and scores of teenagers. Despite the warm weather, the gathered youth wore their hoodies up and woolly scarves pulled across their noses and mouths. But some were familiar, the younger siblings of people I knew from school. They'd come from the poorer bits of the surrounding area – Edmonton, Brimsdown, Ponders End. The main road, usually a gridlocked nightmare of double deckers and Fiat Puntos, was empty but for blue lights and vans from the Territorial Support Group, a police unit responsible for public order. The crowd was arranged in more haphazard clumps than the police in their military formation, but they were taut, tense and purposeful. The Metropolitan Police's German Shepherds were in a frenzy, straining with every sinew against their leashes to get at a bewildered Staffie that one girl had brought with her. I flapped around impotently between the two battle lines, certain that something big was going to kick off, and totally unsure of where to be when it did. When a glass bottle flew through the air, exploding against the door of a police van, I decided it was time to ring mum and ask if she could come and give me a lift.

What had happened? On 4 August 2011, Mark Duggan – a twenty-nine-year-old black man of mixed Irish and Afro-Caribbean descent – was shot dead by the Metropolitan Police in the nearby neighbourhood of Tottenham. The hard stop – a police manoeuvre where armed police stop a vehicle believed to contain dangerous suspects – which killed Duggan was a part of Operation Trident, a police unit set up to address gun crime in London's black community. While the death of Mark Duggan at the hands of police was later ruled lawful by a jury, it reeked of injustice for those with their own experiences of discriminatory policing. All too many in Tottenham had known what it was like to be stopped and searched without cause, raided without justification, roughed up without apology. Many of Tottenham's elders could remember the Broadwater Farm riots of 1985, sparked when forty-nine-year-old mother Cynthia Jarrett died in her home during a police search of the property. Jarrett's death itself came just a week after Cherry Groce, another black mother, was left permanently paralysed after being shot by police conducting a search of her home in Brixton. During those nights of renewed turbulence in 2011 I asked my grandma, a veteran anti-racist organiser who'd lived in Tottenham since the early 1980s, if she was all right: then seventy-four, she brushed me off, remarking that if she didn't have a dicky leg, she too would have been out on the streets giving the cops what for. The bullet which killed Mark Duggan reopened old wounds in the community.

For the neighbourhood's younger residents, the killing of Mark Duggan resonated painfully with their own experiences of police violence and disproportionate targeting for stop and search. Some who knew Duggan remarked on the difference between the Mark they knew and the one depicted by the national media. The photograph favoured by the press, of Duggan glowering at the camera, had been cropped to erase the fact that he was standing by the grave of his infant daughter, a memorial stone held in his hands. Despite being presented as an exceptionally vicious criminal, his only convictions were for cannabis possession and handling stolen goods. As one person who went to school with Duggan and saw him just a few days before he was killed told me: 'In that whole midst of everything, he's the ... top twenty-five gangsters in Europe. Who the fuck made that table up? ... Like, Mark's about but he's not [the top] twenty-five in Tottenham!'[1]

At a protest on 6 August outside Tottenham Police Station, rumours swirled that a teenage girl had been assaulted by police. Although these rumours were never verified and the girl never found, they sparked a confrontation with police. The neighbourhood's youth were ablaze with fury. What followed were five nights of chaos that spread from north London across much of England. Tottenham burned. London echoed with sirens and shattered windows. Disorder spread up and down the country, and the towns and cities of England were rocked by five nights of bleeding. By the riots' end, five people had died and many more had been injured. Thousands had been arrested and over 1,500 people issued with charges. Under the auspices of then-Director of Public Prosecutions Keir Starmer, courts were authorised to run twenty-four hours a day in order to dole out sentences. One man, Anderson Fernandes, was jailed for taking two scoops of ice cream from a burgled Patisserie Valerie in Manchester.[2]

The riots came just a year into the rule of the Conservative–Liberal Democrat coalition government. Though technically in a political partnership alongside the larger Conservatives, the Lib Dems were little more than a fig leaf for the brutal austerity politics of David Cameron and George Osborne. After hundreds of billions of pounds was spent bailing out the banks in the 2007–2008 financial crisis, the UK government had decided that the best way to replenish the Treasury's coffers was to slash spending on healthcare, welfare, education and infrastructure (otherwise known as 'society'). The forlorn mewling of Nick Clegg did little to hold back the axe. Over £11 billion was taken out of the local government budget – meaning that everything from child protection services to elderly care faced massive cuts to their budgets.[3] The government introduced a 'bedroom tax' for people on housing benefits (meaning that if they lived in a property with one or more 'spare' bedrooms, they lost up to a quarter of their housing support payment). Education maintenance allowance, a £30 weekly payment for poor teenagers in further education, was scrapped entirely. Unemployment, homelessness and poverty all increased; and beneath those headline statistics was a devastating human cost. According to research carried out by University College London, there would be 120,000 excess deaths attributable to austerity between 2010 and 2017 alone.[4] Between 2013 and 2018, more than 17,000 sick and disabled people died while waiting for their benefits.[5] Kids started showing up to school hungry with startling regularity, or in unwashed uniforms.[6] Before 2010, food banks were a pretty marginal phenomenon, but by the 2015 General Election, food bank packages topped one million for the first time.[7] To put it bluntly, austerity turned us into a country where the working class went hungry, got sicker and died younger. But it wasn't all bad news. The rich enjoyed a tax cut to the top rate. Britain's wealthiest families doubled their net worth between 2009 and 2015.[8] The bankers even started getting their bonuses again.

There are those who'd say that the riots had nothing to do with these socioeconomic conditions – that police violence, institutional racism, poverty, economic inequality and austerity were all just excuses for opportunistic looting and lawlessness. And hey, if you're one of those people, who think that context has no bearing on events, I'm surprised and grateful that you've made it this far with the book. But when rioters themselves described looting as 'getting our taxes back', arguing that austerity and inequality didn't matter rings hollow.[9]

What I hope to convince you of, over the course of this chapter, is that the riots were a snapshot of a much larger phenomenon. They showed that there's nothing more powerful and dangerous than when working-class people are united in their loathing of the status quo, identifying with each other rather than against one another, and directing their rage at racial injustice and economic inequality simultaneously. But almost all the mainstream media was implacably opposed to viewing the 2011 riots through this lens. Instead they blamed what they perceived to be black culture – hoodies, slang and music – for stirring the nation's youth into a frenzy. The ruling class closed ranks, pinning the blame on minorities themselves, rather than on how the government's austerity policies and endemic police racism combined to drive rioters into a destructive rampage. By looking at the media and political response to the riots, we'll see that the uprising of Britain's youth terrified elites because of the simple fact that black and white were largely united on the streets. The response was a political project to divide the working class along the lines of race and establish the category of a 'white working class' whose interests would be implacably opposed to, and threatened by, calls for racial equality.

In the immediate aftermath of the riots, Britain's elite media marshalled its best and brightest talking heads in order to make sense of the madness. On the BBC's *Newsnight*, historian David Starkey joined author Owen Jones and novelist Dreda Say Mitchell. Peering haughtily over the top of his horn-rimmed glasses, the professor-slash-pundit insisted to a sceptical panel that the riots were 'completely superficial' – more to do with wanting to loot trainers than any meaningful experience of social exclusion.[10] When attempting to explain why white youths across the country had participated in riots sparked by the police killing of a black man in Tottenham, David Starkey offered the following explanation:

> There has been a profound culture change. I've just been re-reading Enoch Powell, the 'Rivers of Blood' speech. His prophecy was absolutely right in one sense. The Tiber didn't 'foam with much blood', but 'flames lambent' wrapped around Tottenham and wrapped around Clapham. But it wasn't intercommunal violence. This is where he was completely wrong. What's happened is that a substantial section of the 'chavs' that you wrote about have become black. The whites have become black.[11]

The whites have become black. According to Starkey, Britain's once rosy-cheeked and Hovis-scoffing white working class had degenerated into something altogether more sinister. Gesturing at Owen Jones, the esteemed professor perhaps missed that his co-panellist's book was less an anthropological study of so-called 'chav' culture than it was a passionate excoriation of the media and political establishment's demonisation of impoverished Britons in the age of austerity. But regardless of whether he'd done the required reading, Starkey's point was clear. Black culture was a social contaminant, and it had polluted the decent and pure white working class. Enoch Powell's apocalyptic vision of the consequences of black and brown immigration to the UK had come to pass.

Powered by a sense of injustice and no shortage of naivety, a group of friends and I spent the subsequent nights of the riots hoofing around Hackney and Tower Hamlets distributing 'bust cards' with legal advice, as if there was much a bunch of arts and humanities students could teach the uprising youth of working-class London about how to interact with the criminal justice system. The disputed circumstances surrounding the fatal shooting of Mark Duggan – lurid media reports of a shoot-out were debunked, after a bullet lodged in a police radio was found to have been fired from a police firearm – combined with longstanding hostility between the Met and those they policed.

The neighbourhoods I'd grown up and gone to school in – Tottenham, Edmonton, Enfield – were discussed by the nation's newsreaders with the kind of grim exoticism reserved for Helmand or Fallujah. Young people in grey tracksuits, scarves tugged up around their mouths, were framed by burning bins and smashed windows to present images of urban menace. 'Thugs and thieves terrorise British streets,' blared the print headline of the *Daily Express*,[12] while both the solidly right-wing *Telegraph* and notionally liberal *Independent* were united in their condemnation of 'mob rule'.[13] A ruffled flock of jour-nalists and minor celebrities (including, weirdly, Pop Idol runner-up Gareth Gates) took to Twitter calling for the military to be deployed on the streets of London.[14] Gizzi Erskine, host of *Cook Yourself Thin* and daughter of the second Baron Erskine of Rerrick, tweeted: 'The LA riots were stopped 6 days [in] when the army started shooting. Hmmmm. Thoughts?'[15] I didn't see her say the same during the 2024 race riots where the far right targeted immigrants and people of colour.

Participants in the riots were written up as yobs and morons, more animal than human. Those who tried to contextualise the nights of violence by drawing attention to the social or polit-ical conditions of the time found themselves ridiculed by the media, who saw their role more as spewing fire and brimstone than fostering the public's understanding of current affairs. 'To blame the cuts is immoral and cynical,' argued the *Daily Mail* in an editorial.[16] 'This is criminality – pure and simple – by yobs who have nothing but contempt for decent, law-abiding people. No, regardless of the propaganda pumped out by the Left-wing establishment, this is not a repeat of the political riots that scarred the early 1980s, which were sparked by mass unemployment and alleged police racism.' The best way to understand what happened, according to the right-wing press, was to believe that Britain's youth had simply turned feral due to their own rotten morality. Two days after the *Mail*'s comment piece, faithful parrot and then-Prime Minister David Cameron repeated their 'criminality – pure and simple' line in the House of Commons.

The attitude amongst much of the media and political establishment was that it didn't matter that unemployment for young black men had doubled in the three years following the financial crisis,[17] nor that black and Asian households amongst the poorest fifth of the population experienced the biggest drop in living standards due to the government's changes to tax, benefits and cuts to public services.[18] It didn't matter that Mark Duggan had been shot in a 'hard stop', a tactic recommended for review by the Independent Police Complaints Commission after the unlawful killing of Azelle Rodney by police in 2005. It didn't matter that black people were six times more likely to be stopped and searched than their white counterparts in 2011/12.[19] You could have been made poorer by a government who bailed out the banks, or witnessed police break the very law they're meant to uphold – but that's no reason to be angry.

England's working-class black youth, according to the prevailing view in politics and the media, had no one to blame but themselves for the riots. What, however, could explain the participation of white people, who made up nearly the same percentage of those charged during the unrest as black people?[20] The media establishment had their answer: the whites, in

Professor Starkey's words, had become black. His comments on that fateful episode of *Newsnight* drew hundreds of complaints (and even the condemnation of Piers Morgan), but there was no shortage of voices in Britain's comment pages agreeing with *what* Starkey said while parping objections to *how* he said it.

Perhaps Starkey's endorsement of Enoch Powell's notorious 'Rivers of Blood' speech – a notorious watershed moment in British race relations – was a bridge too far for a media establishment which loudly condemns Powell as a racist, while perpetuating his ideas in the guise of 'legitimate concerns' about immigration. Or maybe it was his insistence that anyone listening to black MP David Lammy on the radio 'would think he was white' that alienated those who were otherwise his ideological allies. But Starkey's central point that social contamination had taken place – that some kind of cultural rot had spread from black Brits to white ones – did find a sympathetic ear across much of the press.

Casting a beady eye over the furore in *The Economist*, Anne McElvoy wrote:

> Some of Dr Starkey's analysis was downright odd – like his statement that anyone hearing David Lammy, the well-educated, black Tottenham MP speak, would think he was white. Plenty of other British black people speak without resort to Afro-American patois. But he did raise an issue plenty of viewers would think worthy of discussion: the cultural and social factors forming the way that some inner-city youths conduct themselves. Nor could it reasonably be denied that the 'gangsta' culture of hooded young men and contempt for the 'Feds', previously known as the police, played a major role in unleashing some of the violence and disorder, even if others from other social and ethnic backgrounds joined in.[21]

Here, McElvoy distances herself – meaning, the window of reasonable opinion – from the more clumsy and cartoonish bits of David Starkey's riots hot-take. The idea that David Lammy sounds white on the radio is, in McElvoy's words, 'downright odd'. You'd be forgiven for raising an eyebrow here: 'downright odd' would be mistaking David Lammy's voice for Joe Pasquale. 'Racist' would be the correct term for associating being articulate with being white, and being white with moral superiority. Strangely, this word fails to feature even once in her piece, though 'possibly offensive', 'objectionable', 'provocative' and 'controversial' all make appearances. To this day, many journalists are incapable of calling something 'racist' if milder and more verbose options are available. Maybe it's a result of being paid by the word, or perhaps an unwritten condition of being part of the club of Britain's elite opinion formers is that you pull your punches when it comes to a fellow member.

No reasonable person could deny, she argues, that 'the "gangsta" culture of hooded young men and contempt for the "Feds", previously known as the police, played a major role in unleashing some of the violence and disorder, even if others from other social and ethnic backgrounds joined in'. This is an almost word-for-word repetition of David Starkey's argument on *Newsnight*, who also spoke disparagingly of patois. 'A particular sort of violent, destructive, nihilistic, "gangsta" culture has become the fashion,' Starkey harrumphed. 'And black and white, boy and girl, operate in this language together. This language which is wholly false, which is a Jamaican patois, that's been intruded in England. And this is why so many of us have this sense of [being] literally in a foreign country.'

McElvoy and Starkey's comments share the view that there was something inherently degraded, criminal and unworthy about contemporary black pop culture – and that this something was both a leading cause of the August 2011 riots, and explained the participation of white youth in them. This was not an isolated view amongst journalists and commentators at the time: Paul Routledge of the *Daily Mirror* blamed 'the pernicious culture of hatred around rap music' for creating a hatred of authority and police amongst the nation's youth, and called for the broadcasting of such music to be banned.[22] *The Telegraph*'s Graeme Archer complained in Starkey-like terms that the nation's city-dwelling youth had learned to speak 'in a completely made-up accent based on their idea of how gangsters talk', enraptured by 'a musical subgenre that mixes blatant pornography with violent, egotistical lyrical content'.[23] He moved away from London later that year – and like every journalist who experiences a life change, was compelled to write multiple articles about it ('Call that white flight if you like. Call it "white avoidance" if you must. I prefer to call it civilised, bourgeois, suburban safety').[24]

A decade on, it's patently laughable that the commentariat's best explanation for the most widespread rioting this country had seen for decades was slang and music. If you're wondering why rap music was assigned such astonishing power by the nation's pundits (*Parental Advisory: This Album Incites Riots!*), it's because there was a long history of presenting black popular culture as both infectious and dangerous. In 1993, a parliamentary debate was derailed when one MP asked whether it was appropriate for 'left-leaning teachers' to teach rap music in English lessons, kicking off a chain of contributions which culminated in another right honourable member launching into a Latin translation of the Beatles' 'Yellow Submarine'. But some scaremongering was less aware of its own silliness.

In 1950s Britain, newspapers were awash with lurid tales of young white girls falling prey to the twin scourges of cannabis and bebop. Alex Brown, a researcher into drugs and social attitudes, found that police raids on London's jazz clubs would result in a press frenzy over the supposed corruption of white teenagers by black culture. The narcotic effect of weed and the intoxicating nature of jazz was presented as being one and the same. 'The young girls, in particular, abuse themselves in a nauseating fashion before their suppliers, Negroes many of them,' harrumphed one article.[25] 'Sometimes the dealer tantalises his victims, refusing to sell until one of the girls has danced with him. Eyes rolling, body twitching, a sixteen-year-old girl then slides into the motions of bebop in the arms of the black peddler.' This theme of the devious, almost mystical power of black music would be repeated in the pages of the *Spectator* over fifty years later, where one writer castigated 'the musico-industrial complex' for '[making] actual the stereotype of the Jamaican as a man of small brain but large appetites, with a powerful though primitive sense of rhythm'.[26] There's no doubt that the legacy of Jamaica's music scene is certainly powerful: not only is the Caribbean island's international cultural impact unparalleled, but evidently the right dub — played at just the right frequency — can make a British opinion writer spontaneously start measuring skulls.

This racist hysteria was conferred with a sense of legitimacy in the early 2000s, when British politicians began blaming rap music for a particularly nasty spate of violent incidents. After two black teenagers were killed in Birmingham at a New Year's Eve party in 2003, the Labour culture minister Kim Howells blamed the shooting on 'hateful lyrics' from 'boasting macho idiot rappers'.[27] In 2005, the Metropolitan Police introduced Form 696 — a risk assessment specifically for organisers of events that included DJs and MCs, which included questions about the ethnic makeup of the intended audience. It gave specific prompts about music styles likely to be played, including 'bashment, R&B, Garage'. Form 696 was an obvious attempt to police the music scene favoured by black and minority ethnic youth in London; even though it was scrapped by the city's mayor Sadiq Khan in 2017, rap duo Skengdo x AM found themselves legally prevented from playing their own music due to a 'gang injunction' targeted specifically at drill, a hip-hop sub-genre that has become the latest target of this kind of panic.

So it's not a surprise that black music provided a convenient scapegoat during the 2011 riots. Politicians, police and the press have attempted to link black culture to criminality and corruption of the youth since the first days of immigration from the former empire. Indeed, as one scene falls out of fashion and another rises, it's common to see formerly maligned genres being held up as an example of the good old days. The cannabis-wreathed jazz scene is compared favourably to the hedonism of disco; Public Enemy go from dangerous militants to a conscious antidote to gangsta rap. The very same names identified by the commentator David Goodhart as being particularly to blame for the riots (Dizzee Rascal, Lethal Bizzle and Giggs) are now seen as respectable elder statesmen of UK rap. No doubt the carousel will turn again, and the drill MCs currently being blamed for all manner of social ills will be recast as pillars of the community.

As I watched the great and the good talk about the riots on TV, I realised something. There is no accidental idiocy in British media consensus: there are only politically convenient lies. These farcical explanations played a powerful role in shaping public perceptions. A joint study carried out by the *Guardian* and the London School of Economics later in 2011 contrasted what the public thought had caused the unrest with the reasons offered by rioters themselves, to revealing effect. The general public felt strongly inclined to pin the blame on nebulous personal failings like 'poor parenting', 'criminality' and 'moral decline'.[28] But the rioters interviewed in the *Guardian*/LSE study showed a more sensitive understanding of the societal factors that led to such a turbulent summer. They were far more likely than the general public to bring up structural issues such as poverty, policing and government policy.

Interviewees recalled their own experiences of mistreatment at the hands of police. A Muslim teenager in Tottenham recalled when, during a stop and search, one officer mockingly remarked to a colleague 'Mate, why don't you ask him where Saddam [Hussein] is. He might be able to help out.'[29] Other rioters referred to the police as 'the biggest gang out there', whose role is to intimidate the public rather than ensure their safety.[30] Three-quarters of rioters thought the death of Mark Duggan was an 'important' or 'very important' cause of the unrest, but only half of the general public agreed that the fatal police shooting in north London, objectively the catalyst for the civil unrest across England, was a particularly significant factor.

Many of those interviewed talked about being motivated by a sense of injustice; it was their experience of policing, poverty and the government's savage cuts to public spending which brought them out onto the streets. One man in Tottenham said that 'I still to this day don't class it as a riot, I think it was a protest.' Figures of authority – whether the police, the press or the nation's politicians – had taken every opportunity to remind the young, urban poor that they viewed them as scum, that the chronic deprivation they saw all around them was a result of their own moral failings. It was a fiction to believe that you could be treated fairly; if you lived in the 'wrong' neighbourhood, wore the 'wrong' clothes or had the 'wrong' skin colour, you could expect to be treated like a criminal regardless of whether you'd done anything wrong. The killing of Mark Duggan showed just how dangerous being deemed a criminal could be.

Not a single rioter interviewed cited rap, patois or the existence of hooded sweatshirts as a reason for their participation. Which isn't surprising – I don't think anyone would ascribe the fall of the Weimar Republic to the rise of bias-cut dresses. But the joint political and media operation to misrepresent the riots as the senseless violence of a feral underclass was an overall success. Pundit gum-flapping about gangstas, feds and cultural decline wasn't only the familiar hysteria of an older generation being confronted by a youth that they find scary and incomprehensible. In part, what we see in the political and media framing of the 2011 riots is a Herculean exercise of blame-shifting.

Forced to explain the most intense rioting Britain had seen for decades, there was a concerted effort by the country's leading lights to direct our understanding away from social and economic factors, towards cultural 'failings' like clothes and slang. It's the government's fault if the streets are ablaze because of poverty, crap housing and institutional police racism. But it's the youth's fault if their allegiance to an 'inferior' ghetto culture that celebrates criminality turned them into mindless thugs. You can see why politicians – and the journalists who prop them up – preferred the latter explanation. No Cabinet minister ever got the sack because people thought the young were listening to too much 140bpm rap.

But there was more at play than simple political calculation. The ludicrous importance attributed to language, clothes and pop culture also reveals a lot about how race and class were being thought about at the time. As Owen Jones argues in his 2011 book *Chavs*, a profound transformation had taken place in how the British working class were framed in politics and media. Once upon a time, so the yarn goes, they were decent – i.e. white, hardworking and deferential to those in power. They doffed caps, said 'wotcher' and no one ever locked their doors. But over a period of decades, this shifted to a portrait of fecklessness, criminality and cultural degradation.

Matt Lucas and David Walliams's Vicky Pollard character, from the massively successful 2000s sketch show *Little*

Britain, summed up this new state of depravity. Vicky was poor, had loads of kids, wore leggings and was out to take what she could get from the welfare state. As Jones writes, the dominant image of the British working class went 'from salt of the earth to scum of the earth'.[31] The nation's opinion pages and the gurning caricatures of *Little Britain* told a unified story. As James Delingpole – who once described himself as part of 'the most discriminated-against subsection in the whole of British society: the white, middle-aged, public-school-and-Oxbridge-educated middle-class male' – wrote in *The Times*:

> The reason Vicky Pollard caught the public imagination is that she embodies with such fearful accuracy several of the great scourges of contemporary Britain: aggressive all-female gangs of embittered, hormonal, drunken teenagers; gym-slip mums who choose to get pregnant as a career option; pasty-faced, lard-gutted slappers who'll drop their knickers in the blink of an eye; dismal ineducables who may not know much about English or History, but can damn well argue their rights with a devious fluency that would shame a barrister from Matrix Chambers.[32]

'Lard-gutted slappers', 'dismal ineducables' – this kind of snarling, vicious tirade against the inherent inferiority of so-called chavs was a staple genre of UK media in the early 2000s. It wouldn't get past an editor now, and it shouldn't have been signed off by one then. It doesn't bode well for *The Times*, one of the most venerable and respected publications in the global media landscape, that Delingpole was ever taken seriously. But even without his expensive education, it's possible to identify some flaws in the argument that a grotesque and exaggerated parody of a working-class woman, as penned and portrayed by Walliams and Lucas (who both attended private schools), was a realistic depiction of life on a housing estate. It's like bringing up Ursula from *The Little Mermaid* to talk about what it's really like under the sea.

But this was a recurring trope in UK media. The *Sunday Mirror* ran a feature on 'THE REAL LIFE VICKY POLLARDS' in 2005;[33] in 2013, the broadsheet *Telegraph* used an image of the *Little Britain* character to illustrate a story about a school allowing pupils to wear jogging bottoms.[34] Most people today would consider it intellectually dishonest, if not downright idiotic, to blur fiction and reality in this way – but for those who don't, there's a successful career in journalism out there for you.

Jones argues that these broadsides against chavs were part of a deliberate project to demonise benefits recipients as scroungers to justify the government's slash-and-burn approach to welfare provision. News stories about criminally deviant working-class people were elevated to the level of national scandal, to create the impression that poor people were a dangerous and feral underclass, rather than victims of government policy. Indeed, the idea that working-class people might be able to argue their case ('dismal ineducables who may not know much about English or History, but can damn well argue their rights with a devious fluency that would shame a barrister') was seen as evidence of just how far society had fallen: *not only do we allow these disgusting people to exist, but we give them rights as well!*

This sentiment was a frequent theme of early 2000s social commentary. Theodore Dalrymple argued that ideas like egalitarianism and determinism – i.e. that equality is good, and that people are shaped by their experiences – had helped create an underclass that constantly sought to excuse its own actions. 'The urban savage has rights,' growled Dalrymple, 'of which he is only too aware.'[35] Should an 'inner-city thug' be denied immediate gratification, claimed Dalrymple, they'd allege that their human rights were being breached. And then, of course, explode into violence. Rather than being the foundation of a civilised and democratic society, the message in the media was that poor people being able to legally or politically stand up for themselves merely allowed them to exploit the system. This narrative blueprint would form the basis of how journalists later explained away the 2011 riots. But the early 2000s obsession with chavs wasn't just about class; it also embodied elite anxieties about race.

If, by 2011, journalists and talking heads were falling over themselves to scaremonger that 'the whites have become black', it was because there was already a strong cultural perception that this was the case. In multiple sketches, the white and Bristolian Vicky Pollard would snap 'God, you're so racist!' when told to cease and desist some kind of antisocial behaviour. This idea that people – particularly, working class people – cynically throw accusations of racism around to avoid accountability had been popularised by Ali G's catchphrase, 'Is it cos I is black?' In both the cases of Ali G (played by Sacha Baron Cohen) and Vicky Pollard (played by Matt Lucas) part of the gag is that obviously, visually, they're not black people. The joke is that Ali G and Vicky Pollard are deluded about who they are. But that didn't necessarily mean that ethnic minorities weren't being ridiculed in either instance.

'Is it cos I is black?' has been thrown at people of colour ever since to pour scorn on their accounts of experiencing racism. The joke of Ali G or Vicky Pollard accusing others of racism is that it's wholly self-serving, a trump card to avoid being held to normal moral standards. Like Delingpole's diatribe against the 'devious fluency' of working-class people arguing their rights, Baron Cohen's catchphrase has become a way to discredit black people doing the same. What's more, Vicky Pollard's abject state wasn't just communicated by the fact she was a single mum: worse still, some of the toddlers she pushed in a phalanx of prams clearly had black or Asian fathers. Part of why Vicky Pollard – symbol of the aggressive, grasping poor – was worthy of national derision was because she was making the working class less white, at a time when the fastest growing ethnic group in the UK was 'mixed race'.[36] If the whites were becoming black, in the words of David Starkey, it was because chavs (embodied by sexually promiscuous and culturally stunted figures like Vicky Pollard and Ali G) were making them become so.

The idea that the white working class felt a kind of connection with black culture was seen as clownish, grotesque and even obscene. What was a joke in the sketch comedy of *Little Britain* and *Da Ali G Show* was taken with remarkable seriousness by the country's establishment media. Melanie Phillips berated the 'underclass which is a world apart from the lives most of us lead' and, perhaps confusing *Little Britain* with a documentary, bizarrely alleged that Britain's cultural decline had led to 'whole communities where committed fathers are so rare that any child who actually has one risks being bullied'.[37] Elsewhere Phillips has argued that the prevalence of single-parent families in black communities is to blame for the over-representation of young black men as victims of knife crime.[38] Vicky Pollard's children of many colours, therefore, aren't just a racist gag about how disgusting it is to have a mixed-race family; they are, rather, evidence of a social contamination between black communities and white people, which turned the once decent white working class into lawless 'chavs'.

The early 2000s media construct of a feral and ethnically ambiguous underclass corroding British civilisation from the inside was a powerful political tool. It meant that social problems could be blamed on those experiencing the sharp end of them. These people were beneath contempt – disgusting, backward, and dragging the whole of society downwards.

Some of the things that politicians said about this so-called underclass had to be seen to be believed. The discourse was vicious, and it emanated from the very heights of power. This is what New Labour kingpin Peter Mandelson said, in the early days of Blair's government, channelling the persona of the left-behind working class:

> We are the long term, benefit-claiming, working-class poor, living through another period of cultural contempt. We are losers, no hopers, low life scroungers. Our culture is yob culture. The importance of welfare provisions to our lives has been denigrated and turned against us; we are welfare dependent and our problems won't be solved by giving us higher benefits. We are perverse in our failure to succeed, dragging our feet over social change, wanting the old jobs back, still having babies instead of careers, stuck in outdated class and gender moulds. We are the challenge that stands above all others, the greatest social crisis of our times.[39]

The racial dimension of this media hysteria meant there was a convenient black/brown bogeyman on which to blame unrest that could otherwise be explained by socio-economic causes. In some way, the response to the riots – and the cultural foundation it was built on – recognised something true about cross-racial solidarity within the working class, even if the commentators put a grotesquely negative spin on it. As one rioter put it:

> We all got together that day, the Asians, the blacks, the whites. It felt like we were like one big gang. We took over Birmingham. Normally we don't get along. [But] we weren't fighting each other, we were fighting the police.[40]

When working-class youth of all races took to the streets after a black man was shot to death by the police, the country was shaken to its core. There was deep recognition among the youth that they had a shared experience. But if shared cultural coordinates like music and language helped facilitate that understanding, it wasn't the cause. It was obvious that they had been marginalised and oppressed by those in power. Impoverished by politicians, ridiculed in the press and harassed by the police, it's no wonder that a significant chunk of England's urban poor felt moved to anger by the killing of Mark Duggan. Though the riots were violent, destructive, frightening and – in some areas – fatal, they were also an expression of class consciousness. Whether you were black, white, Asian or mixed, if you were out on the streets for those nights in August 2011, it was because you felt like you were being screwed over by the same system.

The particular fear amongst the media class of the whites becoming culturally black set the stage for what would happen next in how our political and cultural elites would frame class and race over the following decade. If dangerous and disruptive things could happen when black and white people felt a sense of affinity and shared experience with one another, something would have to be done to break down the bonds of solidarity amongst the British working class.

The Invention of the 'White Working Class'

Something funny began to happen after 2011. After years of media pearl-clutching about multiethnic 'urban savages', 'chavs' and made-up inner-city accents, you just... stopped hearing about it. Something had dramatically shifted. No longer were politicians and pundits talking about the 'perverse failure' of 'losers' and 'no hopers' to succeed in life. Anger was no longer the violent result of feral urban youth being hyped up by hoodies and hip hop. Instead, a new group had appeared, armed with reasonable concerns and well-grounded grievances. 'There is a section of Britain's population that feels as though it is not getting its fair share and it is being left behind,' said Matthew Goodwin in a 2015 documentary about British race relations. 'You know these people are profoundly unhappy, upset and angry about how Britain is changing and evolving. Yes, we call these voters left-behind voters, older, white, not very well educated in comparison to other groups, profoundly angry with politicians in Westminster.'[41] It was as if one day all the Burberry-toting teenage mums with knives just disappeared, and standing in their place was a new object of media fixation: the white working class.

Conceptually, the idea of the white working class displaced that of the chav. Using a simple Google Ngram search, you can see that use of the terms 'chav' and 'chavs' collapses just as use of the phrase 'white working class' absolutely skyrockets. The social meanings attached to the terms were turned inside out. Chavs were supposedly disgusting, feckless and suspiciously interested in black culture. The white working class, however, carries connotations of decency, cultural conservatism, hard work and separate social existence from ethnic minorities. And the very same journalists who decried chavs as nothing less than warts on the arse of society were suddenly very concerned that working-class people had been demonised, disparaged and marginalised by a snooty liberal left.

James Delingpole is one who accomplished a leaping ideological 180° that would put Simone Biles to shame. Delingpole – who, as you'll recall, thought the country was being overrun by 'pasty-faced, lard-gutted slappers who'll drop their knickers in the blink of an eye' and 'dismal ineducables' – found himself a decade later railing against the 'ugly mix of preening superiority and poisonous disdain' levelled at working-class people.[42]

Writing for the *Sun* in 2017, Delingpole was weighing in on a social media micro-scandal about Nottingham-born, south London-based artist Hetty Douglas. The twenty-five-year-old had posted a picture to her Instagram stories of a group of scaffolders queueing in a central London McDonald's, captioning the snap 'These guys look like they got 1 GCSE.' At the time, Douglas didn't have much of a public profile. With the greatest respect to her, no one really knew her beyond the handful of art-world insiders who thought works such as 'sorry for treating you like shit & 4 fingering your best m8' were really Saying Something.[43]

But the post went wildly viral, and not in a good way. A screenshot of the offending Insta story racked up thousands of retweets. Douglas was slammed as a snob, a spoilt rich girl, and amongst some of the more vitriolic comments, as a 'fucking stuck up bitch'. She was seen to embody everything that was wrong with how south London was changing. Gentrification was making areas like Peckham, Camberwell, Brixton and New Cross prohibitively expensive for anyone other than those lucky enough to be bankrolled by Mum and Dad. I almost certainly took the opportunity to stick the boot in — as others have written, the discourse-machine is powerful and the allure of participating in someone else's public shaming is near irresistible. It made me feel virtuous to jump on someone I didn't know and make sweeping judgements about her based on a single Instagram post. I'd like to think I'd be more circumspect now.

Although the controversy had its origins on social media, the outrage wasn't confined to it. Commentators presented Douglas as a symbol of a sneering metropolitan elite who couldn't hide their loathing of the proletariat. James Delingpole was one of the pundits who took to the nation's opinion pages to haul Hetty Douglas over coals. She wasn't just one person who published a particularly obnoxious and mean-spirited thing on Instagram, wrote Delingpole breathlessly: no, the arts graduate was no less than 'the brainwashed product of a culture dominated by a liberal elite which treads on eggshells where any minority is concerned but which thinks it's perfectly acceptable, desirable even, to pour scorn and bile on the white working class'.

This liberal elite was over-educated and underemployed. They supported Jeremy Corbyn and couldn't abide Brexit. They flaunted 'worthless degrees' in 'Teletubbies and Transgender Studies' (citation needed), hated blue-collar workers (citation needed) and had caused the country to be afflicted by more hatred and division than any time 'since the days of the Civil War' (citation – well, you get the picture). Delingpole offered other examples: a vlogger, Suzy Lu, who tweeted that striking fast-food workers should 'get an actual decent job', and an anonymous tweeter who had mocked Bruce Forsyth, as proof that there was a liberal-left conspiracy against the working class. Breaking the fourth wall, Delingpole addressed his reader directly. 'If you're reading this newspaper,' he warned darkly, 'the likelihood is that the liberal elite loathes you with a vengeance.'

But in 2006, James Delingpole had been only too happy to join in with what he called 'a conspiracy against chavs'. In that article for *The Times*, he rebuked the liberal *Guardian* newspaper for defending a 'disgusting, selfish, violent underclass' against upper- and middle-class mockery. Despite having written scathingly about 'dismal ineducables', Delingpole condemned Hetty Douglas for implying that 'people without academic qualifications are inferior' and that 'their supposed stupidity is something she and her doubtless equally tedious chums, the educated people, should have a good giggle over'. Elsewhere, Delingpole defended Jeremy Clarkson when the *Top Gear* host said on BBC One that striking workers should be shot.[44]

There are those who would say there is no difference between James Delingpole's actions and what Hetty Douglas did. They'd be wrong. Hetty Douglas confined her class snobbery to a single Instagram story on her personal social media;

James Delingpole saw fit to stigmatise working-class people in a national newspaper. Douglas offered an apology for her words, admitting that what she'd written was 'not nice and not clever'. Delingpole maintained that the targets of his disdain only got what was coming to them. 'If they weren't quite so repellent,' runs Delingpole's line of thinking, 'we wouldn't need to make jokes about them, would we?'

Hypocrisy isn't new in the business of opinion writing, although this is a particularly egregious example of a journalist denouncing that which he has done himself (only, worse). But what's at play here is an astonishing and calculated act of political projection. It was frankly bizarre to link the YouTuber Suzy Lu, who as far as I can tell is largely apolitical, to Jeremy Corbyn – particularly when he had been vocal in his support of the McDonald's strike. Nor was there any particular evidence to suggest that Hetty Douglas was a liberal lefty, other than the fact that she fitted the age and geographic profile of someone likely to vote that way. Comparing James Delingpole's articles side by side, it's clear that his diatribe against a culture of 'poisonous disdain' towards the British working class more accurately describes his own behaviour, rather than anyone else's.

But Delingpole wasn't alone. Melanie Phillips, the columnist who had harrumphed at length about a fatherless, feckless underclass, popped up again at this point to argue that the nation's moral backbone was found in the 'economically shattered communities with very high levels of poverty and unemployment' who had switched from Labour to Tory in the 2019 general election.[45] Far from the scourge of 'feral children [and] feral parents' that Phillips had described in 2011,[46] the British working class were cast as 'deeply, passionately patriotic and attached to democracy' – no less than 'the very best of Britain'. During the riots, Melanie Phillips found common ground with David Starkey and snarled that the 'disaster of multiculturalism' had dissolved the country's social bonds. The liberal intelligentsia had excused the 'criminal wrongdoing' of British minorities for too long. But by 2019, British working people were 'repelled by identity politics and victim culture and are deeply worried by Muslim immigration and behaviour'. If in 2011 the whites had become black, by 2019 (as Phillips would have it) they wanted to turn back.

In *Chavs*, Owen Jones predicted that the years of insult and social exclusion endured by working-class people would result in a backlash. The far right would claim to speak for the (white British) left behind. But what he couldn't foresee was that *the very same individuals* who had been cheerleading the demonisation of the working class would suddenly transform themselves into tribunes of the much-maligned, forgotten white working class. The British commentariat turned out to be more unprincipled and double-dealing than even Jones predicted.

This phenomenon, however, is not just mere political cynicism. We have to understand why a narrow and ideologically loaded image of the white working class has become so dominant in how we think about race and class. It's not a coincidence that the likes of James Delingpole and Melanie Phillips frame their advocacy for the white working class in exclusively cultural terms. Right-wing populists voting against free school meals provision in Parliament, or Melanie Phillips' continued insistence that welfare payments are to blame for social corrosion, tells you something about how seriously this lot take the material conditions of working-class people. Railing against multiculturalism, or complaining about anti-racist language, doesn't put food on anyone's table (except the columnists', of course). But then again, it was never meant to.

There's a reason why concerns about the cultural influence of anti-racism feature so prominently in these defences of the white working class, whether that's using the phrase 'white privilege', '[treading] on eggshells where any minority is concerned' or valuing multiculturalism. It's not because these things actually impact problems like deprivation, educational attainment or geographic inequalities. It's because the only reason people are talking about the white working class at all is to hit back at decades of progress made in the recognition of racial injustice. The phrase 'white working class' builds oppositionality, a sense of competing interests, into an otherwise diverse socioeconomic group. The contrast being drawn isn't between white working-class and white middle-class individuals. It's between the white working class and immigrants, people of colour, Muslims and their supposed advocates within the all-powerful liberal elite. Put it this way – no one's talking about the *class* bit of white working class. It is, fundamentally, a concept that's intended to stoke the politics of racial resentment.

How has white privilege become such a contentious phrase in modern politics, particularly where class is concerned? If white privilege simply refers to the 'invisible weightless knapsack' which allows white people to move through the world without being discriminated against because of the colour of their skin, this isn't really a controversial idea. Race doesn't play an active role in why white people experience poverty, or any other form of oppression like homophobia, ableism or transphobia.

A white working-class person isn't refused housing because the landlord doesn't want to rent to white Brits. They don't miss out on jobs because someone reads a traditionally English name on a CV and thinks 'no thanks'. And if they can't walk around their neighbourhood without being stopped and searched by police, it's not because cops have a prejudice that white boys are trouble. But people who are white and poor are at the sharp end of housing inequality and police harassment, and they don't get the same job opportunities as their middle-class counterparts.

All these things happen to people who are white and working class *because they are working class.* It is not on the basis of race.

But as Emma Dabiri observes in *What White People Can Do Next*, there has been a bit of conceptual mission-creep. The language of white privilege has become untethered from its original, specific meaning and has been talked about like a jacket that white people can take off at will. They can supposedly 'give up' their advantage, or share it with people of colour. But the absence of racial discrimination isn't a substance you can divvy up and hand out. It's not something you can leave at home. This framing becomes particularly absurd when you consider the experiences of white people who are struggling at school, or in the care system, or having to choose between heating and eating. Talking about how they're not subject to racism is one thing; it is quite another to demand that white people in poverty relinquish a privilege they don't possess in any materially meaningful way.

The idea, on the other hand, that contemporary anti-racism is hell-bent on denigrating white people who are working class doesn't hold water. There are a handful of examples (mostly the odd blog or tweet, invariably from an American) where someone has tried to argue that poor white people are uniformly more privileged than people of colour. But overall, presenting the needs of people who experience racism in opposition to impoverished white people is an extremely marginal position. The bigger problem is that class, and how it cuts across race, isn't really considered much within this new wave of anti-racist consciousness. It's clear though, these self-appointed champions of the white working class aren't trying to highlight a failure of radical strategy. They'd have us believe that activists are marching around telling ex-miners that they're privileged assholes, or trying to obliterate Bruce Forsyth from the historical record.

By presenting anti-racism as a threat to the white working class, two things happen. The first is that the experiences of white working-class people are weaponised. They are wielded as a tool against attempts to diagnose problems of racial inequality, and to delegitimise any proposed solutions. Acknowledge institutional racism? *What about the white working class.* Tackle discriminatory policing? *What about the white working class.* Address the legacies of colonialism and slavery in modern society? *What about the white working class.* This is not a real question, but a mechanism that cuts off a conversation about racial inequalities. It is a dance between mythical enemies that isn't intended to advance the cause of working-class people, but to obstruct racial progress.

The second and most devious effect of this weaponisation of white working-class identity is that it actively inhibits efforts to redistribute wealth to address the scourge of economic inequality. By selectively championing the white working class in order to attack people of colour, the working classes of all races lose out. Blaming an imaginary problem, and an imaginary enemy, creates space for politicians to wriggle off the hook. Those who have overseen more than a decade of cuts to welfare, education and infrastructure mime shock and horror at the plight of the impoverished, all while continuing to pursue the same policies which shifted wealth from the poor to the rich in the first place. All of a sudden it wasn't the government who neglected impoverished communities – it was Black Lives Matter.

But this narrative also strategically reframes economic inequality as a matter of competing identity interests. And indeed, there's a certain irony here. In attempting to roll back the political and cultural impact of anti-racist ideas, the white working class have to be presented as though they themselves are a minority ethnic group. This isn't really a matter of demographic percentages; reports show that the education gap between the white rich and the white poor is biggest in areas which are majority white. Minority status for the white working class isn't based in numbers. It's a vibes-only category.

The feeling is that people of colour have had something about their lives recognised, and that recognition has changed social and cultural norms. The boundaries of what's considered acceptable have changed. The ethnic complexion of the country is noticeably different. You can't, we often hear, say anything any more without it offending somebody. It doesn't matter whether these things are actually true, or whether some of the changes might even be welcome. The prevailing mood is that racial minorities have got their way at the expense of the white working class.

As Julie Burchill tellingly put it, 'the diversity divas have diverted attention from the lack of opportunities for a whole swathe of underprivileged children put beyond the pale of pity by their risibly named "white privilege".'[47] In the attention-economy, recognition is currency – and the 'diversity divas' have picked the pockets of the white working class. In order for the white working class to be acknowledged culturally, they need the authority of being seen as a minority themselves. It's like there's a visibility competition, and the only way you can have your socioeconomic suffering seen at all is for it to be presented in explicitly racial terms.

It's no coincidence that a right-wing journalist like James Delingpole refashioned himself as a protector of the working class in 2017, the same year that left-wing Labour leader Jeremy Corbyn nearly won an election on an anti-austerity platform. Class inequalities between rich and poor are actually quite straightforward to solve, if you're willing to tax wealth, fund welfare and public services, squeeze profits and drive up wages. But if you can reframe class as a kind of ethnicity, then it's possible to redirect working-class anger away from structural causes and towards more nebulous feelings of cultural resentment.

Redistributive policy platforms have struggled to stem the tide of manufactured gripes. So long as the outrage factory is still up and running, there will be a never-ending supply of fuel for white working-class ire. And this means that a promise to improve everyone's living conditions is viewed with suspicion, because the benefit to working-class people of colour has only been framed as white people being sold out. We're not seeing the white working class reject identity politics, as Melanie Phillips says: on the contrary, the entire concept of a distinct white working class, whose interests are incompatible with that of black and brown people, is the distillation of identity politics.

Journalists were not alone in driving this manufactured distinction between the white working class and everybody else. The Tory government jumped on the bandwagon too. It wasn't enough just to talk about the issues and injustices faced by white working-class people. Anti-racism and diversity had to be blamed for it. In 2020, under the premiership of Boris Johnson, a report was released to much media fanfare. Titled 'The Forgotten: how White working-class pupils have been let down, and how to change it', it featured an extended section on use of the term 'white privilege'. 'White privilege' was defined in the report as the 'idea that there is societal privilege that benefits White people over other ethnic groups in some societies, particularly if they are otherwise under the same social, political, or economic circumstances'.[48] The report didn't show any evidence of the term appearing in school teaching material, but observed that in the wake of the Black Lives Matter movement it had been more commonly used in public forums, including in an explainer for parents published by the children's charity Barnardo's.

Nevertheless, the phrase 'white privilege' crops up more than twenty-five times in the report, framed as 'pernicious ideology', 'divisive' and 'alienating'. 'Austerity', or references to funding cuts, features much less frequently. The report failed to produce any evidence that use of the term 'white privilege' has a direct impact on the under-attainment of disadvantaged white working-class children; instead, the report's authors insisted that merely *hearing* that term outside of school could negatively impact white working-class children. Once more, the report didn't offer any evidence – statistic or anecdotal – that such a thing was actually happening. Despite this, the report advised that organisations which receive taxpayer money 'should consider whether the concept of White Privilege is consistent' with their duties under the Equalities Act.[49] How the concept of white privilege might breach the Equalities Act, or what might happen to an organisation's taxpayer funding if they considered the idea, the report did not say.

Not long after 'The Forgotten' was published, Boris Johnson's government followed up with another supposedly groundbreaking report. Commissioned in the wake of George Floyd's murder at the hands of police in the US, the Commission on Race and Ethnic Disparities argued that Britain 'no longer' has a system rigged against people from ethnic minorities. It insisted that geography, social class and family structure were more important than race in determining life outcomes. Tony Sewell, chair of the commission, claimed that the report found 'no evidence' of institutional racism.[50] Furthermore, it suggested that talking about 'historic' racism was responsible for creating a 'deep mistrust' amongst people of colour – and that this, in itself, was a barrier to success. Bizarrely, the report recommended that the period of slavery in British history should be discussed as 'not only being about profit and suffering but how culturally African people transformed themselves into a re-modelled African/

Britain'. It's not institutional racism that's stopping black people from having a fair shot at life's opportunities, but their continued failure to look on the bright side of slavery.

The Sewell report has been widely criticised. Jonathan Portes, a Professor of Economics at King's College London, observed that the report categorised racial disparities in such a way as to exclude the possibility that they could be explained by racism at all.[51] 'In 35 years of both producing and consuming government reports, I don't think I have ever seen one where the evidence and analysis has been so comprehensively discredited so quickly and completely,' wrote Portes. 'The report is better viewed as "rhetoric-based evidence making"' than a serious statistical enterprise, he added. Indeed, despite the methodological shonkiness of the report, it was praised by right-wing culture warriors as a 'major blow against institutional wokeness... the sacralisation of historically disadvantaged racial, sexual and gender minorities'.[52] Regardless of whether the Sewell report was a reliable piece of research, it served a powerful political purpose.

'The Forgotten' and the Sewell Report operated as a one–two punch. Both reports were published at a time when the Black Lives Matter movement was top of the global news agenda. Black people and allies of the movement were on the streets and in the papers refusing to let endemic injustice, violence and discrimination be swept under the rug. But what these reports did was establish an antagonistic competition between tackling class disparities and taking on racial injustice. Paying attention to the impact of institutional racism on the life chances and experiences of black and Asian Brits wasn't just an exercise in taking offence, making mountains out of molehills like slavery and colonialism: doing so was actively disenfranchising the white working class. It's a neat trick, when you think about it: white working-class boys weren't being failed by cuts to the education budget, crumbling infrastructure or the wholesale destruction of council housing. It was because too much airtime was being taken up by brown people talking about their problems. Rather than being an opportunity for people to identify with each other across racial boundaries, focusing on the injury done to one was to steal something from the other. Though consciousness of racial inequality was disparaged by the Johnson government as a nasty and divisive form of grievance politics, their version of class consciousness was in fact exactly that. Because you could only talk about the working class *if* they were white – and hostile to the working class of colour.

The shift from thinking of working-class Brits as 'chavs' to the white working class has been potent in repositioning the political right-wing as the cultural custodians of working-class anger. Not only does this displace the political left from its once traditional territory of working-class advocacy, it casts them as the baddies. This doesn't have anything to do with policy, but everything to do with cultural perception. If you live in a city, have progressive values or support anti-racist causes, you've contributed to the neglect of the white working class. It doesn't matter that there are lots of people who are white and working class and who also live in urban areas, are on the left, and want a society free from racial discrimination; the division might be imagined but it has a very real impact on how politics works in the UK. Those changes, which include Brexit and the seismic 2019 general election, were helped along by a transformation in elite cultural opinion.

The right stopped talking about chavs, and loudly beat the drum of the white working class. In the early 2000s, journalists, talking heads and politicians thought about that working class as a deviant, corrupted demographic who had failed to live up to middle-class norms and values. They weren't the rosy-cheeked working class of old, but a new and feral underclass: 'chavs', 'urban savages', 'dismal ineducables', 'real-life

Vicky Pollards'. When the 2011 riots erupted in England, Fleet Street and Westminster united in one voice to blame inner-city culture. Rap, slang and victim mentality had caused the most widespread social unrest the country had witnessed for decades; what's more, these sticky bits of language, music and ideology had wormed their way into the brains of the white poor, turning them black. 'Black culture,' sniffed David Starkey on *Newsnight*. 'It's not skin colour, it's cultural.' Race, when turned into culture, is a dangerously infectious condition.

But today, the 'chav' has been banished to the back of the politico-media store cupboard. Occasionally elements of the stereotype are brought out of retirement to justify reactionary policy decisions (or to obstruct humane ones): in July 2024, arguing that Labour should keep the two-child benefit cap, Sarah Vine played an early 2000s classic blaming people in poverty for their own circumstances: 'if you can't afford to look after your kids, don't have them in the first place'.[53] But overall, there has been a drastic reduction of the gratuitous, gleeful class loathing that was a mainstay of punditry around the turn of the millennium. That doesn't mean that class inequalities have stopped existing – indeed, the gap between rich and poor in the UK has widened – but it's no longer the done thing for privately educated columnists to harp on about the 'lard-gutted slappers' that haunt their imaginations.

This isn't simply because the boundaries of social acceptability have changed; there has been a revolution in the right's propaganda strategy. Once loud-and-proud snobs have transformed themselves into tribunes of the forgotten – elites have found a useful weapon in the image of a white working class. This white working class isn't defined by the conditions of those who happen to be both white and working class, but is the product of certain political, social and cultural priorities. Anti-racism is cast as a conspiracy against impoverished whites, and the cause of the working class is held back by a never-ending visibility competition. The left, in valuing both racial and socioeconomic justice, is recast as a gaggle of traitors of the white working class. You can vote to take food off the tables of the nation's poor, as long as you promise to wage war on anyone, real or imagined, who might accuse them of having 'white privilege'.

David Starkey was clearly nuttier than a slice of baklava when he argued, during the 2011 riots, that 'the whites have become black.' His view was founded on racist ideas of cultural contamination, and on a belief in the inferiority of black popular culture. But what Starkey and all the other commentators who tried to blame music and tracksuit bottoms for the unrest could at least acknowledge was that the white working class have a lot in common with their peers from black, Asian and minority ethnic descent. As the rioters themselves said, there's a lot of shared material experience in terms of poverty, housing inequality and a profound lack of trust in the justice system. That overlapping material experience also had a cultural dimension: white young people, just like they've done for generations, found something of themselves in art that originated in working-class black communities. When sparked by an instigating moment, like the fatal shooting of Mark Duggan, those shared coordinates can blaze into something capable of disrupting the established social order. But partitioning the working class into metropolitan elites on the one hand and the white working class on the other severs those imaginative connections. It warps people's perception of their social reality; it stops them finding common ground across race, culture and geography.

Illusions are powerful, and they are malleable. A Gestalt switch is where you can see two different images in a single picture, depending on perspective. Whether you see a rabbit or a duck, a vase or two faces leaning in for a kiss, is simply a matter of what your brain deigns to emphasise at any given moment.

The shift between seeing one image and suddenly perceiving another can be disorienting, uncanny, and weird. Stranger still, in a Gestalt switch, you can oscillate between seeing each image, like being caught in the prongs of a tuning fork.

Social class, and its synonyms, are Gestalt images. Depending on your perspective, London is either the seething underbelly of Britain, an urban hellhole riven by violence and poverty, or it's a land of ivory towers from which peer the delicate noses of the liberal elite. 'Inner-city' and 'metropolitan' literally mean the same thing; socially, they have dramatically opposed connotations. Yesterday's chav, incapable of being taught, has become today's working-class white lad languishing at the back of a classroom. What unites these images is the cynicism of those who deploy them – the purpose is not to shine a light on inequality, but to stifle the means by which we talk about it. That the very same individuals in politics and media found it so easy to shift from complaining about the inner-city underclass to railing against the metropolitan elite leaves us with the faintly queasy feeling of a Gestalt switch. The image dissolved and recomposed itself before our very eyes, but nothing materially had changed.

6

Demographic Panic

'Can a woman have a penis?' Once upon a time, this was the kind of thing you'd expect to find scrawled on a toilet wall. Then, all of a sudden, in the spring of 2022, it was all over political media. We'd graduated from asking 'what is a woman?' to peering quizzically down people's trousers. Any time a frontbench politician went on LBC, or Sky News, or TalkTV, they could expect to be asked whether they think a woman can have a penis. Troupes of MPs – including Ed Davey, Rishi Sunak and PM-in-waiting Keir Starmer – were marched into studios and pressed on what precise constellation of genitalia a woman can have. Just in case that was too classy, some journalists combined their knob-preoccupation with toilet talk. 'The trans woman with a penis would use which lavatory?' barked LBC's Nick Ferrari at then-Shadow Education Minister Bridget Phillipson during the 2024 general election campaign. 'She's got a door with a woman on it, she's got a door with a bloke on it, which one does she go in?'[1] It was like the keeper of the Bridge of Death had taken a particularly lewd turn.

There is no clearer example of an issue where minority rights are presented as being in conflict with, or threatening to, majority rights than the 'transgender issue'. Even that phrase, reducing an entire community to a political problem, is inherently dehumanising. It's misleading to try and boil the entire terrain of the conflict to a single issue, like self-identification, puberty blockers, gender recognition certificates or pronouns. All of these issues are various fronts in the same war – one where the very existence of trans people, being able to live as themselves, is at stake. Transgender people are consistently presented as a dangerous minority, seeking to impose their ideology – and their bodies – on others. Whether it's the NHS using trans-inclusive language or young people socially transitioning, the story is always framed in the same way – trans people are a malign influence and want to corrupt otherwise 'normal' people and institutions.[2] Once more, we're seeing a minority community – in this instance, 0.5 per cent of the population in England and Wales – being turned into hyper-visible hate figures.[3] And yet again, real, material vulnerabilities are rendered invisible. Trans people experience greater rates of homelessness than the rest of the population, with a quarter of transgender Britons having experienced homelessness at some point in their lives.[4] One in eight trans people report having been attacked while at work, and half of all trans and non-binary people report having to hide their identity from employers because they're afraid of being discriminated against. Transgender people are at the sharp edge of material dispossession, while at the same time being used by the press and politicians as a means of distracting people away from economic issues. It's a classic minority rule strategy of division.

It's not my intention to close down good-faith conversations. It's important to talk openly about where we, as a society, establish the threshold for being legally and socially recognised as your chosen gender. But that discussion has been hijacked by a highly motivated ideological network to clamp down on the rights of transgender people. They don't want to consider the idea that trans people, and transgender women in particular, are just as deserving of respect as they are. And they've managed to conveyor-belt themselves into mainstream media and politics in order to radicalise others and create a hostile policy environment when it comes to trans rights.

Fear and hatred exist in a feedback loop. What this chapter is about is how those primal impulses are nurtured to fuel a sense of panic around demographics, i.e. the composition of the population. In examining the moral panic around transgender people, and racist conspiracy theories around the Great Replacement, I want to show how an obsessive fixation with identity minorities fills the space where class consciousness should be. Though I'll be talking about first one, and then the other, both transphobia and the Great Replacement open up onto the same moral panic – that the 'right' people, i.e. white people, aren't having enough children, and that unless authoritarian measures are taken, a multi-racial nation will emerge in which the dominant group no longer enjoy numerical supremacy. This is a key component of identity formation – defining who you are by creating hate figures out of who you're not.

So back to whether women can have penises. This phrase has its origins in trans-hostile political activism. Stickers in the shape of – well, you can imagine – started popping up around the country in 2018, bearing the words 'Women can't have penises' (an activist called Venice Allan took credit for the design). That same year, I took part in a Channel 4 discussion as part of a show called *Genderquake* alongside Caitlyn Jenner, Munroe Bergdorf and Germaine Greer. Over the phone, producers had assured me that it would be a respectful, collegial debate where all sides of the issue could hear each other out and put their own case across. I wanted to speak from the perspective of being a woman of colour, who didn't always feel welcome or understood in feminist spaces, and who could draw on that experience to empathise with transgender women. I know how it feels not to fit the mould of idealised femininity. But what actually ended up happening was, to use the technical term, an absolute shitshow.

The panellists were literally surrounded, like it was a theatre-in-the-round, by the studio audience. And somehow, anti-trans activists had managed to infiltrate the crowd. Any time that Munroe or Caitlyn (both of them trans women) opened their mouths to speak, they were met by a barrage of vulgar abuse. Trans-hostile feminists screamed the word penis at the top of their lungs – Venice Allan amongst them – even when cisgender women like me were talking. It was later alleged that the audience had been actively encouraged to heckle by producers.[5] Hundreds of complaints were made to OFCOM, the broadcast regulator. But ultimately, the hecklers had the final word – their slogan that 'women can't have penises' was adopted by the mainstream press.

Though many feminist and LGBTQ rights groups condemned the sticker campaign, the slogan became prevalent within a section of the feminist movement who believe that trans people shouldn't be accepted as their chosen gender. 'CAN A WOMAN HAVE A PENIS?' became the standard interrogation for a particular kind of online transphobe, who would inevitably scoff and harrumph if the reply was yes. The only acceptable answer in these online contexts was one which excluded trans people. Journalists like Kay Burley, whether due to ideological affinity or social media osmosis, ended up being mainstream mouthpieces for the talking points of online extremists.[6]

Why even ask whether a woman can have a penis? On the face of it, the 'answer' seems obvious. You cast your mind back to the first thing you learned about men-bits and lady-bits at primary school and manage to splutter out a 'no'. But maybe, just maybe, the intricate tapestry of our world has more to it than what we teach to six-year-olds. Biological sex is complicated. Chromosomes, hormones, reproductive organs, sexual organs and other physical characteristics don't always coalesce neatly around either end of the binary. According to Human Rights Watch, approximately 1.7 per cent of the world's population is intersex, that is, born with some combination of male and female biological traits.[7] For some of these people, their external genitalia might not match up with their other bodily characteristics. It would take an especially cruel and unempathetic person to say that the shape of their genitals defines them more than how they live in the world. So, stopping to consider it, we'd accept that women with intersex conditions – some of whom may have male sexual or reproductive organs – are women. We certainly wouldn't think it's right to dictate what toilets they should use, or which changing rooms to access.

'Sure,' I hear you say, 'but that's a tiny minority of individuals. Most of the time, for most people, whether they have a penis determines which spaces they can access.' But think about it a little more deeply. There are some contexts in which my sexual and reproductive organs really impact how I'm being treated as a cisgender woman. It matters for women who can't get the right treatment for endometriosis, because doctors are dismissive of their pain. It matters for women and girls who can't afford period products. It matters for black and Asian women, who are more likely than their white counterparts to be diagnosed with late-stage breast and ovarian cancers. It matters in contexts of sexual violence, strip searches and other forms of physical violation and degradation.

But most of the time, people aren't treating me as a woman because they've seen what's in my jeans. It's because I outwardly conform to what people think a woman is, through my clothes, build, hair, behaviour and voice. None of these things *define* a woman. There are cisgender women with short hair, muscular builds, deep voices, butch presentation – you wouldn't want them kicked out of the loos for failure to conform. In practice, my gender is being reflected back to me by others on the basis of how I present myself, rather than any intimate knowledge of my body (and thank the Lord for that). The fact is, when I'm in the women's loos, I don't know if the person in the next cubicle over has a penis or not. I'm not peeking under the door, and they're not especially likely to show me. Other people's genitals are generally not something you see in the ladies' toilets. Gender segregation in bathrooms and changing rooms function on the basis of adherence to social norms, rather than biological ones. If someone looks like a woman, and in the words of Nick Ferrari, walks through the door 'with a woman on it', that's usually all there is to it. You're not going to look down their pants to copper-bottom your first impression.

Here's what's tricky about gender: every time we look for a physical characteristic to pin it to, it wriggles and squirms out of our grasp. We find exceptions to every rule, hard facts which turn out to be assumptions. What makes a woman – or more precisely, what makes us willing to *treat* someone as a woman – isn't fixed. We're talking about clusters of characteristics, rather than a definitive list. You might not accept the idea that trans women are women, or that trans men are men, but the fact is that you've probably shared single-gender spaces with them without even thinking about it. Our ability to accept complexity and nuance in the real world is much better than it is when we're debating issues out of context. But questions like 'can a woman have a penis' box politicians in. Unless they give a stupid and reductive response, they're pilloried as being clueless by a media class who were only ever willing to accept 'no' for an answer. Keir Starmer was excoriated for even hinting at the idea that there might be exceptions to the rule that women don't have penises, which prompted relentlessly negative coverage in the *Telegraph*, the *Spectator* and *The Times* and drew the ire of J.K. Rowling. Since then, the Prime Minister has rolled back on trans rights, promising to exclude trans women from female hospital wards and saying that trans women don't have the right to use female toilets. Politicians may get bullied, but it's minorities who pay the price.

I don't think most politicians who get bounced into taking these positions are themselves committed ideological trans-phobes. But they're pushed, through media and other forms of lobbying, by those who are. As Shon Faye points out in her groundbreaking book, *The Transgender Issue*, *The Times* and the *Sunday Times* between them ran more than 300 articles – almost all of them hostile – about transgender people in one year alone.[8] And the impression you'd get from this media coverage was that we were subject to something like an invasion from within. Whether in hospitals, schools, refuges, sports, prisons or even just the census, trans people were apparently popping up like dandelions and disrupting the day-to-day functioning of institutions through their mere existence. Even just recognis-ing that some people might be trans was enough to invite crit-icism: 'Census trans question under scrutiny for "confusion"'[9] went one headline in *The Times*, while another signalled 'Anger at transgender handbook for children in care'.[10] These pieces are fairly typical of the news offering – I'm not even looking at the comment pages. This steady drumbeat of reporting builds up a foreboding sense that trans = bad, and there's just too damn much of it. It's crude, but it's effective at closing down space for politicians to argue for more trans-inclusive policies.

Ideological transphobes seem to live in an alternate dimen-sion, where genitals are central to every social interaction – and trans people want nothing more than to focus your attention on which ones they might have. In February 2023, a Tory councillor named Ruby Sampson alleged that a trans woman in a pub toilet turned around to her and said: 'I'm going to wipe my hands on my penis.'[11] Weird, right? (Not least because I've never heard of an absorbent penis.) 'The close proximity [of the stalls] made it much scarier still,' Sampson wrote in an article for the *Daily*

Mail. 'What if she turned violent?' And look, if someone said that to me in a ladies' loo, I too would be a bit perturbed. 'I felt like I had been flashed,' she said, 'as the penis image was put in my mind by her announcement. It was said to intimidate.'

But just stop and think for a minute. How likely do you think it is that a random person in a bathroom would say, 'I'm going to wipe my hands on my penis,' to an absolute stranger? Much like the average pub toilet, this story didn't pass the smell test for me when it was published. Then, a couple of days later, a transgender woman posted a thread on Twitter. She suspected it had been her in the loos with Ruby Sampson. She'd been attending a vigil for murdered trans teenager Brianna Ghey, and nipped into a nearby pub for a drink with friends afterwards. There was no toilet paper or hand towels in the toilets – and what she said to Ruby Sampson was that she was going to wipe her hands, after washing them, on her *jeans*.[12] Jeans, penis, potato, potahto. I get that people make honest mistakes. But it seems this one was made precisely because someone saw a trans woman enter a public bathroom and was fixated on what their body might be like under their clothes. Indeed, Sampson wrote at length about how she perceived this stranger's appearance: 'She wore a skimpy top which made her shoulders seem bigger. And she spoke with a strikingly deep voice.'[13] It sounded like she was trapped in her own personal version of Kath Day-Knight's lesbian panic – when you're thinking about something obsessively, you suddenly start seeing it everywhere. Nightmares and fantasies are but a hair's breadth apart, and you'll warp your perceptions to fit what you've primed yourself to encounter.

I can imagine that some people reading this book might think that I'm not taking threats to women's safety seriously enough. Whether it's in prisons or toilet cubicles, women are physically vulnerable to those who might abuse that proximity to harm them. Those who describe themselves as 'gender critical' feminists would argue that if the threshold for accessing women's spaces is dropped to simply identifying as a woman, predatory men will do exactly that in order to target their victims. They point to examples of trans women who've committed sexual assault, such as Karen White and Isla Bryson, as evidence that cisgender women are at risk from violence perpetrated by trans people, particularly in prison settings. But would imposing a blanket rule that trans women should be incarcerated in men's prisons really make people safer? The first thing to point out is that we're talking about small numbers of people. According to the latest available data, between 2021 and 2022, only six trans women were housed in female prisons.[14] Between 2020 and 2022, there were no reported sexual assaults carried out by transgender women in women's prisons. The same can't be said for trans victims of sexual assault in men's prisons – in 2019 alone, there were eleven such cases.[15] Though gender critical campaigners, politicians and the media all focus on the risk posed by trans women in female prisons, the fact is that they're far more likely to be victims of sexual assault in men's facilities. Surely that matters as much as the safety of cisgender women inmates?

I don't want to dwell too long on the 'who goes in which prison' question – we incarcerate far too many people for non-violent offences anyway, many of whom could have been prevented from committing crimes if we had a functioning social safety net. Ultimately I think the case-by-case assessment of offenders, where prison officials and psychologists determine where trans offenders should be placed, taking into account both their safety needs and any potential safeguarding risk to others, is probably the best and fairest system. What I think is important here is that a narrow policy discussion about prisons takes up a disproportionate amount of space when we're talking about trans people in general. By virtue of its overrepresentation, we end up with a misleading and distorted image of trans people. It's like only talking about Muslims in relation to terrorism, black people to knife crime, or women to false rape allegations – it demonises and obscures the reality of that entire demographic. Sure, some individuals from these community groups do these things, but they're in a tiny minority. Giving any group greater rights and freedoms involves some degree of risk, because you can't guarantee that nobody will abuse them. Even the most hardline conservative would probably agree that it's bad to punish a whole group of people, to curtail or restrict their rights, based on the actions of a tiny few. But that's exactly the logic of trans-hostile feminists when it comes to transgender people.

For a cause which purports to be sticking up for all women, transphobia is something of an elite enterprise. Kemi Badenoch – a former Equalities minister under the Conservatives – shed light on the strategy behind the rolling back of trans rights in the UK. Key to the project was 'having gender-critical men and women in the UK government, holding the positions that mattered most in Equalities and Health':[16] i.e. stacking decision-making bodies not with independent, evidence-led experts, but with those who were ideologically opposed to transgender inclusion. In 2023, *Vice News* reported that seven senior officials quit the Equality and Human Rights Commission due to the organisation shifting in a more 'transphobic direction';[17] rather than standing up for trans rights, they'd been providing the government with advice on how to exclude most trans people from using the toilets of their choice. Trans-hostile voices are well represented in the mainstream media, from supposedly left-of-centre outlets like the *Guardian* and *Observer* to the right-wing *Spectator*. Meanwhile, transgender newspaper columnists are basically unheard of.

It probably helps that J.K. Rowling – one of the most commercially successful authors who has ever lived – has vocally supported the 'gender critical' cause.[18] Abigail Shrier, a journalist and author, credited Rowling for mainstreaming opposition to puberty blockers for the purpose of gender-affirming care in the UK. What's more is that, according to Shrier, Rowling's political value lies in her ability to drive a wedge on the left ('She helped gender critical feminists pry [sic] away from the progressive left on this issue') – another way in which the relentless demonisation of minority identity benefits the right.[19] Though Rowling has described herself as being 'empathetic to trans people',[20] that empathy has been hard to detect beyond her occasionally professing that it exists. Her preferred terms for transgender women are 'trans-identified males,'[21] 'biological males with gender recognition certificates'[22] and 'surgically altered' men.[23] Her focus is almost always on trans criminality, trans women in competitive sports, or on what she perceives to be the risks of young people taking puberty blockers: she has remarkably little to say about the pervasive discrimination that trans people face in employment, housing and healthcare. Rowling seems proud to be part of a network of like-minded figures, occasionally sharing photos of herself at dinner with other 'gender critical' feminists like Julie Bindel, Joanna Cherry, Suzanne Moore and Kathleen Stock. No longer simply an author of wildly successful children's IP, Rowling has become a political force to contend with. A single article by Rowling forces government ministers to respond in a conciliatory tone. These views, of course, are well within her rights to express. And nobody deserves threats, abuse or harassment for participating in live political discussions online.

What's striking here is how clearly we can see a particularly famous and wealthy person wielding an outsize influence on the policymaking landscape. Despite presenting themselves as under attack by trans activists and their allies, the likes of J. K. Rowling are well networked, well placed and more widely represented than their opponents. Rowling rejects the accusation that she is transphobic. But consistently presenting trans rights as being in conflict with women's safety ('Trans activism demands that women give away their hard won rights to men')[24] contributes to an overall climate of hostility towards transgender people. If your position is that trans individuals can't be accepted in their chosen gender after transitioning as adults, but can't access puberty blockers as youths, aren't allowed in spaces which align with their gender presentation (but aren't safe in spaces of the gender they were assigned at birth either), can't choose how they're addressed, can't play sports, can't use the changing rooms, can't use the toilets – you can't be surprised when others come to the conclusion that 'gender critical' is code for 'anti trans'. What are trans people meant to do, if there's no way for them to be socially recognised as their chosen gender in public life? Never leave the house? Evaporate?

Trans people are objects of fixation and hatred because of transphobia, there's no doubt. They're targets of obsession, abuse and discrimination for no other reason than who they are. But the state of exception they're forced to occupy also serves to roll back on the rights and freedoms of women. In the UK, following the publication of the Cass Review (an independent review of the NHS's youth gender-identity services, published in April 2024), the prescription of puberty blockers to trans and non-binary youth under the age of eighteen was suspended.[25]

Puberty blockers are a treatment which blocks testosterone and oestrogen, and can stop young people from developing periods, facial hair, breasts, etc. For trans young people, taking puberty blockers as they approach puberty can make it easier for them to live as their chosen gender when they reach adulthood. They're not just prescribed to trans and non-binary people – they can be offered to children entering puberty early, or to adults for other health conditions. In 2024, fewer than 100 children and young people were being prescribed puberty blockers by the NHS – and in the UK, trans minors can't have gender transition surgery.[26] But the Cass Review, and the way politicians chose to interpret it, was a game-changer. The report concluded that there is 'no good evidence on the long-term outcomes of interventions to manage gender-related distress'[27] – that advocacy groups tend to cherry-pick the data which suits them about the benefits, or harms, of prescribing puberty blockers to trans and non-binary youth. I'm not a doctor, so that's not an area I'm going to wade into. But what I do want to talk about is bodily autonomy, and how imposing different rules for puberty blockers from other medications puts the rights of women and girls more broadly at risk.

In the UK, there's a principle called 'Gillick competence' (officially known as Fraser guidelines, but I'm sticking with the more common phrase) which states that children can consent to their own medical treatment – including sexual and reproductive healthcare – as long as they are deemed competent to understand what's involved and there aren't any specific safeguarding concerns. The principle of Gillick competence is the reason I was able to access the contraceptive pill as a teenager, even though it would be a while before I had any tangible reason to worry about getting pregnant. Children in this country have the right, albeit caveated, to make decisions in concert with their doctor about medical treatment. Saying that puberty blockers for trans and non-binary youth are exempt from this principle puts a crack in the dam. Indeed, this appears to be the intention of some campaigners. In *Bell v. Tavistock*, a legal case in 2020, it was argued that somebody under the age of sixteen (in this case, Keira Bell) couldn't consent to taking hormones in order to transition their gender. After an initial ruling against Tavistock (a clinic in London which provides gender-affirming care), Bell lost her case at appeal; and in response, her lawyer,

Paul Conrathe, released a statement alleging that the ruling demonstrated that 'The Gillick competency test is no longer fit for purpose.'[28]

Paul Conrathe is an interesting guy. His CV reveals a long history of taking on cases which apparently seek to restrict abortion rights, from a man who tried to get an injunction to stop his girlfriend from terminating a pregnancy back in 2001[29] to a 2005 case in which Conrathe tried to argue that under-sixteens cannot consent to an abortion without their parents' knowledge.[30] He previously acted on behalf of anti-choice groups such as ProLife Alliance and the Society for the Protection of Unborn Children.[31] Transgender people might be a small minority, but the principles which protect their access to healthcare uphold the same for the majority as well. I don't see my freedoms as a woman being threatened by transgender people: I see them as being profoundly interconnected.

I'm not trans, but I know what it's like to trigger outrage just by existing. When I'm reading the newspaper, or opening social media, and there's another scaremongering story about how trans people are invading women's spaces, I can't help but reflect on how people of colour and immigrants are discussed in the exact same way. Maggie Steed, on a special broadcast with the academic Stuart Hall, once said that 'a number is a fact, you can't quarrel with it.' But, Hall continued, 'as soon as you say numbers, it doesn't matter how you wrap it up – there is only one lesson to be drawn, the numbers are growing. There are too many of them.'[32] That's how it feels when you're reading about immigration figures, or birth rates amongst different ethnic groups, or dog-whistle references to 'cultural change': no matter what the number, or the context, there are always just too many of us. It's dehumanising – like reducing trans people to what their bodies might be like under their clothes, it presents race as the single defining feature of who we are. This is the essence of demographic panic – it turns neutral characteristics like skin colour or gender identity into objects of terror. And this feedback loop of fear and hatred is used to justify measures which limit the freedoms of majority groups.

'Yes lads, we're winning'

Have you ever been haunted by something you've said? Perhaps it was an unkind word, or saying 'I love you' to the wrong person at the wrong time. Maybe you confided in someone unwisely, and watched in horror as a secret became common knowledge. At the very least, you must have once called a teacher 'Mum'. I think that, for as long as we've had language, humans have had to wrestle with the fact that words, once uttered, no longer belong to you. They have an unruly life all their own. Me, personally? I'm unable to forget or disentangle myself from four little words: 'Yes lads, we're winning.' Just like that, I'd prodded an exposed nerve called 'the Great Replacement'. And what this throwaway phrase kicked off, having been made into a human dartboard for the far right, gave me an insight into the narrative ingredients which go into creating a sense of demographic panic. I want to get to the bottom of their fear and hatred of people like me. Maybe if I succeed, they'll stop wanting to kill me.

Here's the context. Back in 2016, when I was twenty-four and still working at a pub (we couldn't even pay ourselves at Novara Media yet, and paid for filming kit out of our own pockets), I made a video titled 'Against Integration'.[33] The title was intended to be a bit of a provocation, by taking aim at one of liberalism's sacred cows: the idea that immigrants have a duty to integrate into the host culture. But really, the title was something of a bait-and-switch. In the video, I was looking at some research carried out by an academic on ethnic segregation in the UK, and wanted to prise apart the definition of 'integration' – if the most ethnically homogenous areas of this country are white British, and you tend to find a mix of minority ethnic groups in areas with a high proportion of people of colour, then who is it that's actually failing to integrate? There's a lot I'd do differently now at my ripe old age (not least insisting on a different camera angle, good God). But I basically still back the premise. I think that anxieties around integration often aren't about how you get different ethnic groups to socialise and relate to one another,[34] but about white people not getting too spooked by the melanin percentage in their local areas.

That wasn't the controversial part of the video. About a minute in, I made reference to some demographic statistics that had been in the news a lot at the time – that in the fifteen years between 2001 and 2016, the white British population in London had decreased by 600,000, while the ethnic minority population had gone up by 1.2 million.[35] And then I followed up with the fateful words 'Yes lads, we're winning.'

It's unlikely that anyone who was genuinely riled up by my words is going to be reading this book. But still, I'd like to take the opportunity to make it clear: I was joking. At the time, I thought that it would be patently obvious to anyone watching that I don't think there's some kind of breeding competition between the races in London. The entire video is about how headline figures about ethnic demographics are used to divide people and scaremonger, and I wanted to make fun of how these numbers are presented to convey a misleading and malevolent impression of what's going on. And just to drive home that I was taking the piss, I delivered the line with a little hand flourish and head bob: the universal signal of irony. Nobody, but nobody, could *possibly* think I was being serious – could they?

It turns out that people very much could, would and did. Every few months, that ten-second section goes viral online, clipped and circulated among right-wing networks as evidence of my supposed hostility to white people and/or the existence of an anti-white conspiracy. House of Lords member Baroness Foster condemned my 'divisive, racist comments',[36] while comment writer and Conservative influencer Emily Hewertson implored her followers to 'imagine if the tables were turned and someone said "white people are winning." '[37] She continued: 'Ash would be the first to call them racist and bigoted. [This sort] of rhetoric perpetuates division. There should be no place for it in a united Britain.' Personally I always thought Britain was united by an appreciation of sarcasm, but hey-ho. *Spiked* dubbed me a 'woke segregationist'[38] (not at all hysterical, well done guys), while Dan Wootton hauled me over coals about it on TalkRadio.[39]

Now, while it's a bit frustrating to be misinterpreted and misrepresented by public figures, it comes with the territory. People who have a political interest in making you look bad will (surprise, surprise) try to make you look bad – getting the chance to flip the script and accuse a woman of colour of being racist against white people is just the icing on the cake. But abuse, harassment and threats of violence are another thing entirely. And those were coming next.

Against the advice of my husband (who wanted me to log off, have a glass of wine and talk about Spurs' transfer targets), I had a look at the comments below the line on some recent repostings of the clip. My excuse is that it's research for this chapter, though if I were to be honest I'd have to admit there's an element of morbid curiosity. 'Wow that's brave of her,' says one man on a recent TikTok repost of the video, 'she may get lynched.' 'Ash Sarkar needs to watch herself,' suggests another. In reply is a comment from someone else asking, 'Have you ordered your crossbow?' I scroll down Twitter, and the number of people calling me 'vile', 'racist', a 'twat', a 'bitch' and a 'cunt' seems endless. As the hate stacks up, an odd sense of numbness washes over me. Some primal sense of self-preservation kicks in, and I stop registering emotions like fear, hurt or distress. This isn't the first time that my brain has had to intercede and shut down my nervous system in the face of violent threats and abuse – I get sent material that's racially derogatory on a daily basis. Mostly, it's just a case of muting the account and moving on. But sometimes it's impossible – or imprudent – to ignore what's being said. In 2018, a CNN journalist got in touch to make me aware that Cesar Sayoc (an American right-winger who had been charged with, and later convicted of, mailing pipe bombs to people that were critical of Donald Trump) had sent me death threats and pictures of mutilated animals. I vaguely remembered the posts, but had just scrolled past them at the time. I didn't report it, because those threats were effectively drowned out in the cacophony of hatred.

One of the weirder abuse eruptions was catalysed by an orange lolly. After sharing a photo of myself, captioned with three orange emojis, eating an ice lolly in the park, I was inundated with death threats. People sent me images of nooses, hurled racial slurs, and promised to douse me in petrol and set me alight. Why? Because they'd convinced themselves that the image and emojis were a coded message of support for a stabbing that had taken place, where three people were murdered in Reading.[40] According to these far-right posters, I used orange emojis because they were a symbol of death or violence in Frances Ford Coppola's *Godfather* trilogy – though others insisted that it was because oranges, being one of Libya's chief exports, meant I was making a sly admission of being an Islamist. A few days later, a tweet caught my eye. Someone had seen me buying groceries in a Tesco Express, close to where I lived at the time, and was wondering whether he ought to punch me in the back of the head.

The experience of being turned into a hate figure is incredibly fucking weird. People who've never met you obsess over your every word and action. You don't recognise the image of yourself being reflected back – and even the tiniest scraps of personal information which make it into the public sphere get blown up and warped before your very eyes. 'She chose a white man because she enjoys being colonised,' says one guy on Instagram about my husband. 'Why else would she live in the UK? She would be free from colonial rule in her native country, but she wants to be in the UK so she can be governed by white men.' Over on Twitter, one troubled soul is convinced that I'm 'literally excited about White birthrates going down'. And the lynchpin of my nefarious scheme? 'Dating a White man who may otherwise have a White child.' Speaking as someone who spent years watching Maury Povich – trust me, he still can.

Identify as a Muslim? You're a closet jihadist. Photographed with a pint? You're a fake Muslim. Think that racism is real, and should be fought at every level? You hate white people. In a relationship with a white guy? You're colonised in the sheets. And look, I'm not trying to play the world's tiniest violin here. I get paid to share my opinions, I get public validation, and I'm pretty sure that my tabby Moussa is the most gorgeous cat the world has ever seen.[41] Life is good. But seeing how people are moved to want to kill each other on the basis of lies really bothers me. I've seen firsthand how people are manipulated into believing, with all sincerity, complete hokum. Fear needs to feed itself on symbols, decontextualised facts and outright lies. The right has built an information universe that's powered by nightmares and fantasies of Minority Rule – and through these stories, they justify and advance authoritarian measures which disempower everyone.

There *are* some minorities people are right to be afraid of. In 2022, five individuals took away the right to decide if and when to have a baby from thirty-three million American women. A handful of judges did more harm to women's bodies than the entire global population of trans people ever have. The US Supreme Court voted six to three to overturn *Roe v. Wade*, a ruling that had protected the right to have an abortion in the US for nearly fifty years. Now, at the time of writing, there are thirteen states where abortion is banned in nearly all circumstances;[42] in eight more there are gestational limits of under twenty weeks. As dissenting Supreme Court Justices Stephen Breyer, Sonia Sotomayor and Elena Kagan put it, this ruling in one fell swoop consigned young women to coming of age 'with fewer rights than their mothers and grandmothers'.[43] It's not a surprise that anti-choicers had to bypass the ballot box for their victory: even in deep-red states which voted for Donald Trump in 2020, the electorate consistently backs abortion rights.[44] According to analysis carried out by *POLITICO*, in counties where Joe Biden received less than 20 per cent of the vote in 2020, abortion rights still enjoyed an average of 31 per cent in referendums – an 11 point lead, indicating that reproductive rights outperform the party that claims to be their natural protector.[45] One in four American women will have an abortion in their lifetimes: and all are made safer by knowing it's there as an option if they need it. Abortion rights aren't a minority enterprise, but overturning them was.

Others have written extensively about how overturning *Roe v. Wade* was the culmination of a multi-decade campaign by the Christian right to turn back the clock on sexual freedoms. Almost three-quarters of white, evangelical Protestants think abortion should be illegal,[46] and it was precisely this demographic who were embraced by the Republican Party in order to catapult Ronald Reagan into the White House in 1981.[47] But what I want to focus on here is the relationship between reproduction and racial demographic panic – because if you sincerely believe that the country is turning irrevocably against white people due to birth rates, it becomes imperative to stop people exercising control over when and how they have children. As Heinrich Himmler, one of the Nazi Party's most senior members and one of the architects of the Holocaust, put it: 'A people of good race which has too few children has a one-way ticket to the grave.'[48]

Under the merciless Arizona sun, a blonde woman in blue-tinted glasses paints a picture of apocalypse. 'Five million illegal aliens are on the verge of replacing you,' she warns the gathered rally. 'Replacing your jobs, and replacing your kids in school, and coming from all over the world. They're also replacing your culture,' she says, adding, as an afterthought, 'that's not great for America.' The crowd, too hot to be properly enraged, signal their agreement with a dissatisfied lowing. Marjorie Taylor Greene – congresswoman, conspiracist and self-identifying 'Christian nationalist' – is on the campaign trail during the 2022 US midterms, drumming up support for the Republican Party. Despite the fact that centre-right Republican voters, turned off by Donald Trump's lurch towards populist nationalism, helped deliver Joe Biden the keys to the White House in 2020, the political complexion of the GOP is more extremist than ever. It is Marjorie Taylor Greene, not the moderate wing, who is in tune with the mainstream of Republican opinion.

That same year, on a primetime television slot, the most-viewed news presenter of the most-watched news channel in America tells the story of how democracy was stolen. In 1965, President Lyndon Johnson signed the Immigration and Nationality Act into law, removing the racially discriminatory barriers that made it harder for non-Western and non-Northern European migrants to settle in the US. And this, explains Tucker

Carlson with the demeanour of a high-school history teacher, 'changed America completely and for ever'.[49] The population boomed over the following decades, with birth rates driven by these new immigrants and their descendants.

'Nothing like this has ever happened in this or maybe any other country ever ... It's not natural, it's the product of a policy choice.' The Democrats, from LBJ to Joe Biden, have conspired to replace 'native-born Americans' with 'more compliant, foreign-born voters'. 'The Great Replacement – yeah, it's not a conspiracy theory,' intones the Fox News host. 'It's their electoral strategy.' And tinkering with the racial complexion of the United States of America, he goes on, threatens to tear the very fabric of society asunder. 'The question from day one has always been "What holds everyone together? What is the one thing we all have in common?"' asks Carlson, with no intention of waiting for an answer. 'It's not an ethnic group. It's not a shared history. Now, it's not a language. So what is it? Well, in the absence of glue, things break apart.' Ethnic group, shared history, language: in a single, clip-friendly monologue, Tucker Carlson frames the American republic as an ethnostate under threat.

Demographic change is a fact of human existence. From the first time Neolithic man discovered that you could cotch and cultivate wheat rather than wandering around hoping to stumble across a tuber, populations have fluctuated according to how humankind interacted with natural resources, ecological changes, technological developments and, crucially, one an other. Maybe you have vague memories of seeing a population pyramid at school: wide bases that narrow dramatically indicating a country with high birth rates and high infant mortality, or chunks ripped out of the young male population by war. There is no 'natural' organisation of human society, untouched by our ability to shape the conditions in which we live. Healthcare improves, infant mortality falls, people have fewer children and they live longer, and so the population ages. Social attitudes to having children outside of marriage evolve, divorce becomes more widely available, gay people are given the legal right to marry, care costs prompt elderly parents to move in with their adult children, and you begin to see a greater diversity of family structures in a society (lone parent, same-sex, blended or extended). Perhaps the only constant thing in the entirety of human history is that we must continually adapt to changes of our own making.

Demographics refers to anything relating to a given population, and the particular groups you find within it. But what those groups are, how we define their boundaries, and what social, political and cultural meanings we assign to them, are all products of what kinds of difference we deem meaningful in society. When did race become an important way to understand the differences between humans? And more importantly, what even is it?

Race is something that looks natural, but isn't – the genetic differences within racial groups are bigger than the differences across racial groups. Fundamentally, race is a way of grouping together human beings by physical or social attributes that are (or at least, are said to be) hereditarily transmitted; that is, shared by people with biological ties and passed down through the generations through bloodlines. We tend to describe how these attributes cluster by region (Asia, Africa, Europe, Oceania, Native American) as race. And it's true, many of the things we think of as racial characteristics are inherited ones: I have the same skin and natural hair colour as my birth parents, and that would be the same no matter what country or social environment I was raised in. These differences in observable physical traits, called phenotypes, are determined by alleles, which are the variant forms of a particular gene (like the ones which determine eye colour, or hair texture). But if race was biological in origin, you'd expect there to be massive differences in alleles between regional groups, and very little difference within them.

In reality, research into genetics has found that there is significant variation within regional groups, and small differences between them. According to a 2002 study conducted by Stanford, more than 92 per cent of 4,000 alleles were found in two or more regions. More than half of them could be found in all seven regions that they examined. And region-specific alleles only showed up in 1 per cent of people from that area – hardly enough to base an entire system for categorising the human species.[50] In short, if race was a matter of mutually exclusive genetics, a Bengali-heritage woman like me probably wouldn't have the same hair colour as someone from Japan, the same eye colour as a person from Italy, or be able to share foundation with my mate whose background is Somali.

'When the first Africans arrived in Virginia in 1619,' writes Theodore W. Allen, 'there were no "white" people there; nor, according to the colonial records, would there be for another sixty years.'[51] That didn't mean that there weren't any people who we would *now* call white in the Virginia colony – but that's not how they would have considered themselves, nor how the law recognised them. '[They] had been English when they left England, and naturally they and their Virginia-born children were English.' It took the passage of half a dozen decades before 'white' 'would appear as a synonym for European-American', and it wasn't until 1691 that it first popped up in Virginia law. The 'white race' had to be invented, argues Allen, in order to stop Anglo and African bond-labourers from uniting and rebelling against their shared oppressors. Whiteness meant that European-Americans, even of the lowest social status, were formally brought together under a system of privileges; Africans, however, were condemned to bondage for their entire lives, a condition passed down to their children.[52] Racial difference was a way of imposing social control.

In an almost comic example of how much race was less about skin colour and more about status, for a time people of mixed heritage could purchase whiteness in Spanish-held territories in the Americas.[53] The process of *gracias al sacar* meant that, in the late eighteenth and early nineteenth century, a small number of mulattoes and pardoes (technical gradations of mixed-race status that were then current in the Spanish Empire) could apply and pay for a royal decree which released them from the 'defect' of non-European origin. The idea was that the crown could dispense with the inherited flaws of someone's *naturaleza*, that is, their natural characteristics. *Gracias al sacar* meant that some individuals with African ancestry could participate in occupations that had previously been closed off to them on the grounds of race, such as surgery and the priesthood, and enjoy privileges that only white people were entitled to, like graduating from university or marrying freely. Race was a method of legally and socially enforcing a class-based society in the Spanish Empire: of course there could be a little bit of leeway for those with money to spend.

Despite race being about as scientifically meaningful as astrology, nineteenth- and twentieth-century thinkers tried to turn it into a science in order to make social, political and economic inequality seem like an outgrowth of nature rather than the work of men. This was the great era of naturalists, intellectuals who studied plants, animals and insects, and established categories for organising the natural world into groupings based on shared characteristics and defined differences. And some of these thinkers dedicated themselves to trying to explain social differences by applying theories from the natural world, often using pseudoscientific methods like measuring skulls as 'proof' that there were biological reasons why black people were meant to be dominated and put to work for white interests, or to rationalise antisemitic beliefs that Jewish people were inherently duplicitous.

Carl Linnaeus, the father of taxonomy, didn't restrict himself to sorting mammals from fishes. Working in the eighteenth century, he also divided humans into races based on skin colour and geographical region, and assigned these races characteristics. So the white 'Europaeus' was deemed the 'light, wise, inventor'; the 'Asiaticus' 'stern, haughty, greedy'; and the black 'Africanus' was reckoned as being 'sly', 'sluggish' and 'neglectful'. This logic, as well as some of the methods involved to justify it, was quite literally dehumanising. Louis Agassiz, a Swiss-born biologist and geologist, travelled to South Carolina in 1850 in order to have photographs taken of enslaved black people.[54] These images, where subjects were often made to pose naked, were intended to demonstrate the physical differences between black and white people – and to prove Agassiz's theory that different races were actually different species. That the horrific conditions enslaved people were subjected to – bad food, backbreaking work, regular beatings and overcrowded housing – might explain some of these observable differences never quite occurred to him.

But it was Charles Darwin's magnum opus, *On the Origin of Species*, that had the biggest impact on the development of scientific racism. This isn't because of anything that is argued in the text; rather, the harm came from how Charles Darwin's ideas were lifted out of the natural world and superimposed on the social one. Herbert Spencer, an English philosopher and a contemporary of Darwin, coined the phrase 'survival of the fittest' to describe how human society evolves through competition for resources: the strong survive and excel, while the weak perish or fall to the bottom. Your place in the social hierarchy was a reflection of how well suited your inherited characteristics were to your environment. Spencer considered traits, like frugality with money, propensity to violence or ability to reason, something that could be passed on, through the blood, from generation to generation. According to Spencer, class and status reflected biological categories, rather than economic or cultural ones, and any attempt to redistribute wealth or power to the poor was interfering with the process of natural selection. Spencer's doctrine became known as 'Social Darwinism' and was used to make inequality seem like a natural part of human development, a symptom of the journey towards the perfection of the species, rather than a consequence of human behaviour.

It's easy to see how Social Darwinism became a means of justifying racism. Even if you didn't believe, as Agassiz did, that different races were wholly separate species, that didn't mean that you had to recognise Jews, Africans, Asians and Indigenous people as your equals. Imperialism was cast as the inevitable result of the inherent superiority of white, northern Europeans over other races, and slavery was simply a reflection of black people's inferiority. Indeed, this became such a popular view in the nineteenth century that differences in social status within races began to be explained as racial differences. John Langdon Down, a doctor in Victorian-era London, diagnosed patients who had Down's syndrome with 'Mongolian Idiocy'.[55] He argued that people with Down's syndrome had regressed to an earlier, East Asian form of humanity; the derogatory UK slang term 'mong', meaning stupid person, is a legacy of this racist and ableist pseudoscientific myth. The urban working class of Victorian England were thought to be evidence of backwards evolution, whose continued reproduction in the smoke and gloom of newly industrialised towns risked breeding 'a puny race unfit to maintain themselves'.[56] Race wasn't just a way of explaining differences in skin colour – it was a way of explaining differences in *everything*.

Some of Herbert Spencer's contemporaries took this idea even further. If the poor, or disabled, or racially 'other' were languishing at the bottom of society because nature was in the process of shuttling them out of the gene pool, why not speed up the process? Francis Galton – a cousin of Charles Darwin – coined the term 'eugenics' in 1883 to describe the process of trying to improve the human population by encouraging the reproduction of those deemed superior and discouraging (or worse) that of those deemed inferior. In Galton's view, society ought 'to give to the more suitable races or strains of blood a better chance of prevailing speedily over the less suitable than they otherwise would have had'.[57] This was of particular urgency for the British, thought Galton, 'for we plant our stock all over the world and lay the foundation of the dispositions and capacities of future millions of the human race'.[58] In short, because Britain had an empire, several settler colonies to its name and was up to its elbows in the savage work of ethnic cleansing, it was imperative that the nation as a whole strove towards an impeccable bloodline.

The eugenicists who followed in Galton's footsteps were responsible for some of the gravest human rights abuses of the twentieth century. In America, compulsory sterilisation laws were enacted, targeting disabled people, African Americans and Native Americans. They influenced American immigration policy, effectively throttling the ability of non-Europeans to move to the United States and introducing mandatory IQ tests at Ellis Island to weed out people with learning difficulties. In the majority of American states, mixed-race marriage was outlawed. As James Q. Whitman observes in *Hitler's American Model*, these measures would serve as inspiration for the Nazi regime's programme of discrimination, sterilisation, euthanasia and extermination. In order to 'preserve' the bloodline of the Aryan race, the Third Reich carried out 400,000 forced sterilisations and over a quarter of a million instances of involuntary euthanasia. The murderous pursuit of racial purity resulted in the deaths of six million Jews, and up to half of the entire Roma community in Europe. Many of the groups targeted for eradication by the Nazis had been classified as undesirables by earlier eugenicists: as Rudolf Hess put it, the Nazis considered their supremacist ideology simply a matter of 'applied biology'. It's not a million miles away from transphobes insisting that biology is destiny.

Racial thinking is bound up in the projects of imperialism, enslavement and genocide in which it was mobilised. Even after the horrors of the Nazi regime were known to the world and the process of decolonisation accelerated, racial thinking endured. In some places, like apartheid South Africa and the segregated American South, it was on the basis of explicit white supremacy. Indeed, the world's disgust at the discovery of human experimentation conducted by the Nazis did not stop the United States Public Health Service from pushing forward with the 'Tuskegee Study of Untreated Syphilis in the Negro Male', a forty-year research project which concealed syphilis diagnoses from hundreds of black American men, and withheld effective treatments even after they became available. But in Europe, the countries which once held vast territories in Asia, Africa and the Caribbean were now reckoning with the migration of formerly colonised subjects to the imperial motherland. The UK government actively encouraged people from Commonwealth countries to move to England and help rebuild the country after the devastation of the Second World War. The twin crises of losing its empire and having to rely on migrant labour caused a conundrum in the British political imagination. As Kojo Koram and Kerem Nisancioglu put it, 'How do you generate the mythology of a "Great" British nationalism in a context where – through decolonisation – it was having its arse handed to it by peoples it had imagined to be racially inferior?'[59]

Enter, stage right, Enoch Powell. In 1968, the then-Shadow Defence Secretary for the Conservative Party made a speech that has now become one of the most notorious pieces of oratory in British history, one we have already encountered in an earlier chapter. Powell had come to the Midland Hotel in Birmingham to speak against the Labour government's introduction of the Race Relations Act 1968, the remit of which was to establish the Community Relations Commission and to outlaw discrimination on the grounds of race in the delivery of public services, housing and employment. Powell then used the speech to rail against what he called the 'preventable evil' of migration from Commonwealth nations to the United Kingdom. In his words, the flow of people from those parts of the world that Britain had formerly colonised to the post-imperial motherland was 'like watching a nation busily engaged in heaping up its own funeral pyre'.[60]

Powell, with his background in poetry and classics, painted a vivid picture of demographic catastrophe. It's the allusion to Virgil's *Aeneid* that most people remember: 'As I look ahead, I am filled with foreboding. Like the Roman, I seem to see "the River Tiber foaming with much blood".' But Powell's most cunning rhetorical trick was to offer himself as a mere vessel for the vox populi: his most direct appeals to racist paranoia are purported quotations from his Wolverhampton South West constituents, including the famous prophecy that 'in this country in fifteen or twenty years' time the black man will have the whip hand over the white man.' Though his incendiary words were condemned, and he was forced off the Conservative front bench, 'Rivers of Blood' became a cultural touchstone in the UK immigration debate. As Stuart Hall wrote, 'Rivers of Blood' deftly wove 'magical connections and short-circuits... between the themes of race and immigration control and the images of the nation, the British people and the destruction of "our culture, our way of life".'[61] These images have been embedded in the national unconscious ever since. Powell's great innovation was to establish the rhetorical use of 'immigration' as a euphemism for being swamped by racial others, who were no longer defined necessarily as inferior, but simply fatally incompatible with white Britons. He, as an individual, may have been defeated, but his legacy thrived.

It's a mistake to cling to the idea of race as an identity: it's more like a technology, invented to govern, dominate, exploit and eradicate other human beings. It was conjured into being so that the transatlantic slave trade could function, so that the powers of Europe could justify their colonies, and to set up hard limits on social mobility so that the white-skinned poor could look upon those who had it worse with a measure of disgust and relief that they at least weren't the lowest of the low. Of course, the impact of race on centuries of history – the movement of people around the globe, the experiences of our ancestors and family members, the conditions of the present day – has a profound impact on how we think about ourselves and those around us. Its social impacts are real, despite the logic of race itself having little basis in reality. But if we try to see race as a mirror to ourselves, treating its distinctions as though they really reflect who we and others are, we will fail to appreciate our full humanity. We will have renewed racism's diabolical grip on our lives and our politics.

What's laid out here is only a partial account of how race became part of our social fabric: and if you're interested, there are brilliant books which describe how the Irish in America went from being seen as a kind of ape to being understood as white, or examine how the notion of European identity was shaped by conflict within Christendom, and also the Ottomans bossing around the Mediterranean. But the point is that race is not natural or fixed – what race is, and what defines racial categories, has changed according to what else happens to be in the intellectual, cultural and economic environment. Race isn't born, it's created. It has to be reproduced with each generation, reinscribed through our social and cultural scripts so that we forget that it's manmade in the first place. But if we pay careful attention, we can see that we use 'race' when we want to make distinctions between human beings – whether geographic, cultural, religious or class-based – seem natural. This is particularly important when it comes to present-day litigation of what constitutes racism, or indeed, who counts as a minority.

If the greatest trick the devil ever pulled was convincing the world he didn't exist, the greatest trick racism ever pulled was convincing generations of us that if you don't explicitly mention skin colour, you can't be racist. Anxieties about race are rendered colourblind by talking about immigration, nationality and cultural compatibility. Islam isn't a race, but the fact that Islamophobia casts a net wide enough to snare people of colour *regardless of whether or not they're actually Muslim* tells us that it's not merely an anti-religious sentiment either. Judaism is quite clearly a religion, but Jewish people (regardless of whether or not they're religiously observant) have been persecuted in the name of racial purity. A person who is a member of a racially marginalised group may also hold characteristics that enable them to be accepted as white in some circumstances and participate in the racial exclusion of others. Race is a slippery beast: it is relational, not fixed, and does not operate the same way across time, place and context. The one constant is that the history of race *is* the history of racism: we have never had an idea of racial difference that isn't used to justify huge imbalances of power, exploitation, conquest or mass murder. It is not 'real', but its various impacts on our lives most certainly are. And understanding that race has been used not to describe differences amongst humanity, but to enforce inequality amongst humanity is perhaps the single most important thing to bear in mind when we try to think about the work that it does in contemporary society.

Weren't we supposed to be past this? The horrors of Nazi Germany and apartheid South Africa, the successes of the civil rights movement in ending segregation, the Universal Declaration of Human Rights – these were all things that were meant to eject racial thinking from the political gene pool. In the 1990s, after the collapse of the Soviet Union invited some optimistic souls to declare the 'End of History' and the final victory of Western liberal capitalism, there was some hope that racism had stopped being a meaningful way of explaining why society functions the way that it does. Racism might exist in the sense of isolated pockets of individual prejudice, but it was no longer relevant to talk about systemic or structural factors. Jim Crow was dead, empire was over, and with neoliberalism in the ascendant, distinctions between citizens melted away in an orgy of consumerism. All men are equal before the eyes of the cash register.

The claim that society had reached the post-racial horizon, or was at least approaching it, was adopted by some sanguine liberals – but more often it was bellowed to the high heavens by conservatives. In 1995, Dinesh D'Souza – an Indian-American conservative commentator, who's now best known for pushing unfounded conspiracy theories about election fraud and his conviction for breaking campaign finance law – published a book called *The End of Racism*. The book didn't simply claim that racism was no longer a force in American society; it claimed that it was wrong to say that racial discrimination, segregation, and even slavery, were wholly or mostly motivated by racism. D'Souza argued that taxi drivers refusing to pick up black male customers was a form of 'rational discrimination';[62] that segregation had been 'a compromise on the part of the Southern ruling elite seeking, in part, to protect blacks';[63] and that, since forms of slavery have been practised in many parts of the world during many historical periods, transatlantic slavery couldn't be considered a racist institution.[64] 'The American slave was treated like property,' he wrote, 'which is to say, pretty well.'[65] Leaving aside the millions of enslaved people who died during the Middle Passage, the high mortality rate amongst captive Africans acclimatising to their new lives in the Americas, rape and sexual violence, and the brutal physical punishments meted out to enslaved people which included whipping, beatings, hangings and shackles, D'Souza's claim crumbles under scrutiny. Would you describe a person being turned into property – being bought and sold, forcibly separated from their children, unable to shape their lives as they chose – as someone that's treated 'pretty well'?

In *The End of Racism*, those who described enduring injustices suffered by African Americans, whether political, social or economic, were branded 'racism merchants'.[66] D'Souza's reasoning was tendentious, his engagement with his critics almost nil: that is to say, the book was total horseshit. But that didn't prevent him being taken seriously at the time. Dinesh D'Souza's book was praised, in an otherwise critical review in the *New York Review of Books*,[67] as 'the most thorough, intelligent, and well-informed presentation of the case against liberal race policies that has yet appeared', and granted two whole episodes of discussion on PBS's *Think Tank*. His central thesis, that differences measured in the life outcomes of black people are the result of their own cultural inferiority and not racism, became immensely popular on the political right, and formed part of the ideological environment that led to liberals and conservatives alike embracing the racist trope of black criminal 'superpredators'. By wrongly declaring the end of racism, D'Souza actually helped create the political cover needed for racism to reinvent itself once more. The conversation was able to transform from a belief in black people's genetic inferiority, to an insistence of their civilisational one. As Barnor Hesse writes, the point of claiming that society is post-racial – that is, post-*racist* – is to create an environment where 'race is no longer represented as a political formulation'. The claim that we've all collectively evolved beyond explaining social ills through the lens of racism means that really, the post-racial narrative is just 'an alibi for the perpetuation of racism'.[68] But if you can't talk about it in public, and elites are united in denying its existence, it can thrive in the dark. Racism is as stubborn as knotweed, permeating the centuries, and as changeable as a chameleon. It can change with the historical moment, adapting itself to its context in order to survive for another generation.

In recent years, the explicit language of racial thinking has made a comeback on the right. Whether it's from populist firebrands on *Fox News* or elite chin-strokers in the *Spectator*, demographics and birthrates have been keeping right-wingers up at night (indeed, spare a thought for the journalist Charlotte Gill, who was so stressed out by 'demographic changes' in London that it made her dread coming back from holiday).[69] And though these opinion leaders are always careful to assert up top that they're talking specifically about immigration, like Enoch Powell before them, they're quickly drawn into images of racial apocalypse. Take, for instance, this 2021 article by bestselling author Lionel Shriver. She begins by noting that more than a third of UK births 'now involve at least one foreign-born parent'; but quickly, the gears shift, and she's talking about ethnic demographics.[70] We're hit by a battery of statistics noting that a third of British schoolchildren are from ethnic minority backgrounds, that there are cities in the UK with non-white majorities, and that the 'ethnic transformation' of the country is destined to rapidly accelerate. Just to be clear, Shriver stopped talking about 'immigration' as a standalone policy area the minute she started talking about ethnicity, because these statistics refer to both foreign and British nationals.

'Even delivering those dry statistics feels dangerous,' she writes, perhaps unconsciously channelling Stuart Hall ('as soon as you say numbers, it doesn't matter how you wrap it up... There are too many of them'). Though Shriver (who, incidentally, is not herself British, but American) says that white Britons are under pressure to 'keep their traps shut' about the fact of rising ethnic diversity in the UK – under pressure from whom, she never says – 'that proscription is socially and even biologically unnatural'. We can't overcome the power of racial difference. 'For westerners to passively accept and even abet incursions by foreigners so massive that the native-born are effectively surrendering their territory without a shot fired,' she writes, 'is biologically perverse.' Now that's what I call demographic panic.

Lionel Shriver is not the first, and most certainly won't be the last, right-wing writer to glide smoothly from expressing concerns about immigration to sounding the alarm on racial demographics. Douglas Murray's *The Strange Death of Europe*, beloved by the more headbanging factions of the Conservative Party and press, similarly bemoans that London has become a 'foreign country' due to the fact that black and brown Brits live here. But there was something so visceral, even apocalyptic, in Shriver's writing. Her persistent invoking of what's 'biologically' unnatural makes it seem as though our very blood rebels against being in community with people from other ethnic backgrounds. This, really, is the core of the Great Replacement nightmare – that it is disgusting, immoral and perverse to accept the idea of multi-racial citizenship. Lamenting that white Brits (whose 'lineages... in their homeland commonly go back hundreds of years') allowed black and brown people to live here without literally trying to gun them down is proper Nazi, blood-and-soil stuff. It's that exact violent fantasy which drives people to wonder out loud about what it might be like to murder me.

I don't believe this is representative of how most people think about their fellow citizens. But it is gaining political traction. Take India for example. The world's largest democracy is governed by a party that explicitly believes in Hindu supremacy, but strategically cultivates a climate of misinformation and paranoia, to scare India's Hindu majority that they are being culturally and demographically threatened by its Muslim minority. Extremist Hindu nationalists and the BJP have pushed the 'love jihad' conspiracy theory, which alleges that Muslim men are hoodwinking or forcing Hindu women into marriage for the purposes of religious conversion so that Islam may rule over India. Despite the Indian Supreme Court having rejected the obviously nonsensical notion of 'love jihad', numerous Indian states have introduced legislation which makes it much harder for interfaith couples to get married, and has led to the arrest of over 200 Muslims between November 2020 and August 2021.[71] Far-right rhetoric about British Muslims appears to have influenced Hindu-supremacist messaging in India. One former BJP MP cited the Rochdale abuse scandal[72] as evidence that 'love jihad' is a universal feature of Muslim community presence: 'Now we have confirmation from the UK as well that "love" is a ruse to trap "kafir" girls to either sexually exploit or convert them to Islam or both,' he claimed. 'Most of such inter-religious alliances are sans any love and are just a part of "jihad".' If people falling in love and having children with each other is 'jihad' – and if for native populations to accept it is 'surrendering their territory' – then violence and authoritarianism becomes not just morally acceptable but morally necessary.

Anti-trans hostility, the Great Replacement and attacks on abortion rights are all part of the same demographic panic. It's all about controlling who gets to determine the composition of the nation. By claiming that the increase in openly transgender people is the result of 'social contagion' (rather than, you know, society being a bit less queerphobic than it used to be), it opens up an avenue for state control of people's bodily autonomy. You can't let one person be trans in peace, lest it leads to dozens more. And if your overriding priority is to boost the population of the white breeding stock, of course you'll clamp down on reproductive freedoms and turn back the clock on LGBTQ rights. Because unless people's ability to live their lives in the way of their own choosing is drastically reined in, who knows what kind of nation they'll produce? Ethnic diversity will increase inexorably, and the dominant group, whether it's white people in Europe and America or Hindus in India, will cease to enjoy the advantage of numerical superiority. Racism, however, has never been a simple numbers game. Whether it's the apartheid regime of South Africa or Israel's control of the West Bank and illegal settlement construction, some societies have chosen forms of *de jure* minority rule over multi-racial society. Such nations define themselves by supremacist ideology – and implement ever more authoritarian means in order to uphold it. That's the choice facing societies across the world: embracing multi-racial democracy, or the myth of identitarian supremacy. But division along identity lines is more useful to the ruling class – it keeps people from recognising their majority class status and shared material interests. There has been a wealth grab, on historic levels, the world over. And this class of planet-spanning landlords want nothing more than to make sure that we don't notice it.

7

Planet Landlord

I will put a very simple proposition to you: namely that today,
all politics is about real estate.
Fredric Jameson

The Price of Air

Imagine that, at some point in the not-too-distant future, the
government makes an announcement: the air that you breathe
is going to be privatised. In a way, you can see the thinking.
For years, air pollution has been getting worse. You've noticed
it when you leave the house, a horrible taste lingering in the
air. Colds hang around for longer, and though you no longer
smoke or vape, a gnarly cough haunts you for weeks after you'd
normally be feeling better. Every blown nose results in a sticky
dark sludge left in the tissue. Children in low-income neighbourhoods have suffered disproportionately from asthma and
respiratory problems, and in one particularly tragic case, a smil-
ing nine-year-old girl died. Sure, air used to be free at the point
of use, but it wasn't as if people's tax money had been put to
good use ensuring that pollution levels stayed low. The state, it
has been decided, can no longer be trusted to keep the air clean.
Now, with air retailers offering to fit smart oxygen meters free
of charge, households would be charged directly for their air use

('More frugal breathers would be rewarded with lower bills', notes a presenter on BBC Radio 4 approvingly).

The Prime Minister, elected on a pro-growth manifesto, heralds the transfer of the nation's air as the beginning of a new dawn – a chance for the ruthless logic of profit to swoop in, and sweep away all those awful public sector inefficiencies. She explains, from behind the lectern, that businesses have a motive to ensure that air stays clean and breathable: if the quality of the air declines, they'll lose the government contract which gives them the right to sell each region's air. By turning air into a commodity, you incentivise companies to make sure it's of the highest possible standard, for the lowest possible price. 'It's just like any other business,' she chides an enquiring journalist. 'You wouldn't expect a bakery with rubbish cupcakes to succeed, would you?' Markets are shaped by the rational logic of supply and demand: if there is a commercial demand for clean air, then companies will supply it in the pursuit of revenue. Simple as.

A committee of politicians is set up with the specific job of making sure the newly privatised air industry is working properly (some had accepted donations from air companies, but nobody paid that much attention). Promises are made about how the country's polluted air supply would be the world's cleanest in five years, or maybe a decade. We'd be the gold standard for public-private partnerships, a modern economy where the profit motive was put to work in the interest of the collective good.

But cleaner air never seems to arrive. Instead, the government introduces a system of particulate credits, where businesses who had kept their pollution under agreed limits could sell the excess to companies who'd gone over theirs. Foreign investors snap up shares in air companies, meaning that billions of pounds worth of dividends leave these shores to fill the coffers of multinationals based in tax havens. Legislation gets passed giving air companies carte blanche to dump dirty air in rural areas, choking natural beauty spots and wreaking havoc with wildlife. But the profits keep on coming.

One autumn, when a particularly bad fog rolls in and people are warned to stay inside because the air is too dangerous to breathe, some entrepreneurs realise that there's money to be made. Apple designs a battery-powered air filter that fits over your face like a mask, with wi-fi and Bluetooth capacity so you can make calls and listen to music. Home purifier systems are installed in the apartments and houses of the wealthy (though of course, this just makes the air in deprived communities even worse). For a lower price, you can buy disposable oxygen canisters on the go. But unlucky enough to be on the breadline? You've just gotta put up with breathing whatever the air companies deign to provide – and keep paying the bills for it. Politically, the issue seems settled: the leader of the opposition refuses to commit to renationalising the air. But as more children end up with air pollution listed on their death certificates as a reason for their untimely demise, CEOs and shareholders shrug off the criticism: after all, it's not hurting their profit margins and it's not as if the poor can simply stop breathing. They've got the power: a stranglehold on a resource that everyone needs to live.

The idea of air being privatised, becoming super profitable for corporate shareholders, but worse to breathe for all of us, might seem a bit outlandish. But everything I've just framed as speculative fiction is lifted straight out of our recent history. The system of carbon credits, whereby polluters pay off other companies, is how car manufacturers get around lowering their own emissions. Much of the rest of our little fable is drawn from what happened to water in the UK: between 2016 and 2021, private water companies increased the amount of time spent pumping raw sewage into British waterways by 2,553 per cent.[1] We're living in the midst of an unfolding disaster as privatised infrastructure crumbles around us. The things we need to survive are traded as commodities, and we are held captive by a diminished status as consumers, as opposed to citizens. It is nigh on heresy to suggest, as Liberal politician Joseph Chamberlain did in the nineteenth century, that it is impossible 'to combine the citizens' rights and interests and the private enterprise's interests, because the private enterprise aims at its natural and justified objective, the biggest possible profit.'[2] Capitalism was supposed to deliver a property-owning democracy, where everybody had a stake and wealth was fairly distributed. Instead, society has been cleaved in two: there are landlords, the people and corporations who increasingly own everything, and there are tenants. That's everybody else.

Throughout this book, I've been showing you the various methods through which working-class power has been inhibited, splintered and weakened. It's down to how the left has internalised an individualistic and competitive model of victimhood; a media machine that's dedicated to pumping trivial outrage-bait; a political class that's obsessed with chasing headlines; the stoking of anti-immigration moral panics and the hobbling of working-class institutions like trade unions and council housing to shift the window of politics rightwards; and a confected sense of demographic panic which directs antagonism horizontally and downwards rather than up at elites. And if I was a liberal, I'd stop the book here, dash the manuscript to my editor and celebrate the end of a lengthy writing project. But these aren't purposeless, random, disconnected phenomena. The weakening of working-class power is both the result of, and in service to, a historic wealth and resource grab by corporations, financiers and oligarchs.

The prevailing view of most people who work in politics and media is that things are the way they are because people just happen to do things. When establishment opinion-formers are called upon to explain why something bad has happened, you'll often hear that cock-ups are always more likely than conspiracy. It's an individualist explanation of events, rather than a structural one. Society is the way it is because of a series of accumulated accidents, and any attempt to provide a more structural explanation is regarded the same way as the suggestion that aliens shot JFK. There is, of course, an incentive for powerful people to insist that power doesn't really exist, that it doesn't protect and entrench itself at the expense of others. But maybe – just maybe! – there's a middle ground between hollering that societal injustices are the result of an elite paedophile cabal operating out of American pizza parlours, and just waving them away altogether. And rather than thinking about power as the result of winning arguments, as though political debate happens on a level playing field, we should look at the question of ownership. Because that – not your identity, not your geographic location, not your values – will tell you where you stand in society.

The Enclosure of Almost Everything

How much do you *really* own? Take a moment to think about it. You have a roof over your head, but is that because you're paying rent to a landlord? If your name is on the deed, is that because you own your home outright, or are you paying off a mortgage? If your home could be repossessed if you ended up in arrears, are you that much different from a renter? What about a car – did you get it on finance? That phone you're using, are you paying off the price of the handset as well as for data and calls? You might have a wardrobe full of clothes and a bin full of takeaway boxes, but did you get any of them using a buy-now-pay-later service? Do you own the data, and not just the content, that you generate for Google, Facebook, WhatsApp, Instagram or TikTok? We live in an age where we have a lot of the items that used to indicate wealth, like exotic foods and fashionable clothes, but we own remarkably little. If you want to work out whether you're part of the landlord class, or a member of the great mass of renters, ask yourself what would happen if all of your debts were called in tomorrow – your credit card, your student loans, your mortgage, if you have one. Would you be able to draw on your savings, to earn enough money in a short enough period of time, or to sell possessions which have increased in value since you bought them, to keep yourself afloat? Would you still have a home to live in, food to put on the table, money to cover your care needs and those of any dependants, and the general cost of living? If the answer is 'no' or 'probably not', then congratulations: you're part of the renting class. And what we experience as culture wars is really the social scaffolding that holds up rentier capitalism.

So what is rentier capitalism? Well, 'rentier' is really just a word for landlord. Basically, rentier capitalism describes an economic system in which the dominant economic activity is income that's derived primarily from 'the ownership, possession or control of scarce assets and under conditions of limited or no competition'.[3] Think about collecting rent on real estate, charging interest on loans or being able to profit from controlling the flow of natural resources like water, energy and land. In a rentier capitalist system, the ownership class are able to generate their income without actually contributing to the production of goods or services, which leads to a concentration of wealth and power in the hands of that small elite. Think about the private rental market: landlords don't build the houses or keep prices low for those who can't afford to buy. When it's contract renewal time, and your rent goes up, it's not because your landlord has decided to renovate the kitchen or add another bedroom – it's because they want to keep up with what the rest of the market is doing. Rentier capitalism is extractive – it is defined by the upward flow of money from those who don't own assets, to those who do.

As Brett Christophers explains in *Rentier Capitalism: Who Owns the Economy, and Who Pays for It?*, there are different modes of rentierism. There are literal landlords who extract ground rent, but also firms which take over natural monopolies like telecommunications and digital platforms which control the flow of information. And recent decades have seen the rise of corporations whose job isn't even really to *do* anything. Outsourcing giants like Serco specialise in winning government contracts, from security to contact-tracing during the pandemic, and then subcontract the actual delivery of those services to other, smaller companies. The profitability of outsourcing firms comes from the fact that their size means they can bully smaller companies out of the competition for contracts, but then use their position in the market to squeeze favourable terms (i.e. cut prices on wages and costs) from them as they outsource downwards. Shareholder dividends don't come from the fact that they can deliver quality goods and services, argues Christophers, but from the fact that they've become very good at extracting taxpayer money, suppressing smaller firms and throttling workers' pay. They extract 'rent' in the form of service fees, often having won contracts in circumstances where the state can't even offer a better deal to itself through insourcing.

The argument for shifting the responsibility for public goods into the hands of rentiers is that their duties towards their shareholders mean that they're compelled to offer better and more efficient services. But we're surrounded by examples where the precise opposite has happened. Take Thames Water, for instance. At the time of writing, the firm is teetering on the edge of collapse. It's not because they pumped seventy-two billion litres of sewage into the river between 2020 and 2023,[4] nor is it because they had to warn hundreds of households in May 2024 not to drink the tap water because it had been contaminated with a vomiting bug.[5] And just to be clear, it's not because the people of London and the surrounding areas spontaneously stopped needing water in order to live. It's because their owners made too much money from it. Between 2006 and 2017, Thames Water was owned by a consortium led by an Australian bank called Macquarie. Over that period of time, Thames Water went from having £3.4 billion in debt to £10.8 billion – while shareholders, including Macquarie, were paid out £2.7 billion in dividends.[6]

If that looks, sounds and smells like asset stripping, that's because it is. Macquarie moved in, loaded the company with debt, extracted a tonne of loot and then fucked off before it all came crashing down on their heads. In 2024, Thames Water is sitting on a growing debt mountain of at least £16.5 billion – and customers are being threatened with bill increases of nearly an extra £100 a year just so the company can sort out its finances.[7] The price of water doesn't just reflect its scarcity or abundance: it measures how badly private owners have messed up. Oh, and just in case you were worried that Macquarie would be pariahs in UK markets after their reckless stewardship of Thames Water, don't worry. In 2021 they were allowed to buy a majority stake in Southern Water,[8] and in July 2024 – in the early weeks of Keir Starmer's new government – announced that they would take full control of Britain's gas network.[9] It may be the case that by the time this book comes out, Thames Water will have screwed up so royally that the government is compelled to take it back into public ownership. That would be great news – apart from the fact that other failing water companies like Southern Water, SES Water and South East Water would all still be in private hands.

Others have done the debt-loading trick in different sectors. When the Glazer family, who made their fortune owning and renting out American shopping malls, took over Manchester United in 2005, the football club was debt-free. But now, nearly twenty years later, the club owes £653.3 million in debts, and has already forked out £772.5m in interest charges.[10] The Glazers, meanwhile, helped themselves to more than £150 million in dividend payments between 2016 and 2022.[11] And just like the water companies who've extracted vast sums of money while infrastructure crumbles, the iconic stadium of Old Trafford falls deeper into a state of disrepair. On rainy days – which are pretty frequent in Manchester! – water pours in through holes in the roof. I'm not a Manchester United fan, and as a supporter of a rival club, their anguish does please me on some level. But there's something obscene about how a coterie of extremely rich people can come in and ruin something that people adore by loading it with debt. Buying something doesn't necessarily mean you're meaningfully invested in it. There's no love in corporate takeovers.

There's an idea that ownership results in a sense of responsibility. And in some ways, that's true. If you have a dog,[12] a car or a home, it's likely you feel a sense of obligation towards looking after it precisely because it's yours. But that's not something which scales up – and that's because your feeling of value and care towards something is a reflection of its importance in your life. You rely on that dog for companionship or protection, you need that car to get around, and home is the place where you can inhale a whole tube of Pringles by yourself and nobody can judge you. When a resource is defined solely in terms of making money, when you no longer need it for the nourishment of your life or conditions, it becomes less valuable in every way but its price-tag. Privatised water companies can pump faeces into rivers, preside over contamination of the supply and hike prices for consumers because they don't view water as a public good. Your need for water creates an imbalance in power and leverage which they can exploit for profit. The pipes which take water into your home are secondary to the ones which flow money upwards and outwards to shareholders.

Don't believe me? Listen to what these private corporations have to say for themselves. Avanti West Coast, the British train operating company which you may remember ruining your day when you foolishly tried to get from one major city to another without bankrupting yourself, runs an absolutely abysmal service. The railways used to be in public hands in the UK, until British Rail was sold off piece-by-piece in the 1990s. Different companies – themselves often owned by foreign corporations, and indeed, by other countries' transport operators – competed for the contracts to run passenger services along different routes. Avanti West Coast is particularly rubbish. Between 2023 and 2024, the equivalent of one in every fifteen trains they ran were cancelled;[13] three-quarters of the Manchester-to-London trains run late.[14] But Avanti West Coast executives aren't at all embarrassed or chastened about it. In January 2024, Novara Media's very own Polly Smythe revealed that bosses at one meeting joked about how they were raking in taxpayer cash: 'Roll-up, roll-up, get your free money here!' read one Powerpoint slide.[15] Avanti's executives were literally laughing about how much dosh they get from the Department of Transport, and how little they have to stump up for investment. They then followed up by bragging that they still get the money even if they don't meet all of their targets, and an extra bonus if they do meet them.

Similarly, in 2021, then-CEO of BP Bernard Looney was delighted. Sure, ordinary families might be struggling to pay for heating, food, petrol and other costs, but he and his shareholders were having a grand old time. 'When the market is strong, when oil prices are strong and when gas prices are strong, this is literally a cash machine,' bragged Bernard Looney to the *Financial Times*.[16] Shareholders could expect a boost to their returns, while in some parts of London over a fifth of households were in fuel poverty.[17] This was before Russia's invasion of Ukraine, which prompted an inflationary crisis across much of Europe, pushed people into penury and signalled a massive payday for the likes of BP. Since February 2022, when the invasion began, BP's payments to shareholders tot up to approximately £22.3 billion in dividends and buybacks.[18] For them, it's a 'cash machine'; for you, it's a cost-of-living crisis.

As discussed in Chapter 4, Marxists define a class as those who have common material interests, are conscious of those interests and work collectively in some way to advance those interests. Macquarie's debt-loading of Thames Water, or Avanti and BP's grotesque boasts, aren't the result of bad people spontaneously deciding to do bad things. They're behaving as a class. It's because they know what their interests are, and they work to advance them at every opportunity. Their ability to do so is made possible by the asymmetry of power between those needing a resource, and those controlling access to it. Without collective class consciousness, and collective class action of our own, we have no counterweight to that power. And like a bad landlord hiking your rent because they know you don't have anywhere else to go, these corporate giants are able to leverage your need – whether it's to catch a train, or to heat your home – to extract the maximum amount of profit for themselves.

The examples I've cited here – water, energy, rail and even football – are areas where corporate landlords have taken over infrastructure and services which they didn't themselves make. That's perhaps the defining feature of neoliberalism, a global project of massive privatisation where public goods have been transformed into profit-extracting enterprises. Margaret Thatcher, the Prime Minister whose iron will (and police force) broke the miners' strike, and who sold off council housing and privatised state assets, famously said that the problem with socialism is that 'they always run out of other people's money'.[19] But it should be said that the problem with neoliberalism is that they always run out of other people's assets. These corporate landlords do not create, they do not build and they rarely improve. All they know how to do is extract money for shareholders until the company goes under, and another buyer – or indeed, the state – has to step in again. And if I was a social democrat, I could end the book here. All you need is a bit of taxation, some strategic renationalisation, and perhaps some anti-trust laws here and there. Manuscript finito, and it's off to the pub for me, to join the liberal version of me, who's already several drinks in.

That, however, would fail to take into account how profoundly neoliberalism has changed in the last fifteen or so years. In the first financial quarter of 2007, the top five biggest publicly traded corporations by market capitalisation were Exxon-Mobil, General Electric, Microsoft, Citigroup and AT&T. In the first quarter of 2024, only one of those companies is still in the top ten. Microsoft, Apple, Nvidia (a software and semiconductor chip manufacturer, specialising in AI), Alphabet (Google's parent company) and Amazon are now the five largest by market capitalisation with Meta following close behind. The wealth controlled by these corporations is gargantuan. In March 2021, Apple's market capitalisation was bigger than the US budget deficit – only seven countries had GDPs which were bigger than Apple's market value.[20] And sure, these companies make useful products: phones, laptops, graphics-processing units, search engines and more. But trying to explain these tech giants solely in terms of the products they make is wholly inadequate.

Is Amazon really a retailer? Sure, there are Amazon-branded products like cat food and shampoos. But they make up a small percentage of its sales.[21] Let me take you through my last few orders. Amazon don't make the tub of gochujang I bought yesterday (CJ Haechandle, or the food factory they contract, does that). They don't make the hydrating face mist I ordered

(BYOMA, or the factory they contract, does that). They don't make the lightbulbs I purchased for the bathroom, the D-lock I got for my bike or the sewing kit I bought with every intention of learning how to darn. These physical goods are just the tip of Amazon's revenue iceberg. Amazon Web Services – which makes up nearly a third of the world's cloud infrastructure market – made more than $25 billion in the twelve months leading up to April 2024.[22,23] As Yanis Varoufakis argues in *Technofeudalism*, these companies who actually make the products you buy on Amazon or Alibaba have the status of vassal subjects beneath their lord or king. He calls the likes of Amazon, or the Apple App Store, 'cloudalists' – they control the space in which commercial transactions take place, and skim off most of the profit margin in the form of rent. He writes that these tech giants operate 'digital fiefdoms': today, 'conventional capitalist manufacturers increasingly have no option but to sell their goods at the discretion of the cloudalists, paying them a fee for the privilege, developing a relationship with them no different to that of vassals vis-à-vis their feudal overlords.'[24]

This is wildly different from the privatisation model discussed above, wherein corporations take over something that already exists and extract money from it. These digital fiefs aren't a 'market' – they regulate everyone else's access to the market, and mediate every transaction within it. And part of the reason why their market capitalisations are so insanely huge is because they've found a way to turn their consumers into labourers. Every time you post a photo, make a TikTok, leave a review, turn location services on, send an email, talk to Alexa, use Google Maps or WhatsApp your mum, you're working for Big Tech without getting paid. We train AI for free by interacting with it, whether we know that's what we're doing (e.g. mucking around with Chat GPT) or unknowingly when we're shitposting on Twitter.

This isn't privatisation. It's more like enclosure. All the things which spring from our human impulses, like curiosity or desire for social interaction, are captured by the digital infrastructure of Google, Meta, Apple and Amazon. As Jodi Dean, who similarly argues that the economy has taken a feudalistic turn, puts it: our age is one where '[t]he proprietor of the land no longer works it, and those who work the land no longer own it. Craftworkers likewise stop owning the instruments of labour. The tools employ them instead.'[25] Every time you get an Uber, stay in an Airbnb, order a Deliveroo or browse products on Amazon, you are generating and circulating data. And this data rebounds on us in the form of algorithms, shaping and programming our own behaviour. We're all toiling away for digital landlords, without seeing a penny for it. In *Technofeudalism*, Yanis Varoufakis points out that in the old corporate giants of Exxon-Mobil, General Motors or General Electric, workers collected about 80 per cent of the company's income in wages and salaries. But 'Big Tech's workers, in contrast, collect less than 1 per cent of the firm's revenues. The reason is that paid labour performs only a fraction of the work that Big Tech relies on. Most of the work is performed by billions of people for free.'[26] The result? Workers' share of global income is on a downward trend.[27]

How does the centre-left government of Keir Starmer propose to deal with this? When it comes to the old corporate landlords of the railways and the energy companies, there are signs that he's willing to curb their power. He's promised to bring the railways back into public hands when their contracts end, and to set up an energy company which can undercut the likes of British Gas. But when it comes to these new, digital landlords, he's rolling out the welcome mat. When the previous Tory government awarded a patient data contract to Palantir – a US tech giant whose activities span from surveillance and 'predictive policing' to providing the Israeli Defence Force with technology for its genocidal war on Gaza[28],[29] – then-Shadow Health Secretary Wes Streeting's main objection was that it didn't go far enough. 'The NHS has struck gold here, yet it's leaving it in the ground,' he said at a health conference in 2024.[30] Though Streeting has made it clear that patient data will not be sold onwards by Palantir under a Labour government,[31] you can't help but wonder why a company which has developed products that help governments spy on their own citizens would be trusted with sensitive clinical data at all.[32] Though governments are quick to talk about the harms of tech when it comes to misinformation, social media addiction and the possibility of a godlike AI, they're remarkably relaxed about the amount of power being accrued by digital landlords – and how they turn us into digital serfs.

Don't get me wrong, I'm not an anti-technology Luddite. There is no part of me which yearns for a life without wi-fi and pasteurised milk. But there is an alternative to allowing giant landlords of property, infrastructure and information to hoard and control resources which are critical to the public good and human flourishing. There's a reason why I opened this chapter by speculating what it might be like if the very air we breathed was turned into a commodity – it's to get us to connect emotionally to the horror that it's exactly what we've done to everything else. We turned water, land, housing, data, food, energy and even the human attention span into commodities. And in doing so, what have we achieved? People can't afford homes, because landlords buy up the housing stock and property developers land-bank the ground more could be built on. We've allowed companies to asset strip water firms and pay out money which could've been used on cleaning up the supply to shareholders abroad. We've allowed hedge funds and bankers to speculate on the price of food and drive the cost of bread and rice up. We've allowed energy companies to drill for more oil and gas, all while the planet heats, as long as they invest a tiny proportion of their revenues in the odd solar farm. We've ceded our survival to a planet-spanning class of landlords.

Here's why I'm not a liberal, or a social democrat. I believe that the politics that we've got are a reflection of the balance of class forces in society. And on the one hand, we've got billions of people who are splintered on the basis of nation, language, gender, sexuality, race and religion. Even within countries, where we at least notionally share a language and a geographic location, we make a virtue out of what divides us. We look at the idea of solidarity with suspicion, and instead find myriad ways of insisting that people who are set against one another by racism, sexism, homophobia and transphobia are unable to identify shared interests with one another. We embrace the idea of being minorities, despite forming the majority class. And on the other hand our real opponents, the planet's landlords, don't feel the same way. Sure, they might compete with each other for market dominance. They might even play dirty to undermine their rivals. But when push comes to shove, they know where their class interests lie. When it's time to resist regulation or dodge taxes, corporate landlords understand that they're all in it together. The world's elites, the minority of people with real power and wealth, are conscious of being a class. What the rest of us truly have in common with each other is that what we once had as *the commons* has been expropriated from us.

Epilogue

Exactly at the moment when I was supposed to submit this manuscript, much of the UK erupted into racist rioting. Migrant-owned businesses, hotels housing asylum seekers, people's homes and even just men and women on the street who happened not to be white found themselves under attack from Belfast to Rotherham, Middlesbrough to Tamworth. The spark which ignited a week of smashed glass was (as I mention earlier in this book) the brutal and tragic slaying of three children at a Taylor Swift dance class in Southport on 29 July. False claims that the perpetrator was Muslim and/or an asylum seeker were amplified by the likes of Andrew Tate and Tommy Robinson;[1] according to misinformation expert Marc Owen Jones, social media posts stating or speculating that the perpetrator was Muslim, a migrant, a refugee or a foreigner garnered at least twenty-seven million impressions.[2] The man arrested and charged by police turned out to be a Cardiff-born seventeen-year-old.

It would be wrong, however, to mistake this catalyst for being the cause. The public were primed to think of asylum seekers as criminal, backward and vicious long before Twitter was a glint in a tech bro's eye. When was the last time you heard of refugees talked about as anything other than a problem? Alongside far-right staples like 'Oh, Tommy Tommy!'[3] and 'Who the fuck is Allah?',[4] rioters could be heard chanting 'stop the boats'[5] – a slogan which had been emblazoned across Prime Minister Rishi

Sunak's lectern. Decades of relentlessly negative coverage of the asylum issue had done its work to dehumanise asylum seekers – and the Blair-era policy of dispersal, housing asylum seekers in the poorest parts of the country, might as well have been designed specifically to provoke division and resentment. Systematically stripping the opportunity, optimism and infrastructure from a town isn't generally conducive to making it more welcoming to outsiders.

According to the *Financial Times*, seven out of the ten most deprived areas of the country witnessed rioting between 30 July and 5 August 2024.[6] As rioters made their way through the criminal-justice system a few weeks later, and details of their lives were made public, a throughline emerged. Whether in Southport,[7] Sunderland[8] or Bristol,[9] many of those being sentenced were unemployed and/or of no fixed address.

One John Cann, convicted of violent disorder, was no stranger to the courts: he had twenty-four convictions for thirty-nine offences, mostly non-violent.[10] His childhood was, by anyone's standards, absolutely horrific. In mitigation, the court heard that Cann was taken into care at the age of six. In 1992, he fell ninety-five feet and severely injured his leg, resulting in him being in a coma for a short while, and subsequently requiring a prosthetic. Nothing screams 'functioning social safety net' like a care-experienced child growing up to be a habitual offender without a permanent home. I'm not saying that having a hard life gives you a pass on racist rioting. But it's easy to see how being treated as disposable by society would make a person nihilistic, disdainful of the law and callous to the suffering of others. If there's a parallel to be drawn between the riots of August 2024 and the riots of August 2011, it's this: happy communities with ample economic opportunities generally don't set their own towns on fire.

But – and this is important – it's also not right to paint the riots simply as the violent cri de coeur of the dispossessed. In

Manchester's Piccadilly Gardens, a lone black man was attacked by a mob of white men, for no other reason than his race.[11] In Belfast, a child holding her mother's hand was filmed skipping down the street, chanting 'Pakis out'.[12] In Tamworth, rioters broke into a hotel housing asylum seekers, tried to set it alight with people inside, and scrawled 'FUCK PAKIS' on the walls with spray paint.[13] The racist intentions of rioters were plain for all to see. It wasn't all about immigration, and it wasn't all about poverty. Dan Evans' petty bourgeoisie feature heavily amongst those being sentenced too – like the director of a kitchen-fitting business from Darlington, who cried in court when remanded in custody.[14] The woman credited with being the first person to share the false information that the Southport suspect was an asylum seeker named Ali Al-Shakati wasn't exactly part of the great unwashed: according to *The Times*, she 'lives a well-to-do family life in a £1.5 million house in the rural north of England'.[15] Those who had whipped up hatred and suspicion against Britain's minorities in Britain's newspapers aren't poor, and often aren't working class. Douglas Murray, in November 2023, wrongly predicted that Muslims protesting against the genocide[16] in Gaza would 'defile the Cenotaph and the statues of our dead and our war leaders', and that if the army would not be sent in 'then the public will have to go in, and the public will have to sort this out themselves and it'll be very, very brutal'.[17] He's an Eton alumnus. Anti-migrant, anti-Muslim and anti-minority sentiment can't all be attributed to class inequality.

I genuinely hope that I haven't bummed you out. Maybe you've read this book, and you feel a sense of despair. Or perhaps you feel I've got it all wrong – maybe there's a centre-left government in Downing Street, and you're thinking that I'm just being salty for the sake of it. And look, I'm not going to sit here and pretend that there's absolutely no difference between wet liberals being in power, or white nationalists being in power. When Donald Trump goads black journalists by falsely claiming that Kamala Harris only 'happened to turn black' a few years ago,[18] or Nigel Farage says that a growing number of Muslims don't share our values,[19] it has a profoundly emboldening effect on racists everywhere. It does matter if culture wars are being stoked by a head of government, who is able to turn both the might of the state and the zeal of their followers on vulnerable minorities. But (as the 2024 riots showed) a centrist government with no real idea of how to combat racist ideas – and indeed, taking an active role in anti-migrant crackdowns – isn't a particularly strong bulwark against the far right.

A change of government between establishment parties is not the same as movement in the direction of real equality. While corporations and oligarchs are able to commodify, privatise, enclose and control the essential ingredients for human survival and flourishing, we exist under a true minority rule. It's always worth bearing in mind which way big business will tip in a straight political conflict between the racist far right and the redistributionist left: in June 2024, when Marine Le Pen's far-right party Rassemblement National vied with the left's New Popular Front for control of the French National Assembly, bankers and businesses were rooting for RN.[20] If liberal technocrats are unavailable, capitalists are more than happy to jump into bed with fascists. Kick in the heads of asylum seekers, drive trans people out of public life, whatever – just don't touch my profit margins.

So, if you can't trust the political custodians of the status quo, should you instead allow yourself to be overwhelmed by despair? There are plenty of good reasons to. I'm writing this just a week after Earth's hottest day since records began.[21] That abstract statistic means these concrete things. It means that a few days ago, in Canada, the premier of Alberta (who previously pushed conspiracy theories that wildfires were driven by an uptick in arsonists, rather than climate change) tearfully helmed a press conference announcing that an out-of-control wildfire was tearing through a picturesque mountain town.[22] It means that the basic, not-even-extra-virgin supermarket olive oil that I buy is 260 per cent more expensive than it was just a couple of years ago.[23] And it means that earlier this spring, a deadly heatwave in West Africa and the Sahel saw temperatures surge above 45°C.[24] We've probably missed the boat on holding global temperature changes at 1.5°C, and we're looking down the barrel of a world where floods, fires, food insecurity and temperatures which are literally too hot for people to survive will become even more frequent and extreme.

You can look at any one of the crises surrounding us – whether it's the climate emergency, the genocide[25] in Gaza or rising inequality – and just see a reason to give up the hope that human beings are capable of bettering ourselves as a species. But the odds have always been stacked against justice. You'd never have bet on the success of the abolitionists, or the suffrage movement, or the civil rights struggle, or the fight for abortion access. But courage and collective action are capable of wondrous things. We have an obligation to resist the temptation of passivity and despair, while also seeing the scale of the challenge around us clearly. Others have done exactly that, even in the most abject of circumstances. When imprisoned by Mussolini's fascists, the Marxist philosopher Antonio Gramsci wrote that he was 'far from feeling beaten';[26] but he was not in denial about his situation either. In a letter penned in his cell, he identified as 'a pessimist because of intelligence, but an optimist because of will'.[27] If he could do it, so can you.

What I've hoped to show over the course of this book is that how we think of ourselves, our fellow human beings and the world around us isn't just the random, organic product of our individual perceptions. Our very thoughts are moulded by the work of institutions, the discourses they pump out and the conditions they create. If we feel alienated, disempowered or lonely, it's because a project of intense atomisation has made us that way.

The neoliberal right deliberately crafted and pursued this strategy. As Margaret Thatcher said, 'Economics are the method, the object is to change the heart and soul.'[28] And indeed something at the very core of us has been transformed by decades of rentier capitalism and ideological neoliberalism. We've lost faith in our ability to change things. We've come to doubt the value of working with people who don't perfectly resemble us. We're suspicious and punitive, building barriers and trip-wires to confirm that other people are not to be trusted. We make sameness the condition of solidarity. This pervasive feeling of woundedness and wariness is a product of the left's historic defeats over the past forty years – we're like this, because we've been losing. But it's also time to admit that we've been losing because we're like this. We can't achieve anything while minoritising ourselves.

That doesn't mean throwing away identity-based struggle, and ignoring the brutal injustices of racism, sexism, ableism, homophobia and transphobia. But if we continue to insist that minorities can fight alone, we're consigning ourselves to losing alone. We can no longer afford to disappear into the solipsism of feelings; it's imperative that we pull our heads out of our arses and refocus on the material harms which exist outside of individual subjectivities. Nothing frightens those hoarding power and wealth more than when people are able to overcome their differences, and hone their anger on a single, upwards target.

While we're shaped by forces larger than ourselves, we still have agency. We can make choices – and I'm not talking about individual ones, where we dedicate ourselves to policing the boundaries of our own moral purity. We can make choices which bring us into community with other people, as the highest source of good. We can organise in our neighbourhoods, friendship circles, schools and workplaces. Is it an uphill struggle? Well, duh. We're working against the prevailing direction of our material conditions, which aim to keep us separate. But, as the hundreds of thousands of people who globally poured out onto the streets in condemnation of Israel's bombardment and starvation of Gaza in 2023 and 2024 has shown, there are moments of acute moral urgency in which people work in concert with each other despite profound differences in identity and outlook. It can be done: it just needs to be scaled up.

The stakes are high. But we have so much more to gain than just economic fairness. When we are conscious of ourselves as a majority class, we can begin to take back all that was stolen from us – including our sense of comradeship with one another.

NOTES

INTRODUCTION

1 The Office of National Statistics, 'Private rent and house prices, UK: May 2024', https://www.ons.gov.uk/economy/inflationandpriceindices/bulletins/privaterentandhousepricesuk/may2024

2 Michael Savage, 'Alarm at growing number of working people in UK "struggling to make ends meet"', *Guardian*, 21.04.2024.

3 Nuffield Trust, 'Peak leaving? A spotlight on nurse leaver rates in the UK', 30.09.2022, https://www.nuffieldtrust.org.uk/resource/peak-leaving-a-spotlight-on-nurse-leaver-rates-in-the-uk#:~:text=How%20many%20are%20leaving%20the,these%20staff%20left%20the%20register

4 Sally Weale, 'Eight in 10 primary teachers in England spending own money to help pupils', *Guardian*, 05.06.2024.

5 Philip Whiteside, 'Half of young mothers skip meals for their children', *Sky News*, 28.03.2017.

6 'Public opinions and social trends, Great Britain: personal well-being and loneliness', Office for National Statistics, 16.08.2024.

7 Rob LaFranco, Grace Chung and Chase Peterson-Withorn, 'World's Billionaires List', *Forbes*, 01.04.2024.

8 'Unpaid care, England and Wales: Census 2021', Office for National Statistics, 19.01.2023.

9 'Unpaid Eldercare in the United States – 2021–2022: Data from the American Time Use Survey', Bureau of Labor Statistics, 21.09.2023.

10 Throughout this book, I will call the actions of Israel in Gaza since 7 October 2023 a genocide. At the time of writing, at least 1,410 Palestinian families have been wiped out from Gaza's civil registry: https://www.middleeasteye.net/live-blog/live-blog-update/

israeli-massacres-wiped-out-1410-palestinian-families-civil-registry. According to Gaza's health ministry, an additional 3,463 families in Gaza have lost all but one family member. The UN defines genocide as 'a crime committed with the intent to destroy a national, ethnic, racial or religious group, in whole or in part'. It is my belief that Israel's 'concerted policy to destroy the health-care system of Gaza' (see the *Report of the Independent International Commission of Inquiry on the Occupied Palestinian Territory, including East Jerusalem, and Israel*, p. 18, https://documents.un.org/doc/undoc/gen/n24/262/79/pdf/n2426279.pdf), Israel's use of 'starvation of a weapon of war' against Palestinian civilians (see *Report of the Special Committee to Investigate Israeli Practices Affecting the Human Rights of the Palestinian People and Other Arabs of the Occupied Territories*, p. 2, https://documents.un.org/doc/undoc/gen/n24/271/19/pdf/n2427119.pdf) and Israeli airstrikes on designated humanitarian zones (see https://www.nbcnews.com/news/world/palestinians-killed-israeli-strikes-safe-zones-exclusive-nbc-report-rcna148008 and https://www.bbc.co.uk/news/articles/cwyx9znxl4eo), constitute genocidal acts. Furthermore, it is my view (and that of South Africa's legal team, given in the presentation of their case against Israel at the International Court of Justice) that statements made by Israel's President Isaac Herzog, Prime Minister Benjamin Netanyahu, and former Minister of Defence Yoav Gallant demonstrate genocidal intent: https://www.icj-cij.org/sites/default/files/case-related/192/192-20231228-app-01-00-en.pdf, p. 60. I agree with UN Special Rapporteur Francesca Albanese that an analysis of Israel's policies, patterns of violence and their impact on the Palestinian people of Gaza meets the threshold of genocide (see *Anatomy of a Genocide: Report of the Special Rapporteur on the situation of human rights in the Palestinian territories occupied since 1967*, https://www.ohchr.org/sites/default/files/documents/hrbodies/hrcouncil/sessions-regular/session55/advance-versions/a-hrc-55-73-auv.pdf). But beyond the legal case, I believe that we all have a moral obligation to call what's going on by its proper name – even if international courts have yet to deliver their final verdict. You don't need anyone's permission to speak as your conscience dictates.

11 Yes, I know it's been renamed X. But who *actually* calls it that?
12 Greg Petro, 'As Amazon Turns 30, E-Commerce Share of Retail Is Flattening: Is It A Trend?', *Forbes*, 21.02.2024.

13 John Stepek, 'UK Houses Haven't Been This Unaffordable Since 1876', *Bloomberg*, 17.02.2023, https://www.bloomberg.com/news/newsletters/2023-02-17/uk-houses-haven-t-been-this-unaffordable-since-1876

14 Charles Hymas, '"Exit from ECHR is the only way to solve small boats crisis"', *Telegraph*, https://www.telegraph.co.uk/politics/2024/04/05/exit-from-echr-is-the-only-way-to-solve-small-boats-crisis/

15 Stuart Hall, 'The Neoliberal Revolution', *Soundings*, Issue 48, 04.08.2011, p. 17.

16 W.E.B. Du Bois, *Black Reconstruction*, p. 701

17 Melanie Phillips, 'Islamophobia is a fiction to shut down debate', *The Times*, 07.05.2018.

18 Melanie Phillips, 'Jeremy Corbyn is not the cause of left-wing Jew hate, he's the result of it', *Jewish Chronicle*, 18.10.2018.

19 https://iep.utm.edu/fouc-pol/

1 HOW THE 'I' TOOK OVER 'IDENTITY POLITICS'

1 Holly Holtz, 'The Trotsky House', *Institute of Doctoral Studies in the Visual Arts*, https://www.idsva.edu/articles/the-trotsky-house

2 'THE COMBAHEE RIVER COLLECTIVE STATEMENT', The Combahee River Collective, 1977.

3 Ibid.

4 Ibid.

5 Ibid.

6 Emma Dabiri, *What White People Can Do Next: From Allyship to Coalition*, Penguin UK, London, 2021, p. 15.

7 Linda Villarosa, 'The Disturbing Truth About Hair Relaxers', *New York Times*, 13.06.2024.

8 Yolanda Moses, 'Is the Term "People of Color" Acceptable in This Day and Age?', *Sapiens*, https://www.sapiens.org/language/people-of-color/

9 E. Tammy Kim, 'The Perils of "People of Color"', *New Yorker*, https://www.newyorker.com/news/annals-of-activism/the-perils-of-people-of-color#:~:text=The%20phrase%20%E2%80%9Cpeople%20of%20color,kinds%20(%E2%80%9Ccoloureds%E2%80%9D)

10 NPR, *Code Switch*, https://www.npr.org/transcripts/918418825

11 Quoted in Shereen Marisol Meraji, Natalie Escobar and Kumari Devarajan, 'Is It Time To Say R.I.P. To "POC"?', NPR, 30.09.2022.

12 'Did Anne Frank Have White Privilege? The Most Online Discourse of 2022 | Offline with Jon Favreau', *Pod Save America*, 18.12.2022.

13 'Touch Grass Ableist', *Know Your Meme*, 28.11.2020.

14 Since writing this, gal-dem has sadly shut down. As of November 2024, their website is in the process of being digitally archived by the British Library.

15 'White Panther Party 10-point Program', *Ann Arbor Sun*, 05.12.1968.

16 Graham Lee Brewer, 'How Black women coined the "say her name" rallying cry before Biden's State of the Union address', Associated Press, 11.03.2024.

17 Quoted in Lakeisha Goedluck, 'From #SayHerName to "woke", is the language of Black liberation being looted?', *gal-dem*, 21.02.2023.

18 Sandee LaMotte, 'Robin DiAngelo: How "white fragility" supports racism and how whites can stop it', CNN, 07.06.2020.

19 Robin DiAngelo, *White Fragility: Why it's so hard for white people to talk about racism*, Beacon Press, London, 2018, p. 70.

20 Daniel Bergner, '"White Fragility" Is Everywhere. But Does Antiracism Training Work?', *New York Times*, https://www.nytimes.com/2020/07/15/magazine/white-fragility-robin-diangelo.html#:~:text=In%20early%20June%2C%20Robin,describes%20it%2C%20antiracism%20consciousness%20raising

21 Jade Bremner, 'Coca-Cola faces backlash over seminar asking staff to "be less white"', *Independent*, 24.2.2021.

22 'Mexico's deadly Coca-Cola addiction | Unreported World', YouTube, 03.10.2021, https://www.youtube.com/watch?v=hqnUohxXVoI

23 Oscar Lopez and Andrew Jacobs, 'In Town With Little Water, Coca-Cola Is Everywhere. So Is Diabetes.', *New York Times*, https://www.nytimes.com/2018/07/14/world/americas/mexico-coca-cola-diabetes.html

24 Tsedale M. Melaku, Angie Beeman, David G. Smith and W. Brad Johnson, 'Be a Better Ally,' *Harvard Business Review*, Nov–Dec 2020.

25 Ibid.

26 'Humans of CIA', YouTube, 08.04.2021, https://www.youtube.com/watch?v=m7_PGYgmcP0

27   'Humans of CIA', YouTube, 25.03.2021, https://youtube.com/
      X55JPbAMc9g?si=4E2DtkbXvUzdFQTy

28   Joshua Bloom and Waldo E. Martin, *Black Against Empire: The
      history and politics of the Black Panther Party*, University of California
      Press, Berkeley, 2016, p. 43.

29   Ibid., p. 310.

30   adrienne maree brown, *We Will Not Cancel Us*, AK Press, Chico,
      2021, p. 18.

31   Ibid., p. 26.

32   Bowler, Danielle, 'Identity Politics Returning to the Source', *Moya
      Magazine*, Issue 02, 24.02.2022.

33   David Batty, '"Skinny, bendy and blonde": women of colour
      challenge racism in UK yoga', *Guardian*, 21.06.2022.

34   Since writing this, the posts or accounts have been taken down.

35   Ryan Shocket, 'This Woman Tweeted About Having Coffee Every
      Day With Her Husband – The Internet Tore Her Apart', Buzzfeed,
      24.10.2022.

36   Yes, I am aware that this is a ridiculous sentence to write, and rest
      assured I loathe myself for it.

37   Jon Silman, 'Feline internet celebrity Jorts the Cat slammed over
      ableist Instacart comments', *We Got This Covered*, 18.10.2022.

38   @DisabledUndem, 'Jorts account doubling down on ableism isn't
      what I had on my eugenics bingo card for today', via Twitter,
      18.10.2022.

39   David Baddiel, *Jews Don't Count: How Identity Politics Failed One
      Particular Identity*, HarperCollins, London, 2021, pp. 81–82.

40   @Baddiel, 'Questioning the idealisation of Churchill is fine, but
      doing it in such extreme language just fucks up the parameters of
      language itself: calling WC a white supremacist mass murderer leaves
      no room to describe, say, Hitler. A "worse white supremacist mass
      murderer?"', via Twitter, 30.01.2019.

41   @Baddiel, 'Also, there's an unconscious anti-Semitic effect here: a
      woke instinct to highlight, correctly, the not talked-about-enough
      historical suffering of POC has somewhere in it, I think, an unspoken
      critique of the conventional sense of the singular evil of The
      Holocaust', via Twitter 30.01.2019.

42   Maggie Baska, 'UK's first trans-inclusive birthing language
      guidelines[...]', *The Pink News*, https://www.thepinknews.com/

2021/02/10/chestfeeding-brighton-sussex-nhs-trust-
trans-non-binary-birthing-language-guidelines/

43 Ghada Abdulfattah, Fatima AbdulKarim, and Dina Kraft,
'"This is what the war has done": How October 7 forever
changed Israel and Gaza', CHRISTIAN SCIENCE MONITOR, https://
www.csmonitor.com/World/Middle-East/2024/1007/
october-7-israel-gaza-one-year-later

44 'A Year of Israel's Devastating War on Gaza', *Al Jazeera*,
https://www.aljazeera.com/gallery/2024/10/7/a-year-of-
israels-devastating-war-on-gaza

45 Jessie Yeung, Radina Gigova and Mohammed Tawfeeq, 'More than
10 children losing legs in Gaza every day as dire health crisis grows,
aid groups say', CNN, 07.01.2024.

46 MEE Staff, 'Israel "undoubtedly" committing genocide says
Holocaust scholar Amos Goldberg', *Middle East Eye*, 29.04.2024.

47 Emma Farge, 'UN expert says Israel has committed genocide in
Gaza, calls for arms embargo', Reuters, 26.03.2024.

48 See Introduction, note 10

49 Max Fisher, 'This chart shows every person killed in the
Israel-Palestine conflict since 2000', *Vox*, https://www.vox.
com/2014/7/14/5898581/chart-israel-palestine-conflict-deaths

50 'Translate Hate: "From the River to the Sea"', American Jewish
Committee.

51 Charles Hymas, 'Prosecutors criticised for not charging protesters
over "from the river to the sea" chant', *Telegraph*, 19.10.2023.

52 Arj Singh, 'Keir Starmer suspends senior Labour MP Andy
McDonald over "river to the sea" speech', *Independent*, 31.10.2023.

53 Noah Zatz, 'PALESTINIAN FREEDOM, ANTISEMITISM
ACCUSATIONS, AND CIVIL RIGHTS LAW', The Law and
Political Economy Project, 20.11.2023.

54 European Legal Support Centre, 'VICTORY: "From the river to the
sea" is protected speech, Dutch court rules!', 18.10.2023, https://
elsc.support/news/victory-from-the-to-the-sea-is-protected-
speech-dutch-court-rules.

55 Hymas, 'Prosecutors criticised', *Telegraph*, 19.10.2023.

56 'Gaza health ministry: 3,785 Palestinians killed in Israeli strikes since
Oct. 7', Reuters, 19.10.2023.

57 Simon Childs, 'Prestigious Science Institute in Meltdown Over
"Alleged Peaceful" Palestine Cake Sale', Novara Media, 27.06.2024.

58 Harriet Sherwood, 'London hospital takes down artwork by Gaza schoolchildren after complaint', *Guardian*, 27.02.2023.

59 Zvika Klein, 'More than 1,000 global entities adopted IHRA definition of antisemitism', *Jerusalem Post*, 17.01.2023, https://www.jpost.com/diaspora/antisemitism/article-728773

60 'Labour must reject biased IHRA definition that stifles advocacy for Palestinian rights', Open Democracy, 28.08.2018.

61 See Introduction, note 10

2 TALK IS CHEAP

1 *Good Morning Britain*, ITV, 15.05.2023.

2 Nick Ferrari, LBC, 29.07.2024.

3 Ben Rumsby, 'England shirt fiasco two years in making – and Nike "originally proposed rainbow colours" ', *Telegraph*, 22.03.2024.

4 Matthew Smith, 'Where does the British public stand on transgender rights in 2022?', YouGov, 20.07.2022.

5 Ibid.

6 *Good Morning Britain*, ITV, 03.03.2020.

7 *Good Morning Britain*, ITV, 10.03.2020.

8 In 2016, the IOC guidance for transgender athletes competing in the Olympics changed. While it's true that athletes no longer had to undergo gender-affirming surgery or hormone therapy, there were still some restrictions in place. Transgender women athletes had to declare their gender and not change that assertion for a period of four years, and demonstrate testosterone levels within particular limits for at least one year prior to competition and throughout the period of eligibility.

9 Luke Tryl, Tyron Surmon, Arisa Kimiram and Conleth Burns, 'Britons and Gender Identity: Navigating common ground and division', More In Common, 16.06.2022.

10 Mason Walker, 'U.S. newsroom employment has fallen 26 per cent since 2008', Pew Research Center, 13.07.2021.

11 'Breaking News? The Future of UK Journalism', House of Commons Communications and Digital Committee, 27.10.2020.

12 Alex Barker and Alastair Gray, '*Guardian* to test paywall on news app in reader payments push', *Financial Times*, 09.04.2022.

13 Freddy Mayhew and Charlotte Tobbit, 'Covid-19 crisis leads to more than 2,000 job cuts across UK news organisations', *Press Gazette*, 14.08.2020.

14 Kate Dennet, 'BBC director-general Tim Davie warns staff of job cuts after freezing of licence fee for next two years that will lead to £285m black hole', *Daily Mail*, 20.01.2022.

15 Jim Waterson, 'Hundreds of jobs to go as BBC announces World Service cutbacks', Guardian, https://www.theguardian.com/media/2022/sep/29/hundreds-of-jobs-to-go-as-bbc-announces-world-service-cutbacks

16 Charlotte Tobitt, 'Buzzfeed to cut 15 per cent of overall workforce in restructure feared to affect UK', *Press Gazette*, https://pressgazette.co.uk/news/buzzfeed-to-cut-15-per-cent-of-overall-workforce-in-restructure-feared-to-affect-uk/

17 Sara Boboltz, 'BuzzFeed Announces Deep Cuts To HuffPost Staff After Acquisition', *HuffPost*, 09.03.2021.

18 Matthew Moore, 'BBC staff twice as likely to be privately schooled', *Times*, 18.09.2019.

19 'Elitist Britain 2019', The Sutton Trust, 24.06.2019.

20 Robert Gordon, 'The Fight That Changed Political TV Forever', Politico, 04.08.2015.

21 Ofcom, 'News Consumption in the UK: 2024', chrome-extension://efaidnbmnnnibpcajpcglclefindmkaj/https://www.ofcom.org.uk/siteassets/resources/documents/research-and-data/tv-radio-and-on-demand-research/tv-research/news/news-consumption-2024/news-consumption-in-the-uk-2024-report.pdf?v=379621#:~:text=In%202024%2C%20seven%20in%20ten,it%20as%20a%20news%20source]

22 'News Consumption in the UK: 2021', OFCOM 27.07.2021.

23 Richard Seymour, *The Twittering Machine*, The Indigo Press, London, 2019, p. 38.

24 Ibid., p. 44.

25 Statista, 'Most popular social media platforms in the United Kingdom (UK) as of the third quarter 2023, by usage reach'. 26.03.2024, https://www.statista.com/statistics/284506/united-kingdom-social-network-penetration/

26 Moya Lothian-Mclean, 'Twitter is strictly for the birds: never am I more disconnected than when plugged in', *Guardian*, 03.04.2022.

27 Ewan Somervile and Nick Gutteridge, 'Gary Lineker retweets call for Israel to be banned from international football', *Telegraph*, 14.05.2024.

28 Matt Murphy and Sean Seddon, 'Gary Lineker: BBC boss Tim Davie "sorry" after sport disruption in Lineker row', *BBC News*, 12.03.2023.

29 Chris Stokel-Walker, 'Inside the Rise of the Niche Twitter Expert', *Vice*, 24.03.2022.

30 Oliver Pritchard-Jones, 'Corbynista uses England's Euro 2020 success for shameless dig at Churchill', *Daily Express*, 10.07.2021.

31 Oliver Pritchard-Jones, 'Left-wing activist sparks Twitter storm with "classless" jibes after Prince Philip's death', *Daily Express*, 11.04.2021.

32 Mary-Ann Russon, 'Elon Musk's Twitter algorithm changes are "amplifying anger and animosity", say researchers', *Evening Standard*, https://www.standard.co.uk/news/tech/elon-musk-twitter-algorithm-cyberbullying-discrimination-cornell-uc-berkeley-b1084490.html

33 William Davies, 'The Reaction Economy', *London Review of Books* (Vol. 45, No. 5), 2 March 2023.

34 'Jameela Jamil supports Will Smith amid "punch" drama with Chris Rock. Writes "It's a bit yikes to me"', Anindita Mukherjee, *India Today*, https://www.indiatoday.in/movies/hollywood/story/jameela-jamil-supports-will-smith-amid-punch-drama-with-chris-rock-writes-it-s-a-bit-yikes-to-me-1930538-2022-03-28

35 Louise Lavigueur, 'Jameela Jamil stands up for black women after Will Smith's Oscars outburst', *Mirror*, https://www.mirror.co.uk/3am/celebrity-news/jameela-jamil-stands-up-black-26574456, 28.03.2022

36 'Rees-Mogg plays Rule, Britannia! in Commons to celebrate Proms U-turn', PA Media, *Guardian*, https://www.theguardian.com/politics/2020/sep/03/rees-mogg-plays-rule-britannia-commons-celebrate-proms-u-turn

37 'Glossary of Poetic Terms: objective correlative', *Poetry Foundation*, https://www.poetryfoundation.org/education/glossary/objective-correlative

38 Piers Morgan, *Wake Up: Why the 'liberal' war on free speech is even more dangerous than Covid-19*, HarperCollins, London, 2020, p. 77

39 Ibid., p.2.

40 Culbert, Michael, 'SU adopts BSL clapping to replace traditional applause', The Oxford Student 23.10.2019: Web. Accessed 13.07.2022.

41 Morgan, *Wake Up*, p. 11.

42 'Why PETA Wants You to Stop Saying "Pet"', PETA UK, 04.02.2020.

43 Morgan, *Wake Up*, p. 2.

44 Steerpike, 'UKTV's bizarre Fawlty Towers ban', *Spectator*, 12.06.2022.

45 @SwainITV, 'Not just statues but reporting on the removal of a #faultytowers episode from #UKTV', via Twitter, 12.06.2020.

46 @Vicibox, 'That this couintry has is beyond decadent and gone to the dogs; our history, culture and way of life is under threat from militant racist groups and Government needs to get a grip to re-assert the rule of law while lockdown still has some force' [sic], via Twitter, 11.06.2020.

47 @JohnCleese, '...That's why they're so cowardly and gutless and contemptible I rest my case', via Twitter, 12.06.2022.

48 Laura Cox, *Daily Mail*, 22.01.2013.

49 'Cancel Me: John Cleese to present Channel 4 show on "woke" thought', *Guardian*, 24.08.2021.

50 Lizzie May, 'No Pride, lots of Prejudice: Stirling University ditches Jane Austen from English Literature course in bid to "decolonise the curriculum"', *Daily Mail*, 05.04.2022.

51 James Lee, 'Parents fury as primary school policy bans staff using the terms "Mum" and "Dad"', *Daily Express*, 19.02.2022.

52 'Our schools are NOT "scrapping", "banning" or "cancelling" the words "mum" and "dad"', Brighton & Hove City Council, 22.02.2022.

53 Piers Morgan, 'OK. That's it. It's time to tell these woke wastrels to f*ck off and end this nonsense', via Twitter, 23.01.2023.

54 @Dominiquetaegon, 'No. It's pretty much standard for newspapers to have ghost writers for guest columnists, and I thought because I'd never written for them before it would be fine. Eventually when it came to the Carnival article and I been published by them multiple times, I'd had enough and wanted to write it myself for this particular topic', via Twitter, 03.09.2023.

55 @Dominiquetaegon, 'The outrage fest about Notting Hill Carnival is tiresome and to be honest manufactured. I was asked to be the face of a ghost-written, negative, verging on racist piece by the Daily

Mail paper last year and eventually turned it down because it was a complete misrepresentation of what I witnessed whilst I was there. The violence etc that happens is of course not acceptable but it's estimated that 2 million people attend the festival every year', via Twitter, 02.09.2023.

56 *Voice*, 'Investigation launched into Daily Mail ghost-writing', https://www.voice-online.co.uk/news/uk-news/2023/09/08/ investigation-launched-into-daily-mail-ghost-writing/

3 THE LOBBY

1 Christopher Hope, 'In full: Chopper's Politics with Suella Braverman | Conservative Party conference', *Telegraph*, 04.10.2022.

2 @dril, 'turning a big dial taht says "Racism" on it and constantly looking back at the audience for approval like a contestant on the price is right", via Twitter, 15.03.2017.

3 David Hendy, 'The History of the BBC: Broadcasting Parliament', BBC.

4 'The Election. The Statistics. How the UK voted on May 1st.', Politics 97, *BBC*, https://www.bbc.co.uk/news/special/politics97/ news/05/0505/stats.shtml

5 @Nigel_Farage, 'Over 100 migrants illegally entered the UK by small boat today. The invasion is on', via *Twitter*, 16.05.2020.

6 'Channel migrants: Small boats "major threat to UK"', *BBC News*, 22.05.2020.

7 Quoted in Millie Cooke, 'Nigel Farage condemned for response to Southport stabbings as Reform MP accused of "inciting a riot"', *Independent*, 31.07.2024.

8 Kate Nicholson, 'Minister Says Nigel Farage Is Mainly A "Commentator" And Calls Out His Absence In Parliament', *Huffington Post*, https://www.huffingtonpost.co.uk/entry/ minister-calls-farage-out-for-absence-from-parliament_ uk_66ac7eeae4b0bc1c990d0ea5

9 Alix Culbertson, 'George Floyd death: Labour leader Sir Keir Starmer takes a knee in support of Black Lives Matter movement', *Sky News*, 09.06.2020.

10 Elliot Chappell, 'WATCH: "Defund the police" demand is "nonsense", says Starmer', LabourList, 29.06.2020.

11 Jon Stone, 'Priti Patel says fans have right to boo England team for "gesture politics" of taking the knee', *Independent*, 14.06.2021.

12 Alex Young, 'Priti Patel: Up to fans if they boo England team taking the knee, it's "gesture politics"', *Standard*, https://www.standard.co.uk/sport/football/priti-patel-england-take-knee-euro-2021-euro-2021-b940499.html

13 Jessica Murray, 'Tory MP to boycott England games in row over taking the knee', *Guardian* 06.06.2021.

14 Ailbhe Rea, 'Inside the Lobby: Westminster's political journalists', Politico, 27.05.2022.

15 Quoted in Carole Walker, *Lobby Life*, Elliot & Thompson, 2021.

16 Freddy Mayhew, 'Interview with Journalist of the Year Laura Kuenssberg: "I would die in a ditch for the impartiality of the BBC"', *Press Gazette*, 09.12.2016.

17 Gary Younge, 'A "No 10 source" is the voice of power. Too many journalists simply parrot it', *Guardian*, 25.10.2019.

18 Arthur Butler, 'The History and Practice of Lobby Journalism', *Parliamentary Affairs Volume XIII*, August 1959, p. 54.

19 'Allegra Stratton resigns over No 10 Christmas party row', *Guardian News*, via YouTube, 08.12.2021.

20 'Allegra Stratton "humiliates" single mother on benefits in resurfaced Newsnight clip', *Independent*, 08.12.2021.

21 Quoted in Robbie Purves, 'Allegra Stratton's 27,000 complaints when she worked at Newsnight', *Birmingham Live*, 08.12.2021.

22 @FraserNelson, 'Allegra Stratton's resignation shows a sense of responsibility absent from those who made Covid rules that didn't work – and are now giving us more. My Telegraph column:-', via Twitter, 09.12.2021.

23 Fraser Nelson, 'Would we rise up against another lockdown?', *Telegraph*, 08.12.2021.

24 Jane Merrick, 'While Cummings and Hancock clung on after rule-breaking, Stratton quit despite apparently breaking no rules', *i*, 08.12.2021.

25 @Peston, 'I've known @AllegraCOP26 for years. She was a brilliant colleague on the show. As I would expect, she has done the honourable thing, and swiftly resigned. Whatever you think of what she said in the clip obtained by @itvnews, she is a model for many in modern politics…', via Twitter, 08.12.2021.

26   'Private school fees go past £20,000', *Guardian*, 18.11.2002, https://
      www.theguardian.com/uk/2002/nov/18/publicschools.schools

27   @AllegraStratton, 'The Readout: the Tory race just cranked up with
      @rishisunak. (Some think slick vid took months of prep, but appaz
      script done at tea time ydy). With backing of widely liked former
      chief whip @Mark_Spencer, known simply as "The Chief", it's a
      good start', via Twitter, 08.07.2022.

28   Steerpike, 'Watch: Boris Johnson's model buses', *Spectator*,
      24.06.2019.

29   James Walker, 'Talkradio's Ross Kempsell becomes second
      ex-chicken to enter Downing Street', *Press Gazette*, 31.07.2019.

30   Camilla Turner, 'Rival dossiers set out the case to save or sack Boris
      Johnson', *Telegraph*, 06.06.2022.

31   Jim Waterson, 'Dale Vince sues Guido Fawkes owner for libel over
      Hamas claims', *Guardian*, 02.07.2024.

32   Alex Wickham, 'One Third Back UKIP on "Chink" and "Poofter"
      Comments', *Breitbart*, 24.12.2014.

33   'Cross Question', LBC, 26.07.2022.

34   Quoted in Sienna Rodgers, 'Bermondsey Labour MP Neil Coyle's
      texts to Jeremy Corbyn revealed', *LabourList*, 04.09.2020.

35   @elenicourea, 'Labour MP: "Coyle has form at being abusive and
      obnoxious in the Strangers' Bar but these racist remarks take it to
      another level" "This should be investigated thoroughly by the party
      and the whip should be removed while that takes place"', via Twitter,
      10.02.2022.

36   Toby Helm, 'I saw for myself just how hostile many voters were to
      Jeremy Corbyn', *Observer*, 14.12.2019.

37   Noam Chomsky, 'Interview With Andrew Marr', BBC, 14.02.1996.

38   Rivkah Brown, 'How the Guardian Lined Up Behind Starmer',
      Novara Media, 16.07.2024.

39   Andrew Neil, 'ANDREW NEIL: Our university bosses will rue the
      day they failed to stand up to the posh pro-Hamas student protestors
      wallowing in their own stupidity', *Daily Mail*, 20.05.2024.

40   'BBC News, coverage of the pro-Palestinian marches, October 2023',
      BBC News, 27.10.2023.

41   Rosa Prince, 'Rishi Sunak and friends seek a path to peace',
      Politico: *London Playbook*, 23.10.2023.

42   Bill McLoughlin, 'Arrests made after "100,000" people protest in central London for pro-Palestine march', *Evening Standard*, 21.10.2023.

43   @BenChu_, 'I calculate that this #LabourManifesto fiscal package (tax rise/spending pledges) amounts to around 0.2% of GDP. Here's how that compares to the 2024 Tory and Lib Dem manifestos – and also the Labour 2017 and 2019 manifestos...', via Twitter, 13.06.2024.

44   'Sunday Times Rich List: Rishi Sunak leapfrogs King Charles in latest rankings', *Sky News*, 17.05.2024.

45   Fintan Smith, 'Three quarters of Britons support wealth taxes on millionaires', YouGov, 23.01.2023.

46   'Major Tory Donor to Back Labour', *BBC Newsnight*, 18.06.2024.

47   Paul Kelso, 'Chief executives praise Labour's plans after investment summit – but there's a caveat', *Sky News*, https://www.politico.eu/article/uk-pm-boris-johnson-aide-ross-kempsell-gets-plum-place-in-house-of-lords/

4 ECONOMICS ARE THE METHOD

1   Genevieve Holl-Allen, 'How Lib Dems rolled out "Operation Cinnamon Bun" to win support', *Telegraph*, 11.07.2024.

2   'Half of us: Turnout patterns at the 2024 general election', IPPR, 12.07.2024.

3   'Voter Volatility: Statistics from the British Election Study', *British Election Study*, 08.10.2019.

4   Personally, I can't stand the term 'unskilled worker'. Unless you've spent a season picking 30 kilos of strawberries an hour, all without bruising the fruit or doing your back in, you can shut up about 'unskilled' work.

5   Giulia Giupponi and Xiaowei Xu, 'What does the rise of self-employment tell us about the UK labour market?', Institute of Fiscal Studies, 19.11.2020.

6   Dan Evans, '"Mortgage man": Why the petty bourgeoisie is the UK's most influential class', openDemocracy, 20.02.2023.

7   Ibid.

8   Daniel Boffey, 'Labour is miles away from government, says man out to replace Corbyn', *Observer*, 17.07.2016.

9   Helen Pidd, '"Imagine the state we'd be in if Corbyn had been in charge": the view from the "red wall"', *Guardian*, 08.07.2020.

10 Quoted in Kirsteen Paton, 'A Sociology of Class Without Feeling',
    Sociological Review, 07.04.2021.

11 Ian King, 'Sky Views: How do you decide if someone is working
    class in 2019?', *Sky News*, 13.09.2019.

12 Rowan Moore, 'Housing in crisis: council homes were the answer in
    1950. They still are', *Guardian*, 30.04.2016.

13 '1957: Britons "have never had it so good"', *BBC On This Day*,
    20.07.1957.

14 Quoted in Roland Butt, 'MRS THATCHER: THE FIRST TWO
    YEARS', *Sunday Times*, 03.05.1981.

15 Want to raise your blood pressure? Over 40 per cent of properties
    sold off under Right to Buy are rented out by private landlords.

16 @JamesKanag, 'Everybody knows about the Conservatives +
    Liverpool. Less so about the electoral roadblock stretching across the
    North West + Yorkshire, a conurbation of 4m+ people where anti-
    Conservatism is still entrenched. Most of Lab-Con gains (see below)
    where here in 2017 (10/16)', via Twitter, 14.08.2019.

17 Ben Butcher, 'The eight seats that show how divided Britain is',
    Telegraph, 06.07.2024.

18 Patrick Wintour, 'Dominic Cummings: genius or menace?',
    Guardian, https://www.theguardian.com/politics/2013/oct/11/
    dominic-cummings-genius-menace-michael-gove

19 'Irregular Migrant, Refugee Arrivals in Europe Top One Million in
    2015: IOM', The International Organization for Migration, 22.12.2015.

20 Sandra Laville, 'Raw sewage discharged into English rivers 375,000
    times by water firms', *Guardian*, https://www.theguardian.com/
    environment/2022/mar/31/sewage-released-into-english-rivers-
    for-27m-hours-last-year-by-water-firms#:~:text=Data%20
    released%20by%20the%20EA,14%2C707%20overflows%2C%20
    or%2089%25

21 James Button, 'Out of Africa, the traffic wardens take revenge',
    17.02.2007, *Sydney Morning Herald*, https://www.smh.com.au/
    national/out-of-africa-the-traffic-wardens-take-revenge-20070221-
    gdpii2.html

22 Ibid.

23 Quoted in Anne Karpf, 'We've Been Here Before', *Guardian*,
    08.06.2002.

24 'UK Politics Straw: Asylum is "European problem"', *BBC News*,
    26.08.1999.

25 'Swamped immigration officials are kicking out just TWELVE new bogus asylum seekers a month – out of 3,200 who should be sent packing', *Sun*, 14.02.2001.

26 Quoted in Ciar Byrne, 'Sun's Mr Men spoof prompts accusations of racism', *Guardian*, 21.01.2003.

27 Quoted in '*Sun* accused of Swan Bake "myth-making"', *Press Gazette*, 12.12.2003.

28 'Halt The Asylum Tide Now', *Sun*, 18.08.2003.

29 Sandra Smith, 'What they said about ... immigration', *Guardian*, 20.08.2003.

30 Quoted in Fran Abrams and Anthony Bevins, 'Murdoch's courtship of Blair finally pays off', *Independent*, 11.02.1998.

31 'Tony Blair "is godfather to Rupert Murdoch's daughter"', *Channel 4 News*, 5.09.2011.

32 'Phone-hacking trial: Blair "advised Brooks before arrest"', *BBC News*, 19.02.2014.

33 Michael White, 'No 10 "worked with Sun to manage news"', *Guardian*, 24.05.2004.

34 Will Somerville, 'The Immigration Legacy of Tony Blair', Migration Policy Institute, 10.05.2007.

35 Alan Travis, 'Blair targets huge asylum cuts', *Guardian*, 08.02.2003.

36 'Best Party On Key Issues: Asylum and Immigration', Ipsos, 20.04.2015, https://www.ipsos.com/en-uk/best-party-key-issues-asylum-and-immigration

37 Somerville, 'The Immigration Legacy of Tony Blair'.

38 Roy Greenslade, 'Asylum madness? Look who's talking', *Guardian*, 03.02.2003.

39 Paul Harris, 'Mythical refugees help BNP win white suburb', *Guardian*, 11.05.2003.

40 Ibid.

41 'Asylum: Attacks and deaths 2001 - 2003', *BBC News*, http://news.bbc.co.uk/1/hi/uk/3087569.stm

42 Jon Burnett, 'The new geographies of racism: Peterborough', Institute of Race Relations, 2012, p. 3.

43 Ibid., p. 8.

44 Ibid.

45 Mishal Husain, 'EU referendum: The immigration question', *BBC News*, 14.06.2016.

46 Mariña Fernández-Reino and Ben Brindle, 'Migrants in the UK Labour Market: An Overview', Migration Observatory, 10.06.2024.

47 'New analysis reveals UK continues to fall behind rest of world as zero-hour contracts reach record numbers – and it's young people bearing the brunt', The Work Foundation at Lancaster University, 21.03.2024.

48 Abby Maclure, 'Leeds Census 2021: We speak to residents in the most and least deprived areas of the city', *Yorkshire Evening Post*, https://www.yorkshireeveningpost.co.uk/news/people/leeds-census-2021-we-speak-to-residents-in-the-most-and-least-deprived-areas-of-the-city-3938620

49 Lucy Thornton and Kelly-Ann Mills, 'Leeds riots: Did this shocking video showing children being dragged from home spark violence?', *Mirror*, 19.07.2024, https://www.mirror.co.uk/news/uk-news/leeds-riots-shocking-video-showing-33282725

50 Robyn Vinter, '"We're in it together": how unrest in Leeds escalated – and was defused', *Guardian*, 19.07.2024.

51 Craig Gent, '"We're All Getting Attacked": How Disorder Broke Out in East Leeds', Novara Media, 19.07.2024.

52 Archie Mitchell, 'Nigel Farage sparks anger over "inflammatory" Leeds riot comments', *Independent*, 20.07.2024.

53 @TiceRichard, 'Disgraceful scenes in London and Leeds tonight Rioting on massive scale Multiculturalism has more than failed – this is the consequence of people with no respect for Britain', via Twitter, 18.07.2024.

54 @TRobinsonNewEra, 'Harehills in leeds right now, Muslims are rioting, police are running away!', via Twitter, 18.07.2024.

55 @TRobinsonNewEra, 'This was the spark that set off riots in Leeds last night. Social services and police remove children from an imported family, clearly a safeguarding issue. So the other imported families, to prove they're respectable and responsible, burn down the area', via Twitter, 19.07.2024.

56 @TRobinsonNewEra, 'Lone British girl stands up for her community in Leeds, telling the imports that they've been handed everything by this country, and their behaviour is not acceptable following a night of riots. (Side note, they're not Romanians, but Punjab origin gypsies)', via Twitter, 19.07.2024.

57 @Nigel_Farage, 'The migrant hotel protest in Knowsley happened because many local parents are concerned for the safety of young

schoolgirls. They are decent, honest people with genuine worry — and certainly not "far right"', via Twitter, 13.02.2023.

58 Quoted in Sian Norris, 'What the Knowsley Riot Tells Us About the Far Right Today', *Byline Times*, 13.02.2023.

59 Allison Pearson, 'I'm sick of people with an ounce of common sense being labelled "far-Right"', *Telegraph*, 14.02.2023.

60 Owen Hatherley, *Red Metropolis*, Repeater Books, London, 2020, p. 239.

61 Trust for London.

62 Barrow-in-Furness Borough Council.

63 Rushanara Ali, 'Broken Britain: Bethnal Green and Bow — the constituency where child poverty is becoming the norm', *House Magazine*, 31.01.2023.

5 ONE BIG GANG

1 Recording of the author's conversation with the speaker, October 2018

2 Richard Wheatstone, 'Looter Anderson Fernandes jailed after having one lick of ice cream faces deportation', *Manchester Evening News*, 21.02.2013.

3 Stuart Hoddinott, Darwin Kim, and Nick Davies, 'Fixing public services: Local government', *Institute for Government*, https://www.instituteforgovernment.org.uk/publication/fixing-public-services-labour-government/local-government

4 J. Watkins, W. Wulaningsih, C. Da Zhou et al., 'Effects of health and social care spending constraints on mortality in England: a time trend analysis', *BMJ Open*, 2017.

5 May Bulman, 'More than 17,000 sick and disabled people have died while waiting for welfare benefits, figures show', *Independent*, 15.01.2019.

6 Richard Adams, 'Schools have become "fourth emergency service" for poorest families', *Guardian*, 15.03.2019, https://www.theguardian.com/education/2019/mar/15/schools-have-become-fourth-emergency-service-for-poorest-families

7 'Foodbank use tops one million for first time says Trussell Trust', The Trussell Trust, 22.04.2015.

8 Juliette Garside, 'Recession rich: Britain's wealthiest double net worth since crisis', *Guardian*, 26.04.2015.

9   'Clapham looter: "Getting our taxes back"', *Sky News*, 09.08.2011.
10 *BBC Newsnight*, 12.08.2011.
11 'David Starkey tries to talk about the UK Riots on Newsnight.', YouTube, 13.08.2011, https://www.youtube.com/watch?v=ZhSYfoO6Cdw
12 John Twomey and Mark Reynolds, 'FLAMING MORONS: THUGS AND THIEVES TERRORISE BRITAIN'S STREETS', *Daily Express*, 09.08.2011.
13 'UK riots front pages – in pictures', *Guardian*, 09.08.2011.
14 The tweet has since been removed: https://x.com/Gareth_Gates/status/100703858103291904
15 @GizziErskine, 'The LA riots were stopped 6 days on when the army started shooting. Hmmmm. Thoughts?', via Twitter, 08.08.2011.
16 Daily Mail Comment, 'No excuses for this wanton criminality', *Daily Mail*, 09.08.2011.
17 James Ball, Dan Milmo and Ben Ferguson, 'Half of UK's young black males are unemployed', *Guardian*, 09.03.2012.
18 Sarah-Marie Hall, Kimberly McIntosh, Eva Neitzert et al., 'Executive Summary', *Intersecting inequalities: The impact of austerity on Black and Minority Ethnic women in the UK*, 10.10.2017.
19 'Stop and search: the racial imbalance', Full Fact, 25.02.2014.
20 Paul Lewis, Tim Newburn, Matthew Taylor et al., *Reading the Riots: Investigating England's summer of disorder*, Guardian Shorts, 01.12.2011.
21 Anne McElvoy, 'When black is white', *The Economist*, 16.08.2011.
22 Paul Routledge, 'London riots: Is rap music to blame for encouraging this culture of violence?', *Daily Mirror*, 10.08.2011.
23 Quoted in Dan Hancox, 'Rap responds to the riots: "They have to take us seriously"', *Guardian*, 12.08.2011.
24 Graeme Archer, 'Graeme Archer: Come fly with me', *Conservative Home*, 04.11.2016.
25 Quoted in Alex Brown, 'Cannabis in the 1950s British Tabloids', *Points*, 10.09.2020.
26 Theodore Dalrymple, 'Bum rap for Jamaicans', *Spectator*, 09.08.2003.
27 'RAPPERS UNDER FIRE', *NME*, 06.01.2003
28 Lewis, Newburn, Taylor et al., *Reading the Riots*, p. 11.

29   Ibid., p. 19.
30   Ibid., p. 18.
31   Owen Jones, *Chavs: The Demonization of the Working Class*, Verso, London, 2012, p. 86.
32   James Delingpole, 'A conspiracy against chavs? Count me in', *The Times*, 13.04.2006.
33   Sarah O'Grady, 'The teenagers who just can't speak proper', *Daily Express*, 13.12.2006.
34   Victoria Ward, 'School criticised for allowing children to wear jogging bottoms', *Telegraph*, 08.07.2013.
35   Theodore Dalrymple, 'Sick, thick and dangerous', *Spectator*, 23.08.2022.
36   Lucinda Platt, 'Royal wedding: The UK's rapidly changing mixed-race population', *BBC News*, 15.05.2018.
37   Melanie Phillips, 'Why Shannon is one more victim of the folly of "lifestyle choice"', *Daily Mail*, https://www.dailymail.co.uk/columnists/article-536528/Why-Shannon-victim-folly-lifestyle-choice.html
38   Melanie Phillips, 'We need to talk about absent fathers and crime', *The Times*, 03.03.2020.
39   Quoted in Harris Beider, *White Working-Class Voices: Multiculturalism, Community-Building and Change*, Bristol University Press, Bristol, 2015, p. 18.
40   Lewis, Newburn, Taylor et al., *Reading the Riots*, p. 23.
41   In 'Things We Won't Say About Race That Are True', Channel 4, 04.03.2015.
42   James Delingpole, 'Hetty Douglas' "1 GCSE" post demonstrates shameful snob culture of the liberal lefties who hate the working class', *Sun*, 14.09.2017.
43   Ashleigh Kane, 'Dazed 100 2017', *Dazed*.
44   James Delingpole, 'James Delingpole: All those going on about Jeremy Clarkson's silly comments should be ... shot!', *Independent.ie*, 01.12.2011.
45   Melanie Phillips, 'The British working class saves Britain ... and its Jews', *Jewish News Syndicate*, 13.12.2019.
46   Melanie Phillips, 'Britain's liberal intelligentsia has smashed virtually every social value', *Daily Mail*, 10.08.2011.
47   Julie Burchill, 'So much for education, education, education', *Spectator*, 11.06.2016.

48 'The Forgotten: how White working-class pupils have been let down, and how to change it', House of Commons Education Committee, 16.06.2021, p. 14.

49 Ibid., p.16.

50 Jemma Crew, 'Britain is not institutionally racist, landmark report chief says', *Evening Standard*, 31.03.2021.

51 Jonathan Portes, 'RACE REPORT: Sewell Commission Couldn't Find Something It Wasn't Looking For', *Byline Times*, 09.04.2021.

52 Eric Kaufmann, 'Why the Race Equalities Report is so subversive', UnHerd, 31.03.2023.

53 Sarah Vine, 'SARAH VINE: Axe the two-child benefit cap? No, if you can't afford to look after your kids, don't have them in the first place', *Daily Mail*, 17.07.2024.

6 DEMOGRAPHIC PANIC

1 Nick Ferrari, LBC, 27.06.2024.

2 Richard Adams and Aletha Adu, 'Trans guidance tells English schools to consider social media influence on pupils asking to transition', *Guardian*, 19.12.2023.

3 Holly Bancroft, 'Over 250,000 trans people in UK, as census data reports gender identity for first time', *Independent*, 06.01.2023.

4 Chaka L. Bachmann and Becca Gooch, 'LGBT In Britain: Trans Report', *Stonewall*, January 2018.

5 Jess Glass, 'Exclusive: Genderquake audience were allegedly "encouraged to heckle" trans panellists during Channel 4 debate', *Pink News*, 10.05.2018.

6 @KayBurley, "Can a woman have a penis?"Sir Keir Starmer struggled to answer yesterday... here's what the Labour deputy leader, @AngelaRayner, had to say #KayBurley SR;, via Twitter 29.03.22.

7 '"I Want to Be Like Nature Made Me"', Human Rights Watch, https://www.hrw.org/report/2017/07/25/i-want-be-nature-made-me/medically-unnecessary-surgeries-intersex-children-us

8 Shon Faye, *The Transgender Issue: An Argument for Justice*, Allen Lane, London, 2022, p. 6.

9 James Beale, 'Census trans question under scrutiny for "confusion"', *The Times*, 10.10.2023.

10   Mike Wade, 'Anger at transgender handbook for children in care', *The Times*, 11.05.2023.

11   Ruby Sampson, '"I was frozen to the spot in shock... it was said to intimidate": How a friendly chat in the ladies of a London pub turned menacing and plunged a Tory councillor, 22, into the clash between trans rights and women's safety', *Daily Mail*, 25.02.2023.

12   @sophie_frm_mars, 'and I paused for a sec to understand she meant to dry our hands and then I said "Oh I'll just wipe my hands on my jeans"', via Twitter, 27.02.2023.

13   Ruby Sampson, *Daily Mail*, 25.02.2023.

14   Richard Wheeler, 'Minister: No sexual assaults by trans inmates in women's prisons since reforms', *Independent*, 21.02.2023.

15   Danny Shaw, 'Eleven transgender inmates sexually assaulted in male prisons last year', *BBC News*, 21.05.2020.

16   @KemiBadenoch, 'The third reason was having gender-critical men and women in the UK government, holding the positions that mattered most in Equalities and Health. You only need to look at what the SNP did in Scotland to see what would have happened had we not intervened. The Cass Review would **never** have been commissioned under a Labour govt. Labour did not want to know. We had incredible opposition from the system on everything. It was when the ministers changed that everything changed', via Twitter, 08.06.2024.

17   Ben Hunte, 'Exclusive: Senior Officials Quit Britain's Equalities Watchdog EHRC Over Transphobia', *Vice News*, 13.04.2023.

18   https://x.com/jk_rowling/status/1544635367650885632

19   Abigail Shrier, *Real Time With Bill Maher*, 08.06.2024.

20   @jk_rowling, 'The idea that women like me, who've been empathetic to trans people for decades, feeling kinship because they're vulnerable in the same way as women – ie, to male violence – "hate" trans people because they think sex is real and has lived consequences – is a nonsense', via Twitter, 07.06.2024.

21   @jk_rowling, 'The statistics don't lie. Some – not all – trans-identified males have committed sexual and violent offences against women and girls. Some male predators have capitalised on gender identity activism to claim a trans identity they never espoused pre-conviction or assault. ⅔', via Twitter, 02.03.2024.

22   @jk_rowling, 'Do biological males with gender recognition certificates have the right to enter women-only spaces? It's a simple yes/no question, @UKLabour. Given that you intend to make it

easier for men to gain said piece of paper, women have the right to an answer', via Twitter, 29.06.2024.

23   https://x.com/jk_rowling/status/1862076497806160251

24   Source: https://x.com/jk_rowling/status/1847649265260089752

25   Denis Campbell, 'Children to stop getting puberty blockers at gender identity clinics, says NHS England', *Guardian*, 12.03.2024.

26   Ibid.

27   Hilary Cass, *Independent review of gender identity services for children and young people: Final report*, 10.04.2024, p. 13.

28   Quoted in Ash Sarkar, 'The anti-abortion lobby is on the rise in the UK. We can't get complacent', *GQ*, 04.07.2022.

29   '"I Want to Be Like Nature Made Me"', *Human Rights Watch*, https://www.hrw.org/report/2017/07/25/i-want-be-nature-made-me/medically-unnecessary-surgeries-intersex-children-us

30   Gaby Hinsliff, '"I want to wake up this nation's conscience"', *Guardian*, https://www.theguardian.com/science/2005/feb/27/genetics.theobserver

31   Ibid.

32   Stuart Hall, *It Ain't Half Racist Mum*, 01.03.1979.

33   Ash Sarkar, 'Against "Integration"', Novara Media, 01.06.2016.

34   I've yet to find an ethnic group that doesn't love Jermaine Stewart's 'We Don't Have To Take Our Clothes Off', but perhaps that's a theory for a different book.

35   Anushka Asthana, 'Britain becoming more segregated than 15 years ago, says race expert', *Guardian*, https://www.theguardian.com/world/2016/may/23/britain-more-segregated-15-years-race-expert-riots-ted-cantle

36   @jfoster2019, 'Divisive, racist comments .. and not for the first time from @AyoCaesar ...She plays the "shock" game .. but we're not shocked ..', via Twitter, 28.10.2022.

37   @emilyhewertson, 'Imagine if the tables were turned and someone said "white people are winning." Ash would be the first to call them racist and bigoted. This is the sort of rhetoric perpetuates division. There should be no place for it in a united Britain', via Twitter, 08.03.2020.

38   Fraser Myers, 'Ash Sarkar: Woke Segregationist', *spiked*, 09.02.2020.

39 Gerrard Kaonga, 'Leftie Corbynista Ash Sarkar SHUT DOWN in furious row over "inappropriate" joke', *Express*, 10.03.2020.

40 Alice Peacock, 'Journalist Ash Sarkar gets death threats for photo of her enjoying lolly in park', *Mirror*, 21.06.2020.

41 Citation? Just look at him.

42 Allison McCan and Amy Schoenfeld Walker, 'Tracking Abortion Bans Across the Country', *New York Times*, 01.07.2024.

43 '"Fewer rights than their grandmothers": read three justices' searing abortion dissent', *Guardian*, https://www.theguardian.com/commentisfree/2022/jun/24/supreme-court-roe-v-wade-breyer-sotomayor-kegan

44 Miranda Alice Ollstein, Megan Messerly and Jessia Piper, 'The Supreme Court dismantled Roe. States are restoring it one by one', *Politico*, 11.09.2023.

45 Ibid.

46 Carter Sherman, 'US support for abortion rights up four points to 60 per cent since fall of Roe v Wade', *Guardian*, 14.05.2024.

47 Clyde Haberman, 'Religion and Right-Wing Politics: How Evangelicals Reshaped Elections', *New York Times*, 28.10.2018.

48 Heinrich Himmler, 'Speech to SS Gruppenführers', February 1937.

49 @TuckerCarlson, 'This is too much change. Throw in millions of new people who have no connection to America—who broke our

laws to get here, who don't speak our language and have no idea what the Constitution says and don't care—and you have a recipe for social collapse.', via Twitter on 20.07.22

50 Quoted in Vivian Chou, 'How Science and Genetics are Reshaping the Race Debate of the 21st Century', Harvard University Graduate School of Arts and Sciences, 17.04.2017.

51 Quoted in Theodore W. Allen, 'Introduction to the Second Edition', *The Invention of the White Race*, Verso, London, 2021, p. xv.

52 Ibid., p. 24.

53 Ann Twinam, *Purchasing Whiteness: Pardos, Mulattos, and the Quest for Social Mobility in the Spanish Indies*, Stanford University Press, Stanford, 2015.

54 Brian Wallis, 'Black Bodies, White Science: The Slave Daguerreotypes of Louis Agassiz', *The Journal of Blacks in Higher Education*, no. 12, 1996, pp. 102–6.

55 O.C. Ward, 'John Langdon Down: the man and the message', *Down's syndrome, research and practice: the Journal of the Sarah Duffen Centre*, vol. 6, no. 1, 1999, pp. 19–24.

56 James Cantile, 'Degeneration Amongst Londoners', 27.01.1885.

57 Francis Galton, *Inquiries Into Human Faculty and Its Development*, Everyman, London, 2001, p. 17.

58 Francis Galton, 'Huxley Lecture, Anthropological Institute', *Nature*, Nov. 1901.

59 Kojo Koram and Kerem Nisancioglu, 'Britain: The Empire that Never Was', *Critical Legal Thinking*, 31.10.2017.

60 Enoch Powell, 'Rivers of Blood' speech transcript, *Telegraph*, https://www.telegraph.co.uk/news/0/enoch-powells-rivers-blood-speech/

61 Stuart Hall, 'The Great Moving Right Show', *Marxism Today*, January 1979, pp. 19-20, https://f.hypotheses.org/wp-content/blogs.dir/744/files/2012/03/Great-Moving-Right-ShowHALL.pdf

62 Dinesh D'Souza, *The End of Racism: Principles for a multiracial society*, Free Press, New York, 1995, p. 24.

63 Ibid., p. 170.

64 Ibid., p. 22.

65 Ibid., p. 91.

66 https://archive.org/details/endofracismprincoodsou/page/n7/mode/2up

67 https://www.nybooks.com/articles/1995/10/19/demonizing-the-american-dilemma/?lp_txn_id=1590244

68   Barnor Hesse, 'Self-fulfilling prophecy: The postracial horizon,' *South Atlantic Quarterly*, vol. 110, no. 1, 2011, p. 156.

69   @CharlotteCGill, 'Back to the UK tomorrow. I've never had such dread about Britain. Coming back to London and knowing how unpleasant it'll be. The demographic changes and feeling that is most against Brits. The lack of functional media. The feeling something big has to happen to restore order', via Twitter, 20.07.2024.

70   Lionel Shriver, 'Would you want London to be overrun with Americans like me?', *Spectator*, 28.08.2021.

71   Hannah Ellis-Petersen and Ahmer Khan, '"They cut him into pieces': India's 'love jihad' conspiracy theory turns lethal', *Guardian*, https://www.theguardian.com/world/2022/jan/21/they-cut-him-into-pieces-indias-love-jihad-conspiracy-theory-turns-lethal

72   Balbir Punj, 'No love, only jihad', *Daily Pioneer*, 03.12.2014.

7 PLANET LANDLORD

1   Adele Robinson, 'Huge increase in raw sewage released into UK waterways and sea, data reveals', *Sky News*, 22.08.2022.

2   Kent Buse and Kate Bayliss, 'England's privatised water: profits over people and planet', *BMJ*, 2022, p. 378.

3   Brett Christophers, 'The rentierization of the United Kingdom economy', *Environment and Planning A: Economy and Space*, 11.09.2019, pp. 1,438–70.

4   Helene Horton, 'Thames Water pumped at least 72bn litres of sewage into Thames since 2020', *Guardian*, 10.11.2023.

5   Alexander Butler, 'Thames Water warns hundreds of people in Surrey not to drink tap water', *Independent*, 31.05.2024.

6   Jonathan Barrett, 'As Thames Water sinks, Macquarie Group continues its unstoppable rise', *Guardian*, 10.07.2023.

7   Cahan Milmo, 'Thames Water set to avoid £240m fine from regulator over fears for its finances', *i*, 26.07.2024.

8   Gillian Ambrose, 'Macquarie wades back into UK with majority stake in Southern Water', *Guardian*, 09.08.2021.

9   'Foreign investor that loaded Thames Water with debt takes control of UK gas network', *Telegraph*, 26.07.2024.

10   Dan Sheldon and Mark Critchley, 'Why Manchester United might need more debt to rebuild Old Trafford', *Athletic*, 14.03.2024.

11   Ibid.

12 Cats are excluded from this list, because we don't own them. Rather, we serve at their pleasure.

13 Michael Race and Kelly Austin, 'Avanti West Coast talks over "unacceptable performance"', *BBC News*, 16.07.2024.

14 Jennifer Williams, 'Rail chaos prompts fresh calls to nationalise England's West Coast line', *Financial Times*, 15.04.2024.

15 Polly Smythe, '"Free Money": Executives at Failing Train Company Joke About Making Money at the Taxpayer's Expense', Novara Media, 15.01.2024.

16 Tom Wilson, 'BP boosts buybacks as oil and gas prices create "cash machine"', *Financial Times*, 02.11.2024.

17 'Fuel Poverty Rates 2021', Trust For London.

18 'BP Q1 2024: Shareholders enriched to the tune of £22.3 billion since invasion of Ukraine', *Global Witness*, 07.05.2024.

19 Margaret Thatcher, 'This Week', *Thames TV*, 05.02.1976.

20 Mark Kolakowski, 'At $2.08 Trillion, Apple Is Bigger Than These Things', Investopedia, 17.03.2021.

21 Leon Yin and Adrianne Jeffries, 'How We Analyzed Amazon's Treatment of Its "Brands" in Search Results', *Markup*, 14.11.2021.

22 https://www.statista.com/chart/18819/worldwide-market-share-of-leading-cloud-infrastructure-service-providers/

23 https://www.cnbc.com/2024/04/30/aws-q1-earnings-report-2024.html

24 Yanis Varoufakis, *Technofeudalism*, Vintage, London, 2024, p. 90.

25 Jodi Dean, 'Same As It Ever Was?', *New Left Review*, 06.05.2022.

26 Ibid., p. 84.

27 P. J. Soriano Mena, 'The extent and causes of the declining labour share of income across the globe', *Essex Student Journal*, 2023.

28 Marissa Newman, 'Thiel's Palantir, Israel Agree Strategic Partnership for Battle Tech', *Bloomberg*, 12.01.2024.

29 See Introduction, note 10

30 Laura Donnelly, 'Labour vows to save NHS by sharing data from GP records', *Telegraph*, 19.03.2024.

31 'Sale of NHS data up to government, says tech boss', *BBC News*, 29.11.2023.

32 Denis Campbell, 'Patient privacy fears as US spy tech firm Palantir wins £330m NHS contract', *Guardian*, 21.11.2023.

EPILOGUE

1   Lauren Shirreff, 'The obscure Russian-linked "news" outlet fuelling violence on Britain's streets', *Telegraph*, 03.08.2024.

2   Andy Gregory, 'How lies and disinformation about Southport knife attack suspect led to riots', *Independent*, 31.07.2024.

3   Jabed Ahmed, 'Far-right rioters loot shops and set fire to library and food bank in shameless day of disorder', *Independent*, 05.08.2024.

4   Hannah Al-Othman, 'Factory worker jailed for role in riot at Rotherham asylum seeker hotel', *Guardian*, 20.08.2024.

5   Michael Savage, 'Top Tories fuelled riots with "divisive language" on immigration, say party grandees', *Guardian*, 10.08.2024.

6   Anna Gross, Lucy Fisher and Amy Borrett, 'Far-right riots centred on England's deprivation hotspots', *Financial Times*, 08.08.2024.

7   Jenny Coleman, 'Three jailed for "appalling" rioting in Southport', *BBC News*, 27.08.2024.

8   Anthony France, 'Rioters who brought terror to UK streets named as police condemn violence', *Evening Standard*, 06.08.2024.

9   Chloe Harcombe and PA Media, 'Woman jailed for involvement in "terrifying" mob', *BBC News*, 16.08.2024.

10 Carl Eve, 'Judge savagely puts Plymouth rioter in his place', *Plymouth Herald*, 13.08.2024.

11 John Scheerhout, 'Jailed, the "cowardly" rioter who kicked and punched a lone black man in Piccadilly Gardens', *Manchester Evening News*, 27.08.2024.

12 John Barry, 'At the Front Line of Belfast's Week of Violence', *News Lines Magazine*, 14.08.2024.

13 @RichardGaisford, 'Aftermath of violence in Tamworth shows how a mob smashed their way into a hotel used by asylum seekers, tried to set fire to it with them and staff inside. Petrol bombs, fireworks, bricks and other missiles were thrown at police. The building is covered in racist graffiti. @GMB', via Twitter, 05.08.2024.

14 Rory Tingle, 'Rioters are named and shamed: Sobbing company director, thug who chanted "who the f*** is Allah" and boy, 15, who threw paving slab at man's head among dozens in court – with up to six more rallies tonight', *Daily Mail*, 06.08.2024.

15 Tom Witherow, 'Woman who "first shared fake name" of Southport suspect arrested', *The Times*, 09.08.2024.

16 See Introduction, note 10

17 'Israel, Immigration & Islam | Douglas Murray', John Anderson Media, YouTube, 08.11.2023.

18 Eric Bradner, 'Donald Trump falsely suggests Kamala Harris "happened to turn Black"', CNN, 31.07.2024.

19 Aletha Adu, 'Nigel Farage under fire after saying Muslims do not share British values', *Guardian*, 26.05.2024.

20 Leila Abboud, Adrienne Klasa and Sarah White, 'French businesses court Marine Le Pen after taking fright at left's policies', *Financial Times*, 18.06.2024.

21 Andrew King, 'Last Monday Was the Hottest Day on Record', *WIRED*, 29.07.2024.

22 Leyland Cecco, 'Alberta premier fights tears over Canada wildfires despite climate crisis denial', *Guardian*, 26.07.2024.

23 One litre of Sainsbury's Light Olive Oil was £3 in 2022. I just paid £7.80 for the exact same product last week. And yes, I'm still angry about it.

24 'Deadly heatwave in the Sahel and West Africa would have been impossible without human-caused climate change', *International Federation of Red Cross and Red Crescent Societies*, 18.04.2024.

25 See Introduction, note 10

26 Antonio Gramsci, 'Letter to Carlo', *Letters From Prison*, December 1929.

27 Ibid.

28 Quoted in Roland Butt, 'MRS THATCHER: THE FIRST TWO YEARS', *Sunday Times*, 03.05.1981.

ACKNOWLEDGEMENTS

All intellectual labours are collective efforts, and it would be impossible to name everyone who's had an impact on putting this work together. But here's my best shot.

I don't have kids. But, at the risk of annoying actual mothers everywhere, I reckon that writing a book is a lot like being pregnant. You've created something that everyone will perceive as a reflection of you, and you're paralysed by the terror of what it'll be like when it's out in the world. Will people say it's hideous, dull, stupid or just bad vibes? So, to my editors Alexis Kirschbaum and Jamie Coleman, and my agent Emma Paterson – thank you for your patience, your encouragement, your judicious advice and for wielding the forceps. I couldn't have asked for better doulas. Thank you to Tom Avery, for being the first person to tell me I should write something longer than an article.

To Mesh, Joel, Xalimo, Kerem, Kojo, Aryana, Max, Barney, Sahra and Fran – thank you all for being smarter than me. This book is the product of our late-night conversations, unsayable opinions and deranged hooting. You've collectively been the whetstone against which I've sharpened my ideas, and living proof that being politically committed doesn't mean you've got to be po-faced. To Mr Dips, the Armed Wing – Ruairidh, Charlie, Debs, Hope, Clare and Hattie – thank you for being my comrades and my teachers. To Leila and Nadia, you girls are the heart in a heartless world. Thank you for being there at the worst of times, and for being the architects of the best.

To my colleagues at Novara Media – your thumbprints are all over this book. Thank you for your ambition, political dedication and frankly insane work rate. I'm especially indebted to Aaron Bastani, Michael Walker, Gary McQuiggin and James Butler for their years of political insight and personal advice. Thank you for being such heterodox thinkers. You've never let me rely on assumptions or dogmas, and the left is better for you all being in it. Thank you to Owen Jones for being so generous with your time and your energy, and for never, ever gatekeeping.

To Mum – what could I possibly say that would do you justice? Thank you for keeping books in the house and shoes on my feet, for teaching me the ideas of Frantz Fanon and how to wind my waist. Thank you to Sushi and Anthony, for your love and forbearance as older siblings. You'd have been forgiven for clobbering me a lot more than you ever did. Thank you to Andrew, Sukey, Alex and Maggie for accepting me into your family. To Sara, Ogbonna, Mamoni and David – I wish you could have read this. Thank you for raising me.

And finally, to Joe. I used to think that in order to be happy with a man, I'd have to keep my expectations low. But somehow, I got luckier than I could have ever anticipated. Thank you for being my friend, confidant, husband and co-parent to the most beautiful cat who ever lived. Thank you for believing in me, for nagging me when I needed it and for constantly pushing my sense of the possible. Thank you for loving my family like your own. Thank you for reminding me to be more communist in my writing. Just please, one of these days, would you learn to put the lids back on jars?

INDEX

A NOTE ON THE AUTHOR

Ash Sarkar is a writer, lecturer, journalist and political commentator. A contributing editor of Novara Media, she has written for the *Guardian*, *Independent* and *Huffington Post*, with regular appearances on British television and radio, including *Question Time*, *Good Morning Britain* and *Jeremy Vine*. She has been called one of 'the internet's best left-wing thinkers' by the *Spectator*, and was named Media Personality of the Year by the Asian Media Awards in 2019. Sarkar also lectures at the Sandberg Instituut in Amsterdam, and has taught Global Politics at Anglia Ruskin University. *Minority Rule* is her first book.

A NOTE ON THE TYPE

The text of this book is set in Fournier. Fournier is derived from the romain du roi, which was created towards the end of the seventeenth century from designs made by a committee of the Académie of Sciences for the exclusive use of the Imprimerie Royale. The original Fournier types were cut by the famous Paris founder Pierre Simon Fournier in about 1742. These types were some of the most influential designs of the eight and are counted among the earliest examples of the 'transitional' style of typeface. This Monotype version dates from 1924. Fournier is a light, clear face whose distinctive features are capital letters that are quite tall and bold in relation to the lower-case letters, and decorative italics, which show the influence of the calligraphy of Fournier's time.